Also by Jere Van Dyk

In Afghanistan:
An American Odyssey

CAPTIVE

CAPTIVE

**My Time as a Prisoner
of the Taliban**

Jere Van Dyk

Times Books
Henry Holt and Company
New York

Times Books
Henry Holt and Company, LLC
Publishers since 1866
175 Fifth Avenue
New York, New York 10010
www.henryholt.com

Henry Holt® is a registered trademark of Henry Holt and Company, LLC.

Library of Congress Cataloging-in-Publication Data

Van Dyk, Jere.
   Captive : my time as a prisoner of the Taliban / Jere Van Dyk.—1st ed.
      p. cm.
   Includes index.
   ISBN 978-0-8050-8827-4
  1. Van Dyk, Jere—Captivity, 2008.   2. Taliban.   3. Journalists—
Afghanistan—Biography.   4. Prisoners—Afghanistan—Biography.
5. Afghanistan—History—2001–   I. Title.
   DS371.43.V36A3 2010
   958.104'7—dc22   2009052886

Henry Holt books are available for special promotions and premiums.
For details contact: Director, Special Markets.

First Edition 2010

Designed by Meryl Sussman Levavi
Map © 2010 by Jeffrey L. Ward

Printed in the United States of America
10 9 8 7 6 5 4 3 2 1

To the memory of my mother and father

Contents

Author's Note

In the summer of 2007, I signed a contract to write a book about the border region of Afghanistan and Pakistan. I had a long background in this area, which is now considered the headquarters of al-Qaeda and the Taliban.

I first crossed the border from Afghanistan into Pakistan in 1973, when I drove an old Volkswagen through the tribal areas. I was a young man, exploring the world. Six years later I watched on television as the Soviet Union invaded Afghanistan and knew I would return. In 1981, as a freelance reporter for the *New York Times*, I flew to Pakistan and took a train to Peshawar, the headquarters of the mujahideen, the Afghans fighting the Soviet Union. I had read that these fearless men shouted "God is great" and with old British rifles fought valiantly against a modern superpower. I met their leaders, traveled into the tribal areas, and hiked into Afghanistan, where I lived with the mujahideen along the border.

On Thanksgiving Day 1981, the Afghan army and Soviet forces attacked the mujahideen group I was with. I heard the bullets sing overhead, saw the faces of the young soldiers as they approached us, saw the teenager next to me get shot and the commander wave to me to get back, trying to protect me, his guest. Many men died that day. That night Soviet tanks surrounded our village, and the mujahideen sneaked me away in the night, to save me.

Upon my return to the United States I published several articles in the *New York Times* and wrote a book, *In Afghanistan*, about my time with the mujahideen. I gave speeches, wrote other articles, and worked the politics of Afghanistan in Washington, D.C. I eventually left the country and again traveled the world as a journalist. *National Geographic* sent me to faraway places. I traveled the length of the Brahmaputra River, into western Tibet, hiking alone, foolishly, up a glacier, when the snow gave way but then miraculously held, and I found the river's very source. I made a similar journey up the Amazon River and scaled a mountain to where the stream became a trickle. But still, no matter where I was in the world, I thought of Afghanistan.

In December 2001 I returned to Afghanistan, as a freelance radio reporter for CBS News and WABC television. It was two months after the U.S. invasion and three months following the 9/11 attacks. Over the next six years I returned on several reporting trips for CBS to Afghanistan and Pakistan. Always I was drawn to the border region. I wanted to penetrate deep into the tribal areas, to return to where I had lived with the mujahideen as a young man, to find the leaders I had known from that time, to learn the true story of what was taking place there, in this new time of war.

I returned to Kabul, the capital of Afghanistan, in early August 2007 and began my preparations to travel along the border and to cross into the tribal areas of Pakistan. No Western reporter had done this since the rise of the Taliban a decade earlier. It would be dangerous, but I felt that I could do it. I had contacts that no other journalist had. I knew this region. I knew its culture. There were countless reports that the Taliban had reconstituted itself in the tribal areas of Pakistan and that Osama bin Laden was hiding there. I would go to the men I knew from my recent reporting trips, and through them find the mujahideen I had known twenty-five years before, some of whom were now Taliban leaders.

I let my hair and beard grow. Ramadan, the month of fasting, began in late August, and I began to fast. My goal was to disappear as much as I could into Afghan culture, specifically the culture of the Pashtuns, the people who lived on both sides of the border, in Afghanistan and in Pakistan. I maintained a social life in Kabul, but I kept my work hidden. I began to travel secretly along the border, sleeping in villages, meeting with tribal leaders, mullahs, and the Taliban. I began to cross the mountains into Pakistan. I knew that this was what I was supposed to do, where I was supposed to be. I was determined to push it to the very end.

I kept in touch via e-mail with my editor in New York, my literary agent, a woman I was going out with, my family, and various editors and producers at CBS, but gradually I sent fewer and fewer e-mails. I ate in Afghan restaurants, wore Afghan clothes, and more and more avoided Westerners. I was increasingly on edge and nervous. On January 3, 2008, I wrote a letter to my editor. It would be my last correspondence with him.

CAPTIVE

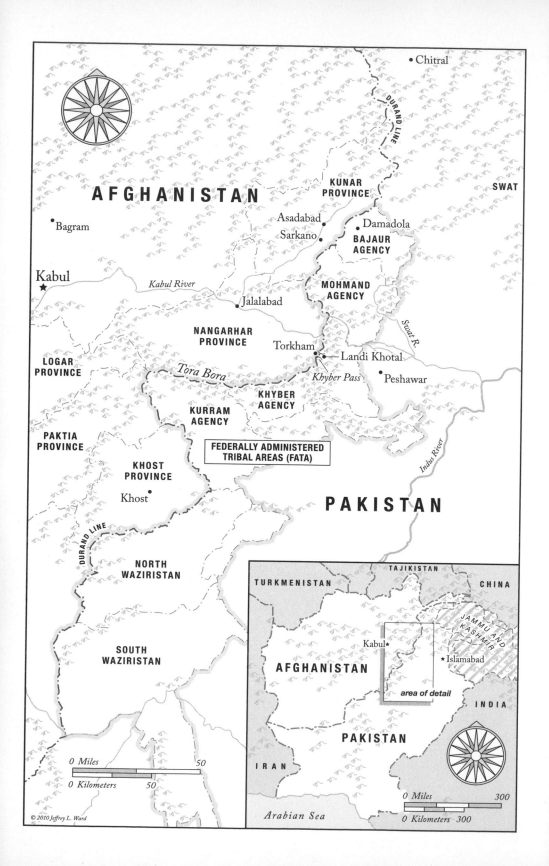

• Chitral

DURAND LINE

KUNAR
PROVINCE

SWAT

AFGHANISTAN

• Bagram

Asadabad •
Sarkano •

• Damadola

BAJAUR
AGENCY

Kabul ★

Kabul River

MOHMAND
AGENCY

• Jalalabad

Swat R.

NANGARHAR
PROVINCE

Torkham

Landi Khotal

LOGAR
PROVINCE

Tora Bora

Khyber Pass

• Peshawar

KHYBER
AGENCY

KURRAM
AGENCY

PAKTIA
PROVINCE

FEDERALLY ADMINISTERED
TRIBAL AREAS (FATA)

Indus River

KHOST
PROVINCE

PAKISTAN

Khost •

DURAND LINE

NORTH
WAZIRISTAN

SOUTH
WAZIRISTAN

0 Miles   50

0 Kilometers   50

© 2010 Jeffrey L. Ward

TAJIKISTAN

TURKMENISTAN

CHINA

JAMMU AND
KASHMIR

Kabul ★

★ Islamabad

AFGHANISTAN

area of detail

INDIA

PAKISTAN

IRAN

0 Miles   300

Arabian Sea

0 Kilometers   300

Prologue

Thursday, January 3

Dear Paul,

Happy New Year. I want to give you an update on the book and to let you know where I am on it at the moment. I am writing a letter because I don't trust e-mails. I am not completely paranoid, but close to it.

I began working on the book at the end of August. I have traveled through most, but not all, parts of eastern Afghanistan along the border. I have a few important places yet to go. I will go to them this winter or later in the spring. I have interviewed a great number of people: tribal leaders, local people, politicians, and mullahs. I have an interview scheduled with President Hamid Karzai on the 10th.

I live in Kabul, but when I am away I live like a Pashtun. I have sneaked four times into the tribal zones of Pakistan, our goal. I have been deep into Mohmand Agency, one of the zones. I went in with very religious drug traffickers. We sneaked past the border post where, a week before, the Taliban killed four policemen.

I have crossed with tribal leaders into Kurram Agency, also in the tribal zones. I have twice been into Chitral, in the north, where Gulbadeen Hekmatyar lives, and where many feel Osama bin Laden may be hiding. I know our goal is to cover the tribal zones, not just eastern Afghanistan.

I have been with the Taliban three times. Once in the mountains, about a six-hour hike south from Tora Bora. The Taliban there came from North Waziristan. They invited me to come with them, on another trip, to their training camps. We shall see. The day after I left, the government came and arrested some tribal people. I don't know if someone recognized me, or learned that a foreigner was there.

Before that I met with a Taliban commander in Kunar Province in the north of Afghanistan, along the border. This meeting represents the first time any journalist has been with the Taliban in eastern Afghanistan, so I am told. A member of al-Qaeda, along with other Taliban, was watching when I interviewed the Taliban commander in Kunar.

The next day the U.S. Army came and attacked them, from the air and on the ground. They did so because the Taliban attacked the army base that night. I was not with them when they attacked the base. I won't do that.

The Taliban leader has since called my translator, and my go-between, a number of times. He wants to take me to their training camps. I haven't agreed to go yet because I am not sure he doesn't want to kidnap me. My go-between is going up into the mountains to talk to him now.

I had one of my biggest scares thus far on New Year's Eve. It is still not over. I sneaked across the border from Kunar, with two guides, and went into Chitral, in the tribal areas. It took a month to arrange this. There I met with a Taliban commander. In every case, thus far, with the Taliban, I have taken a camera and taken their pictures. I take other pictures also.

After I finished my interview—and this man, unlike other Taliban I have been with, was not even remotely friendly—my guides and I took a different route, hiding behind rocks, evading a Pakistani military truck, and sneaked back across the border to Afghanistan. This all happened at night. Most of my trips are at night.

It was a two-part package deal. I was to meet at 3 a.m. the next morning with a Pakistani Military Intelligence officer who would come across the border to meet with me. I wanted confirmation from him of all that I am learning about the military's involvement with al-Qaeda and the Taliban. The tribal chief, who arranged the Taliban meeting, would bring him. He promised that the officer would answer all my questions, including those about Osama bin Laden.

Everything went terribly wrong. I insisted that we meet at dawn, so I could take video of our meeting. I did this for a few reasons. The camera has the recording. I knew I would need proof of such a meeting. The tribal chief decided, because of this, to move us to a different location. At 4:00 a.m., the Taliban commander, and eight of his men, came to where we were originally, to capture or kill us.

The tribal chief was gone to meet with the MI man. My guide and I, and the chief's younger brother, were at another, secret location. I didn't sleep that night. There was machine-gun fire coming from near the U.S. Army base a few miles away. There were helicopters coming and going.

At dawn the next morning, on the way to meet us, the tribal chief and the army man were captured by Afghan intelligence. His men had to get me out of there. We sneaked down the mountain and found another truck. The Afghans risked everything to get me far away from there. Above all a Pashtun will protect to the death a guest. It is part of Pashtunwali, their ancient tribal code, which often takes precedence over Islam. That is why Mullah Omar refused to give up Osama bin Laden. He destroyed his government, his country, and much else all to protect Osama bin Laden. So it was with the men and me.

The tribal chief had given one of his younger brothers to the Pakistanis as a guarantee that he would bring the army man back. He promised the MI officer that if anything happened he would take care of his family for life.

The area where we operated is filled with al-Qaeda and the Taliban. Al-Qaeda had kidnapped a man who worked at the U.S. Army base a week or so before and beheaded him.

A tough nineteen-year-old Afghan, the youngest brother of the tribal chief, and who guided me down a mountain in Chitral and over a stream and back to Afghanistan, and who slept in a room with us to protect us, drove me and my guide fast on a rough track out of the area.

Afghans at a U.S. Army check post stopped us and this time I was discovered, and they took me to the army fire base. The sergeant was as nice as could be, even said he recognized my name and commented on my long experience in Afghanistan, and said he and others had been reading some things I had written. He asked if I wanted anything to eat or to see his commander. All I wanted to do was get out of there, which I did. I was afraid they would find out what had happened.

We rushed on. When we were near a paved road and relative safety, four hours later, I asked the driver to stop. I went down to the Kunar River and washed my face. I came back to see the young Afghan crying softly. He finally broke down. His two brothers were in prison, one being held by Afghan intelligence, the other by the Pakistanis. The full weight of everything hit me. I stood there filled with sadness and, yes, shame.

I was responsible for this trip. I demanded certain things and they followed my instructions. They did everything for me. In return I was going to pay them some money.

My guide is in touch with one of the men who took us to

Chitral, part of the tribal chief's family. I learned last night that the Taliban have now kidnapped the MI officer. I don't know what they are going to do with him. If anything happens to him, the Pakistanis may well execute the tribal chief's brother. The local Afghan intelligence people are keeping this out of the media. Kabul doesn't even know.

The leader of my group is the tribal chief along the border. He was released two days ago by Afghan intelligence. I learned yesterday that a Pakistani MI officer, a friend of the officer with whom I was to meet, had secretly alerted Afghan intelligence that his fellow officer was coming over. It gets even more complicated. It is a very murky world here, a place of ancient tribal ties, betrayal, warfare, double-crossing, and where a man's honor and tribal codes count for everything.

The Afghans I was with are doing everything to keep my name out of it. They promised they would protect me. They have kept their word. This trip is not a game.

I do not have the full answers yet. I am still not out of this. I have to go back to Kunar. I have not yet told you the full story. I am too sick to my stomach. I met with my guide this morning. We do not know what is going to happen to the MI man, and the young man in prison in Pakistan. We worry.

My guide and Taliban go-between are now planning a long trip. It is almost set. I sent trusted men to talk to people to arrange it. The trip will take three weeks to a month, I am told, through many parts of the tribal areas. I am going to go to all the places that you and I discussed. I will go with our enemies. I will leave after my interview with Karzai. A blue suit one day and Afghan clothes the next.

I sent my men back to double-check with the others yesterday. After what happened on New Year's Eve (I forgot that was the date) in Chitral, I am scared.

Everything I am doing costs money. I have about twelve

people on my payroll at different times. I use different men for different tribal areas. A man must belong to the area, and to the right tribe, to do anything. The Pakistanis are using the Taliban, I believe, to try to destroy the tribal structure. They are deeply involved in backing the Taliban. They are, I believe, using U.S. taxpayer money to kill U.S. soldiers. The Taliban get money for what they do. A suicide bomber gets the most, although it goes to his family.

I stay away from journalists here, as much as possible, although I know many people here, because I don't want to talk. I can't tell people what I am doing. I don't really trust anybody. It is too dangerous.

By the way, all the Taliban in the north thought I was a journalist from Nepal. If they found out I was American they would kill me, or so my guides said. I said I didn't look Nepali, but my guides said the Taliban wouldn't know. They are that isolated from the world. I can't believe that the al-Qaeda fighter, who watched me interview his commander in American English, thought I was Nepali.

I have been talking with the U.S. Army about going on an embed along the border, but I have postponed that for now. I was at a dinner the other night, with the deputy commander of ISAF, a three-star British general, who invited me to go with him on a trip whenever I wanted. Maybe, but only after I finish my own work on the ground. I am staying away from the CIA. I do not trust the CIA. I can't afford to let it know what I am doing. I have heard they are along the border. I don't know exactly what is going on between the CIA and the ISI, the main Pakistani intelligence agency, although I have heard that MI is more ruthless. Who knows? I had hoped the Pakistani military intelligence man would have enlightened me about a number of things, but now he is in prison, somewhere, if he is still alive, in part because of me.

I, like every Afghan I have met, am not sure what U.S. goals are here. I will see about talking to U.S. officials after I have completed my work on the ground. I am talking to Karzai now because he will see me, and because I want to use that as leverage with the Pakistanis, including President Pervez Musharraf.

I have a great deal to do, a great number of places to go. I will hopefully still get an official visa for Pakistan, but right now it doesn't matter. I will continue to cross the mountains. Our goal is to understand what is going on, on both sides of the border, which is the center of al-Qaeda, the Taliban, and the "War on Terror."

There is not a tribal chief along the border who believes one word that Musharraf utters. Journalists have written that Afghans and Pakistanis call him "Busharraf," a combination of "Bush" and "Musharraf," meaning that they are both the same, outsiders fighting the Pashtuns, but what they are really saying is "Besharraf," meaning, in Pashto, "a man of no dignity." It is a play on words and, to them, the truth. They all believe that Bush and Musharraf are deceiving the world. One *malik* (tribal leader) called it "a drama." Others agree. I don't have the answers yet. As one malik in Pakistan said, "I have money, men, weapons, and ammunition, but I don't have the ability to make a suicide jacket."

Strange, is it not, that as Pakistan burns, Musharraf can throw lawyers in jail, and judges and politicians, and yet the government has yet to find anyone responsible for one single suicide attack, as they rage across the tribal zones, in Pakistan proper, and here in Kabul.

I know you are concerned about Osama bin Laden. He and al-Qaeda are a big part of this story. I bring him up, whenever I can, in interviews.

I know the manuscript is due in August. I went to see the Pakistanis again last week about a visa. Still nothing. Everyone says they don't trust me. I don't know. I'll get the information one way or another, even if I have to go to Peshawar and Islamabad disguised as an Afghan.

I will continue to stay in touch.

Best wishes,
Jere

PART ONE

The Way of the Pashtuns

Tuesday, February 12

It was midmorning in Kabul, cold and cloudy. Daoud, my translator and guide, called to say that he was waiting outside. I looked out the window at the hills to the west, covered with snow, took my backpack, locked the door to my room, and went quietly downstairs. I wrote a note to the guesthouse manager saying I would be back in a few days. I left the keys on the counter.

I could be gone a few days longer, but it didn't matter. I always left notes like this. I didn't tell anyone else I was leaving. After the attack on the Serena Hotel, in January, the Taliban said that they would now target restaurants and guesthouses where foreigners stayed. I didn't know who was watching.

The taxi was waiting outside the steel gate, thirty yards away, its exhaust spewing in the cold. I had told Daoud never to let the taxi park near the door. We drove through gray, crowded streets with snow and ice on both sides piled up. The driver didn't seem to notice that I was a foreigner. We reached the Jalalabad taxi station, a strip of dirt with a few cars and men standing around. Daoud told me, in English, ruining my cover, to stay in the car. I paid the driver. Daoud found another car, and soon we headed east on the high, cold, windy, dusty, polluted plains of Kabul toward the warmth of Jalalabad.

Once this plain was calm and beautiful; now it was part of an expanding, ever larger, uglier, overcrowded, nervous city, and the Taliban slowly were beginning to tighten the noose around it. We stopped at a police checkpoint, where the driver handed over a small bribe, and began our descent. For a moment I was happy. How I loved this road. Every time I drove it, my mind flashed back, if only for a second, to how happy I was as a young man driving my Volkswagen here. The sun was out, and Afghanistan was romantic. I wasn't afraid then.

In 1973, I bought an old Volkswagen in Frankfurt, a city I knew from when I had been in the army nearby a few years before, and with my nineteen-year-old younger brother drove across Asia to Afghanistan. Kabul was smaller, friendly, and exotic then, the bazaar dark, deep, and mysterious, and long camel caravans came slowly through the empty streets, silent in the afternoon sun. There was the smell of hashish, sewage, and wood-burning stoves. Schoolgirls wore miniskirts with long socks and laughed in the streets. Not once did a child put out his hand to beg, as children did in other poor countries. There was pride here, born of a hard life, I felt, and a wildness and a warmth that drew me in. One evening I watched a bearded old man in a turban with a rifle on his shoulder walk slowly, his back straight, across a street and into the bazaar. To me he was Afghanistan.

We shot down now through the deep, narrow, dark, winding gorge, the layers of rock in some places folded over, rippling like a bodybuilder's stomach. I thought back to that sunny, quiet day so long ago, when I pushed the sunroof back and drove with a smile past the never-ending line of Kuchi caravans, making their way down to their warm, winter pastures in Pakistan, as Afghan kings had once made their way on this same road to their winter palaces in Jalalabad, and before that in Peshawar.

That was before war came again to this land, through which for centuries ambitious men with armies had come and gone. I had seen the mujahideen begin their rise to fight the godless Soviet invader, before the rise of the Taliban and their foreign allies, al-Qaeda, and before Afghanistan lost its soul, at least the one that I knew. The taxi left the gorge and raced down now past wide, brown, empty rolling hills. Men and boys stood by the road holding strings of fish for sale. There were blankets of snow in the shadows. The wide green Kabul River was on our left, its water running east to Pakistan, and beyond it were baked-mud villages in the hills.

Rows of brightly colored pinstriped Pakistani trucks, laden with matériel for the United States and its allies, geared down as they climbed upward, spewing their thick black fumes. We threaded our way through another canyon, and on our left in the east appeared the craggy, snow-covered Tangay Mir Kamon and to the right the Tor Ghar, beyond which lay Pakistan.

I was on my way to cross the border.

I would be going where no Western reporter had gone in years, into the tribal areas of Pakistan, where al-Qaeda and the Taliban were said to be regrouping, and where there was no law except that of Pashtunwali, the ancient, tribal law of the Pashtuns. I would go to Bajaur and Swat and then down into Waziristan. No one else was doing this; no one, to my knowledge, had done this in twenty years. I still had a long way to go. It was so different now from what I had experienced in the 1980s, when I lived with the mujahideen as they fought for their country, and their faith, against the Soviet Union.

I had felt safe with the mujahideen, and I had written a book that brought their story to the people of America. This time I would be traveling with the Taliban and living with them. My life would be in their hands every minute, in Pakistan, where there were no American soldiers. I had to go, and I wanted to do this. I was scared.

I wanted to find out what the Taliban were really like, to see how different they were from the mujahideen. I wanted to learn what they thought and what their goals were. I wanted to go to their training camps. I wanted to explain the Taliban to the outside world. I wanted to go deep into the heart of Taliban country, to get to their leaders, men I knew from the 1980s, and through them perhaps even to find Osama bin Laden himself. I felt that with my contacts, my history with the mujahideen, and my knowledge of Pashtun culture, I could do what no one else could do. I knew these people. We had once been friends.

I wanted, as well, to do something harder and more dangerous than anything I had ever done before. I wanted to really test myself, one last time. Though I was past sixty, I was in pretty good shape, and I still thought of myself as the runner I had been as a young man. I had set a national high school record and had traveled the world on U.S. track and field teams. In college I was a contender for the U.S. Olympic team, and four years later I was a finalist in the Olympic trials. In the U.S. Army I had won my race in the main international military meet in Viareggio, Italy, and I had carried the American flag in the closing ceremonies of a U.S. vs. U.S.S.R. meet in Leningrad at the height of the Cold War. I still ran, even in Kabul, and I did exercises.

The Kabul River rushed over rocks, was calm, and rushed again through canyons with pine trees on either side. The wind was hot and dry now, and we made a rest stop by the road. The driver said there were no mines here. I walked out into the desert and felt the hot, dry wind in my face.

We stopped by a row of small ramshackle shops by the road to have lunch. There were rows of boxes of big red pomegranates, from Kandahar in the south, and oranges from Pakistan. "We will have fresh fish," said Daoud.

A boy brought four ten-inch fish to us. "These are not Pakistani fish, are they?" asked our driver.

"No," said the boy. "Pakistani fish will make a man sick. These are Afghan fish."

Once this land, from western Iran across into India, was ruled by the Pashtuns. Then the British, in their turn, came to conquer.

Afghanistan grew weak from two Anglo-Afghan wars (1839–42 and 1879–80) and was forced to accept two treaties that took away the fertile Afghan land of what would become known as Baluchistan and the Northwest Frontier Province of India, today parts of Pakistan.

In 1893, Sir Mortimer Durand, the foreign secretary of British India, and Emir Abdur Rahman of Afghanistan negotiated, in Persian (the French of Asia), the Durand Line, the border today between Afghanistan and Pakistan. This line, like a sword, cut through the heart and soul of the Pashtun nation, and through some of the most rugged, starkly beautiful land on Earth. Pashtun nationalists today call the region Pashtunistan or Pakhtunkhwa, the land of the Pashtuns, of which Ahmad Shah Durrani, the founder of the Afghan nation in 1747, used to sing, this nation of proud men who worship honor, the Koran, and the gun.

The British wanted this artificial frontier, 1,610 miles long, to extend the formal reach of their empire and to create Afghanistan as a landlocked buffer state to protect British India from the expanding tsarist Russian Empire. In the years following Abdur Rahman's acquiescence, no Afghan government has accepted the Durand Line as a border. Afghanistan was the only country to vote against the admission of Pakistan to the United Nations in 1947, because to do so would have implied recognition of the Durand Line. There are about 14 million Pashtuns in Afghanistan, 42 percent of the country, and about 26 million in Pakistan, 15 percent of the country, mostly living in the Northwest Frontier Province and the Federally Administered Tribal Areas. The Pashtuns are the largest tribal society in the world without their own country.

The three of us sat by the river eating grilled fish, bread, and salad. Afterward, we drove on through a tunnel, and the road kept descending. Boys now appeared selling cellophane bags of chopped sugarcane. We stopped at another police checkpoint, where a man holding a long stick waved us on. We were in Jalalabad. It was

warm and sunny and people walked slowly. The streets were filled
with men and motorized rickshaws.

Daoud and I checked into the Khalid Guest House and went
to our room, on the fourth and highest floor, in the back, away
from people. From the concrete walkway outside our door I looked
down at the barbershop, the parked cars, and the large rusting
boiler and listened to men shouting. Inside our room there were
two cots and a thin mattress on the floor. Daoud found the syn-
thetic prayer mat rolled up under a cot. It is called a *jahnamaz*. *Jah*
means "place," *namaz* means "prayer": a place to pray. A jahnamaz
in Afghanistan is like a Gideon Bible in America. There is one in
every room in every hotel and every guest room in every village.
After he prayed, Daoud turned on the small television, which sat
on a shelf in the corner. An American movie played, this Western
intrusion, the women in it half naked, it seemed, but their bodies
were blurred by the censor, as they and the men fired their guns
and cars piled up on the streets.

I went for a walk and watched a slim young woman, in a blue
silk pants suit and high heels, her ankles showing, her face covered in a *chadari*, walk down the street. She walked with another
woman, also hidden. How elegant she looked, how mysterious and
so much more enticing than the Western women with their guns
on television. A weary young woman about seventeen, with her
chadari back over her head, stood, holding a baby, begging as cars
stopped at a traffic light.

I bought some oranges and returned to the room. Daoud went
to get his hair cut and his beard trimmed. He returned wearing a
white *qwalie*, or prayer cap. He looked like a serious madrassa
student and made me slightly nervous. He went into the bathroom,
performing his ablutions, and prayed. Twice he had prayed now.
He too was nervous.

I had first met Daoud last September. It was Ramadan, the
month when the Koran was first revealed to Muhammad, now

when Muslims fast from sunrise to sunset. I was fasting, too, to understand Islam better, to draw closer to the Afghans than I ever had before, to enter deeper into their world, to be more acceptable to them, to make them more comfortable, especially the Taliban. I needed to do whatever I could. I was going for broke.

I had previously been working with an experienced interpreter, called Sami, along the border. We had started in January 2007, when we had gone up into the mountains to where Pat Tillman, the U.S. soldier and football star, was killed near Khost, near the border. In early September, when I began my book research, we had crossed the mountains into Pakistan into Mohmand Agency, in an old car on a dusty track with drug traffickers, my first trip across, for one day, from dawn until after dark, avoiding the Taliban, and we met with a tribal leader. A month later we met at midnight with the Taliban high up in the mountains, with a Predator buzzing overhead, where Pakistan fell off to one side and Afghanistan to the other, and again Sami was courageous, but he was scared as well. His close friend Ajmal Naqshbandi, a fellow fixer, had been beheaded by the Taliban in April.

Sami's wife didn't want him to go on any more trips across the border with me. I understood. I tried for weeks but couldn't find anyone else to cross over. If I wanted this to work, I had to avoid Afghan, Pakistani, and all foreign intelligence agencies, and all military organizations, including those of the Americans. I had to disappear into Pashtun culture.

I went one hot, dusty afternoon to see Professor Rasul Amin, a former minister of education and the head of the Afghanistan Study Center in Kabul. He was a friend of an old Afghan hand I knew in New York and thus a tie to the past, someone I felt that I could trust. We sat on a sofa in his office waiting for *iftar,* the evening meal to break the day's fast.

I told him a little about my project. One of his assistants, Zarmina, a young Afghan in jeans, came in smiling, shaking my hand, and she sat in an easy chair, her two cell phones ringing constantly. "Don't cross the border again," said Amin. "It's too dangerous for you."

We shared iftar. I said I needed a fixer. Amin asked me to come again and to bring him a copy of my book on Afghanistan, which I had promised him the last time we had met, in 2002. Zarmina and her driver took me back to my guesthouse, talking as if we were old friends. She called a few days later, being friendly, and I wondered why. I saw her again on my next trip to see Professor Amin. I was curious about her. She had grown up in a refugee camp in Pakistan. Her father had died and she was the breadwinner for her family. I admired her. She called again and said there was someone that she wanted me to meet. I was wary. "Please," she said. "He speaks good English. He will be good for you." I sensed that he would be the one. I said okay, grateful to her. She would send him over.

He came the next day. The guard opened the steel door and he entered the compound, smiling brightly, and introduced himself. His name was Daoud. He wore a brown suit, had a short beard, and looked to be about thirty-five years old. We sat at an outside table, where there was no one around. "I want an education," he said, "but I have no facilities. I am looking for help. I can be your assistant." Professor Amin was his uncle. He had worked in the center's library, but he was now a schoolteacher. "I have seen your book. Afghans must see this book. I will translate it into Pashto." I liked his energy and that he wanted to better himself. "I thirst for education. I want to go to Peshawar University, but I need five thousand dollars. The Americans have so much money, and they are giving it away."

I wasn't the U.S. Embassy. Why didn't he go to Kabul University? It was cheap, and it was in Afghanistan. He said that his wife and five children lived in Peshawar. His parents lived in Kunar, the Afghan province along the northeast border. He supported all of them. "I can introduce you to many people in Kunar," he said. This piqued my interest. I asked if he could take me from Kunar over the mountains and across the border to Bajaur Agency, part of the tribal areas, and to Chitral, just north of them. "Yes," he said, smiling again, easily. "No problem. Will you help me get an education?"

One step at a time.

That evening, I asked a friend, Fazul Rahim, the CBS manager in Afghanistan, to run a check on him. I was a consultant to CBS News on Afghanistan and Pakistan. Fazul knew the owner of the school where Daoud taught English. A few days later Fazul called back to report that Daoud seemed okay.

I met with Daoud again. "We'll try it once," I said. "I want to leave as soon as possible." I wondered if he knew how dangerous it was.

"Thank you, sir," Daoud said. "We can cross the border easily." He was too nonchalant about the whole enterprise; what did he know that I didn't know? He leaned forward and looked at me closely. "Can we have an agreement, that my neck is your neck? If anything happens to my children, you will take care of them?" He was serious. He did know. I paused, then said yes. "Thank you, sir. We can do all the things you want."

I smiled to myself. Things always work out.

Three times since then we had met with the Taliban, for a few hours each time, twice in the mountains of Kunar and once across the border in Chitral. Each time Daoud had been scared, even shaking, but each time he had translated patiently. No one else would do what he was doing. He lied to me, always trying to impress me and tell me things he could do when he couldn't. I understood this and overlooked his lies because he was risking his life for me. Now we were going much deeper, to live with the Taliban.

Evening came. I went out for another walk. A warm wind blew, stirring dust and bits of garbage in the streets. The few restaurants were open, and half a dozen young men stood outside, over long narrow charcoal grills, waving fans to keep the embers burning, turning over the kababs, as trucks raced by. The road through Jalalabad was the main route from Pakistan to Kabul. Once it was the main road from India.

I returned to our room. Ahmed, our driver, was there. He gave me a big hug. It was good to see him again. We were all a team. He was a friend of a friend of Daoud's. He was about my height, just under five foot eleven, and solid, probably in his forties, with a short gray beard. He had driven us on dirt tracks through Taliban country to isolated border regions and, once at night, to meet with the Taliban. I trusted him.

My cell phone rang. It was Nazaneen, an Afghan woman I had seen in Kabul a few weeks before. We met six years ago, but she was married. Now she was living on her own. I liked to go to her house and have dinner and sit by a fire and talk. It was a real home. She had a guard, a cook, and a driver, and though they were friendly and kept to themselves I knew they were watching us. I had to protect her honor above all else, and I had to protect myself. One evening, after I had come over almost every night for two weeks, I took a chance and told her briefly of my plans to cross the border and go deep into the tribal areas. I had to tell someone. The tension was building up and I was nervous. She stood by the fire and looked at me for a long time, saying nothing. I wondered what she was thinking. I told her who I was trying to avoid. I was crossing the border illegally, trying to find out what the U.S., Afghan, and Pakistani governments were not telling us.

I was living in an increasingly dark world, in Kabul and especially along the border. I worried about my phone calls and e-mails, about walking down the street and sitting in cafés and restaurants. I had been threatened twice, once in writing. I looked at people closer when they approached. I was becoming like an Afghan, always wary.

But I was determined to make this trip. I was tired of reading what politicians in Congress, the White House, so-called security analysts, intelligence officials, journalists, Pentagon officials, and countless armchair experts from the United States and Europe said about the Pashtuns, the Taliban, al-Qaeda, and the tribal areas, where everyone said Osama bin Laden was living in a cave. They said this was the center of the War on Terror, the center of al-Qaeda and the Taliban.

I didn't believe them anymore. Few if any of them had ever lived with the Pashtuns; few knew, understood, or cared about these people in the mountains, their culture, their tribal codes, and even who the Taliban really were. In the 1980s, the joke was that the United States would fight to the last Afghan; they were wild men with swords in their teeth, good as cannon fodder against the Russians. Nothing had changed. Except America was on the war-path now.

I came to Afghanistan a second time in 1981, a young man with a short letter of introduction from the *New York Times*. I flew to Pakistan and took a train up to Peshawar, carrying a portable typewriter and wearing a seersucker suit. It was romantic then, what I wanted it to be. I met Gulbadeen Hekmatyar, Yunus Khalis, his associate Hajji Din Mohammed, Burhanuddin Rabbani, and other mujahideen leaders. I particularly liked Khalis, an old man with a deep voice, callused hands, a long beard, and a bandolier of bullets across his chest. He reminded me of relatives I had known as a boy, strong, quiet men who wore dark clothes, farmed in Oregon, and read the Bible at night.

I traveled with Khalis's men down through the tribal areas to Waziristan and hiked up into Afghanistan, where I lived with Jalaladin Haqqani, a guerrilla leader under Khalis, and his band of mujahideen. I began to learn about the Pashtuns' code of behavior and the role of Islam in their fight against the godless, communist Soviet Union. I hiked back out in the snow to Waziristan, went south, and crossed scrubland on a motorcycle into Kandahar, where I saw the mujahideen more as normal men who bled and cried, not as fierce, ideological Muslim warriors. I came out with a guide, across a desert, by camel, slept in the sand, and carried a rifle in my saddle. That was enough, then.

I wrote a series of articles for the *New York Times* and a book, *In Afghanistan*. I gave speeches and wrote other articles on Afghanistan. It became my life, but few cared about Afghanistan then. I couldn't forget these men, who, with nothing, said they would fight to the death for their land, their faith, and their families. They had risked their lives to save mine, for I was their guest. They had pleaded with me for something with which to shoot down the Soviet helicopters that controlled the skies. In 1983, I wrote an op-ed article for the *Times*, passing on their plea.

Later on, after the article helped spur action in Congress, I felt guilty for what I had done. I wanted to help the women and children, but I now realized that if the United States gave the mujahideen antiaircraft missiles, the Soviet Union would come in with even greater force, and that more people would die.

A year later, Zalmay Khalilzad, an Afghan-American and a consultant to the State Department, asked if I would be the director of Friends of Afghanistan, a nonprofit organization designed to help the Afghan people. I agreed and later learned that it would be overseen by the National Security Council and the State Department. On March 21, 1984, the first day of spring, the Afghan New Year, I sat in the White House and watched President Ronald Reagan put his arm around an Afghan teenage girl and say, "We are with you." He called the mujahideen "freedom fighters" and said that they were "like our founding fathers."

That summer, the United States and Pakistan brought the

newly formed seven-member Afghan mujahideen government-in-exile to America to present its credentials to the United Nations and to meet with President Reagan. I was their guide in New York. Hekmatyar was the president. He and I spent hours together. Friends of Afghanistan hosted a reception for the mujahideen so they could meet UN delegates. I stood at the door greeting guests when Hajji Din Mohammed entered, smiling. "When are you coming back?" he asked me. I felt warmth spread through me. I was accepted. I didn't know until then how close I had become to these men who had so little but had shared their rice and tea with me and had protected me.

Now, more than twenty years later, Hekmatyar was leading his own faction against the United States. Haqqani was a leader of the Taliban. I wanted to reconnect with them, to learn the truth of what was really going on. I had already seen Khalis, in 2003, before he died, and Hajji Din Mohammed, now the governor of Kabul, a few weeks ago.

"They'll take care of you," Nazaneen told me. "But it would be a good idea to learn a few phrases of the Kalima, just in case." It was the Muslim profession of faith to *al-Lah* (literally, the God) in Arabic, the one true God, not the idols that the Arabs once worshipped in Mecca, the trading center where businessmen hoped that graven images would bring them good fortune, before Muhammad destroyed them. "*Al-Lah-o-Akbar*" does not mean "God is great," but rather "God is greater." The one true God is greater than all the other gods. Christians and Jews also pray to Allah, whom we call God. That evening Daoud and Ahmed taught me the beginning: "*La illaha illalaha Muhammad urrasullalah.*" There is no god but God, and Muhammad is his messenger.

I knew the importance of God in their lives. I understood their fundamentalism. I had grown up in what today would be called a fundamentalist world, but to me "fundamentalists" are political. We were not. We were Plymouth Brethren, a quietest, separatist

deeply Christian group who believe that the Bible is the word of
God and that we are to remain separate from a corrupt and evil
world. I felt that we were separate even within our own small religious community. Most of the men wore dark, somber clothes, and
the women wore modest, self-effacing dresses and hats and veils.
My mother, however, wore bright, almost flashy clothes that she
made herself, and my father wore nice suits. He owned a small
millwork company, and we lived in a modern, distinctive house—at
odds it seemed with our beliefs—overlooking the Columbia River
and the lights of Portland, Oregon, a big city, and all its worldly
temptation. We had horses and went hiking in the mountains and
swimming in forest streams, a wholesome Northwest outdoor life,
and we were deep, thoughtful Christians. We didn't go to movies,
drink alcohol, dance, play cards, or watch television on Sundays.
We prayed before our meals, after which we read the Bible and my
father preached to us.

I felt that because of my own upbringing, I understood a Muslim's deep belief in God, his certainty that he was right, his desire
for purity, his abhorrence of decadence, his fear of sin, of being
tempted by worldly things, which counted for nothing against God
and eternity. I understood his submission to God, ruler of Heaven
and Earth, and to His will, and the knowledge that against God
man is nothing.

The evening news from Pakistan, in Pashto, came on television.
The day before, the Tahreek-e-Taliban, the Movement of the Taliban in Pakistan, had kidnapped Tariq Azizuddin, the Pakistani
ambassador to Afghanistan, near Landi Khotal in the tribal areas.
A massive search operation was under way for the ambassador.

"It's all a game," said Ahmed, laughing. "Everyone knows that.
Pakistan is behind this." He then left to be with his family. We
didn't need him today. The news ended, and it was time for evening prayers. Daoud took out the jahnamaz from beneath the bed
and prayed again. Three times now he had prayed since we arrived.

I sat on my cot eating oranges and studying my Pashto lesson book.

He finished and I asked him, as I had many times that day, to call Abdullah to tell him that we were in Jalalabad, waiting.

I had never met Abdullah, a member of the Taliban, but now I was going to live with him and his men. In September I had gone to a friend, a parliamentarian, who had worked with Yunus Khalis in the 1980s and told him what I wanted to do. He advised me not to go. It was far too dangerous. We shared iftar over a series of evenings outside on a lawn with various Afghan officials. One night my friend introduced me to another parliamentarian called Mullah Malang, who had been a famous mujahideen commander in the 1980s, under Yunus Khalis. He and I talked quietly, away from the others. I showed him my book, my calling card, with its photographs of Haqqani, Hekmatyar, Khalis, and me. Malang said that he knew a man named Abdullah who could help me. He also told me that Abdullah had killed a man in Jalalabad and had had to flee to the tribal areas, where he had joined the Taliban.

The man Abdullah had killed was Hajji Abdul Qadir, a vice president of Afghanistan, and the brother of Hajji Din Mohammed. (*Hajji* is an honorific and means someone who has gone on a pilgrimage to Mecca, one of the five pillars of Islam.) Abdullah wanted to return to Afghanistan under a reconciliation program, and Malang was helping him. He needed Malang and thus, I felt, would not kill me. I felt warm sitting with Malang, and excited. I was part of the Khalis network, a member of this family. I was a foreigner, an infidel, but I had been here with them when their backs were against the wall, fighting the Soviets. They respected me for this and would help me. I could do this.

I met with Malang many times. I had to keep everything secret. I trusted Malang, and he in turn trusted Abdullah. But I was putting my life in the hands of a man who had killed the brother of my oldest friend in Afghanistan. I hated this and hated myself for doing this to Hajji Din Mohammed.

By the time Daoud and I arrived in Jalalabad on February 12, it had taken four months to arrange this trip. Many men had been involved. It was complicated. Abdullah had sent word the day before to come down from Kabul. He was ready. He would send a man from Pakistan to meet us. But Abdullah's phone had been off all day. It was often like that.

Daoud and I walked outside. A warm, soothing breeze again swept down the street. I glanced at a man with dark skin and long hair sitting on the sidewalk. He and another man had been there all day staring at the sun. A few trucks roared by, and then it was silent. The dark, empty streets were eerie. We walked up to a second-floor restaurant, washed our hands in the sink by the door, and sat at a table. A couple dozen men were sitting at tables or on a *meez* (a platform on which Afghans eat sitting cross-legged), eating or drinking tea. The same incessant music was playing from the televisions, hanging from the ceiling; the same tiresome man with long hair and a pasty face sang of love, and the same three women, in red pants suits and saris, sang and danced in the countryside.

Our waiter came over, holding bread over his arm, like a few towels, told us what they had left for dinner, put down some bread, and called out our order. A young man, carrying a large, round, pounded-out metal tray, brought out chicken soup, a salad of onions, radishes, and herbs, a plate of *quabelli* (rice with raisins, nuts, orange peelings, and a few pieces of boiled meat), and *manto* (meat with sour cream and spices cooked in dough). Daoud began to shovel in the manto. I told him not to eat so much. I couldn't stand it. He was getting too fat. We had an arduous trip ahead of us, and even though I pressed him to do some exercise and get in shape, he didn't care about physical fitness. He was a writer, an intellectual. It was beneath him. I tried to contain my anger. He was the only Afghan I could find who was courageous or naive enough to cross with me into Pakistan. His English translation was also better than anyone else's I had worked with.

He ate a plate of custard for dessert. I gave him most of my quabelli. I, the Puritan, was repulsed but said nothing. We had tea and again discussed the plan. Abdullah would send a man to meet us. We were to cross the border with him and meet up with Abdullah and his men. They would take us to Bajaur Agency and Swat; back out, and then down into Waziristan. I had spoken to Abdullah just once. We couldn't talk in any depth, because of my poor Pashto, and we were afraid of the phones.

I kept thinking that Abdullah was involved in the assassination of Hajji Qadir. It was a big operation, involving many men. I wondered if the ISI had been involved, as people said. If so, I was in way over my head. Furthermore, I didn't want to do this to Hajji Din Mohammed. I was betraying him. This haunted me. I kept thinking about it. But there was no other way for me to cross the border.

I was afraid of everything. When I had gone for a walk that afternoon, I had gone through the bazaar, walked down residential streets, and sat in the park watching young men play cricket. Every minute I watched to see if I passed unnoticed. I knew how to dress, how to walk, how to wash my hands, how to eat, how to look at a man and away. If only I could speak decent Pashto.

On the way back from the restaurant I bought a package of cookies at a small stand and a bottle of water, giving myself away, and returned to our room. Daoud took out a worn paperback titled *Political Thought—from Plato to the Present*, which he had bought in Peshawar. I must teach him every day, and he would teach me Pashto. I couldn't refuse his desire to learn. I talked about Plato and explained that *democracy*, in Greek, means "the rule of man." *Islam* means "submission to God."

"I went to a mosque a few months ago," said Daoud. "The imam said in his final prayer, 'Oh Allah, guide the Americans, the other foreigners, and all those against Islam in Afghanistan. If not, destroy them.' The people all said '*Ameen*.'"

"We too say 'Amen' after praying in church," I said.

"It means 'God accept our prayers,'" he said. "The people don't like President Karzai. They say it is better to be a slave of a master than the slave of a slave. They say that the U.S. is the enemy. It is because people have animosities toward one another. They go to the Americans and say they are Taliban, and the U.S. kills many people. The Americans are dependent upon their translators. The translators take cars, motorcycles, whatever they can, as bribes from those who want jobs with the Americans. They tell the U.S. what to do. They have power over the Americans."

I thought back to an old Afghan friend, who told me, "Americans have a hard time in Afghanistan. They don't realize that Afghans never tell them the truth." This didn't apply to me, I thought. I understood Afghanistan. Daoud gave me a Pashto lesson, and we went to sleep.

Wednesday, February 13

There was still no word from Abdullah. Daoud kept calling him, but his phones were off. Meanwhile, Nazaneen called. She was on her way to India for a week to go to a spa. Did I want to go? She laughed. I told her about traveling down to Jalalabad in 1973 and how Afghanistan had changed. I kept looking for the gentleness and the craziness of the past. It made me sad. Children begged now in the streets, pulling on my clothes, angering me, and breaking my heart. "The horses and the men have become wilder the past twenty-five years," she said. "The whole country has become crazy."

I called Asif Durrani, the chief of mission at the Pakistani Embassy in Kabul, and asked about the ambassador. "He didn't show up at Torkham when he was supposed to," Durrani said. "We don't have any information."

Daoud and I went for a walk, past fruit and vegetable sellers behind their carts, automotive repair shops, and young boys washing cars with river water. We walked down a dirt path to a row of low concrete buildings. A sign said ABDUL HAQ PARK. I thought of Haq, a big, friendly man, also a brother to Hajji Din Mohammed, dead now. Daoud and I sat by the Kabul River practicing each other's language.

"Do you have rivers in America?" he asked. I said yes, we had many of them. I told him I grew up on a river. "How does money come here so quickly from America?" he then asked. I explained to him, again, how an ATM worked. I still couldn't get over the idea of ATMs in Kabul, that city of open sewers, few paved roads, and little electricity.

A Westerner, in jeans and a windbreaker, with sunglasses on his head, came and stood near us talking on a cell phone. He had an Australian or New Zealand accent. He talked casually about crossing into Pakistan. "He thinks we are simple Afghans," said Daoud softly. I said he was a fool, talking openly about crossing the border. The man went back into a room in one of the concrete buildings. We walked past it later. He was with a Western woman and an Afghan man. I couldn't imagine the three of them crossing into Pakistan. We walked slowly back to the city. No one looked twice at us.

We watched the news that night on television. The main story was again about the Pakistani ambassador. The anchor, a woman, wearing a scarf, not showing her hair, said that the Pakistani government had announced that the Taliban had kidnapped the ambassador and wanted to exchange him for Mansoor Dadullah, a famous Talib captured by Pakistan. A reporter interviewed a member of the Taliban. "We don't have him," he said. "The Frontier Scouts and the military took him. It's all a game."

The reporter then interviewed an analyst, who posed all the obvious questions. Why was the ambassador driving through the tribal areas? Why hadn't he flown to Kabul, as he always does? Why did he have only one bodyguard? It was a fraud, the analyst concluded. It was the strange game of the ISI.

Later, I gave an interview via telephone to a CBS radio station in Seattle. The host asked me about training camps along the border. I couldn't say that the Taliban had said they would soon take me to them. I went to bed at eleven o'clock. A few minutes later my phone rang. It was Mullah Malang. I had always been the one to call him; this was the first time he had ever called me. He asked where I was. I said that I was in Jalalabad getting ready to go on a trip. "I advise you not to go," he said. "Finish your work there and return to Kabul." My stomach tightened. Why was he warning me? I had to go. I couldn't turn back now. "The Pakistani army is in the border region hunting for the Pakistani ambassador," he said. "It will be very dangerous for you."

Not one Afghan in Jalalabad, it seemed, believed that the ambassador had been kidnapped. It was all a "drama" orchestrated by the Pakistani government to show America how powerful the Taliban were and to get more money from America to fight them. But Mullah Malang was convinced it was real.

The ambassador was said to have been kidnapped on the main road between Pakistan and Afghanistan, the same road over which traveled most of the fuel and matériel for the United States and its allies in Afghanistan. Like scores of other foreigners, I had taken this winding, two-lane paved road through the tribal areas many times in past years. It was the safe corridor through which everyone traveled. Customs officials, now sitting behind computers at the border, insisted that a Frontier Scout accompany foreigners to Peshawar, the first big city on the Pakistani side. When we arrived, he always waited for baksheesh before he got out of the car. We always gave him some money.

I considered it a business. No one ever took a guard from Peshawar. The road passed through an area with electric power lines, glass windows in houses, and large, modern-looking mud compounds. But I had never traveled off the road. Maybe the Taliban knew he was coming and had captured him quickly.

"It is better if you return to Kabul and go later," said Malang. But I couldn't turn back, not now. I was juggling another trip, but I didn't trust those Taliban. This was the best and most complete opportunity that had come yet. It might not come again.

"What about my interpreter?" I asked. I was not to say anything to him, Malang instructed; he was inexperienced. Again, he advised me to return to Kabul. I trusted Malang but I was uneasy. We ended the call, and I turned on the light.

"I heard your conversation," said Daoud. He squinted. His face looked dark and older. I had never seen this look before. "I am not inexperienced," he said. "I've been working with you for three months now."

"I know," I said.

I took out my notebook. *Trust your instincts*, I wrote. I would turn back. I told Daoud that the next morning I wanted him to call Hajji Din Mohammed and set up a different trip. We would go to Tora Bora, where Osama bin Laden had fought the Americans in 2001, and then we would go back to Kabul. I thought of my book. My manuscript was due in August. It took months to set up a trip. I couldn't wait. I had to go now, but I couldn't. Round and round I went in my mind.

Daoud asked what else Malang had said. I didn't answer for a minute, then I said that Malang had advised me to come back to Kabul. He said there were soldiers everywhere hunting for the Pakistani ambassador. Daoud called Abdullah, and this time he got through. Abdullah said there was nothing unusual and would send his man across to meet us.

I sat there. What was I going to do? Why did that ambassador have to get kidnapped now? I turned off the light and tried to sleep. I kept turning. I felt cold and uneasy.

Thursday, February 14

I woke up early and went for a walk. It was a warm, sunny day, with a gentle breeze. The bazaar was busy, the morning air fresh and clean. Men dusted off their wares, others sat drinking tea; men sat on small stools six inches high, behind large steel woks, four feet in diameter, stirring breakfast. Boys and men sat around the wok eating from plates using their hands or forks.

Abdullah had said that his man would call when he crossed the border. There was still no word from him. I went for a longer walk than usual. Every time I was alone I was happy, with a sense of freedom mixed with fear, walking through the city, looking at the array of colors, smelling the spices piled like small pyramids, always trying to understand people talking, constantly watching to see if anyone looked at me closely. I was still afraid that the Taliban who had come across the border from Chitral to capture me, and the Taliban from Kunar, both north of here, were still looking for me. I was afraid they would emerge from the crowd and take me into an alley and I would disappear.

I went to the Internet café. I sat in a small wood cubicle, wondering what kind of jihadi messages had been sent from here. As I paid my bill, the thin young manager asked where I was from. I smiled. He couldn't figure out my accent. I told him, as I did every time, that I came from Kabul. He and another young man smiled as I put on my shoes and walked out into the street, passing deformed beggars shouting for alms; women in chadari, pulling their children; shopkeepers dusting off cameras and radios from China.

I returned by late morning and sat in our small room reading and talking with Daoud. We then went to a bookstore and Daoud took down a small Koran from a shelf, kissed it, and touched it to his forehead. I bought it. I would take it with me on our trip, if we went, part of my disguise as a pious Muslim. Daoud said I must perform ablutions before touching it. I would have to learn how to wash properly. I wasn't Muslim, but I had to be careful, he told me. "Once you begin to read it you will feel something," he said.

We returned to our room. Daoud hadn't yet called Hajji Din Mohammed. I told him to call him immediately. He did. He said that Hajji Din Mohammed said hi. He was my friend. I trusted him. I wished I had talked to him openly when we had met again a few weeks before, but it was impossible. I wanted to go back to him and ask for help. But I couldn't say anything. I was caught in the middle.

"He will have his son take us to Tora Bora," said Daoud. "It's dangerous up there. I don't know if we should go." He didn't want to go. He had never talked like that before. I ignored him.

A man knocked on our door. He wanted the nightly rent, in Pakistani money. I gave him one thousand rupees, about twenty dollars. The room was expensive, but we had a bathroom and Daoud wanted a heater. An hour later, another man knocked. He had a kilo of oranges for us. A man had come by in a land cruiser and said to deliver them to this room number.

Daoud told me to lock the door behind him and went outside with the delivery man. I didn't know if he was overly paranoid or knew things I didn't know. He returned a few minutes later. He wouldn't accept the oranges. He told the manager, who said he would look into it. We must be careful. I thought it was an innocent mistake, but Daoud, who saw a conspiracy in everything, was somber. He was my fixer, my guide, and my interpreter. I had to trust him.

Friday, February 15

I woke up and went outside onto the walkway. It was another warm sunny day, with a tinge of cold in the air. My mind was turning. What was I going to do?

Daoud woke up later, and we had breakfast. He said that he wanted to go to Friday prayers with his family. I didn't know that he had any family members in Jalalabad. I didn't like being left alone, but I wanted to see if I could be alone with no one I knew nearby. I said he could go. He left and I went back out for a walk. It was Friday, the Muslim Sabbath, and most of the shops were closed. The streets were empty. I was anxious. I went again to the Internet café, grateful that it was open and that I could check my e-mail.

I returned to the guesthouse and ate lunch. The waiters were aggressive, asking where I was planning to go. One grabbed my phone and made a call. Who was he calling? I was alone and felt vulnerable. I went for another walk, through a part of the bazaar that was open. Men sat in front of hammers and saws, cans of paint, and bags of cement. I crossed a dirt road, went through an open gate, and entered an olive grove.

An imam was preaching over a loudspeaker. There were men on their knees crowded together in the Amir Shaheed Mosque, in front of which lay the tomb of Hajji Qadir, and hundreds more were outside sitting in the dirt. They began to pray. I took off my *patoo*, the wool shawl that men wear, pray on, sleep under, eat on, and use as a towel after ablutions, and placed it on the ground in the olive grove and tried to pray with them. This was a dangerous thing to do, but I wanted to see if I could pass. I didn't feel anything. I looked around to see if anyone was watching. Four teenagers had put their patoos down next to me. Would they notice that I was a foreigner and didn't know what I was doing? I was nervous. I knelt down.

I had tried to pray or sat in mosques in Cairo, Istanbul, Mashad, and other places, even in Kabul, in deserts and mountains around the world, but never in the United States, curious, searching, always hoping that God, in some way, would appear, but nothing ever happened. But this was different. The boy next to me looked over, and so did the boy next to him. I found myself praying, in a vague way, to the God of my youth. I prayed for my safety even though I thought I no longer believed in God. Then I picked up my patoo and walked back into the bazaar. No one followed me.

I passed through a crowd of about fifty men. Someone was selling cell phones from a cart. I was afraid someone would discover that I was a foreigner. I left them behind and reached the main street and breathed easier.

Daoud called to say that Hajji Din Mohammed's son had called. It was Friday, and he couldn't find anyone to take us today to Tora Bora. Then Daoud called again to report that Abdullah's man had called. He had crossed the border and would be here in one or two hours. I wrote in my notebook, *It looks like we are on. We shall see.*

I returned to the room. Daoud was there, with Abdullah's man, earlier than I had expected to see him. I had met this man before, back in September, shortly after I had met Mullah Malang. Sami, my first interpreter, and I were still working together. Sami had called Abdullah, who had agreed to send his man over immediately to plan a trip into the tribal areas. Sami and I had come down to Jalalabad to meet with him.

It was early afternoon and about ninety degrees, and I was tired from fasting. Sami and I were sitting on plastic chairs on the small lawn under a large pine tree in the front of our hotel when a car drove slowly up the dirt path and stopped. A man in his late forties got out and walked toward us. He was wiry, my height, with a dark beard, wearing a *pakool,* a flat, wool cap, and a simple, off-white *jamay,* the pajama-like clothes that Afghans and Pakistanis wear. I too wore a jamay and a pakool.

We shook hands. His name was Razi Gul. I looked at him nonchalantly, but closely, as he did me. He had a decent, almost kind look about him. He didn't look like a fighter, but Abdullah was a Talib, and so would this man be. He and Sami talked. I couldn't understand the conversation. They kept talking, going on and on, as Afghans do.

Sami turned to me and said, "He is ready to go today."

I perked up. So quickly, so easily? We can cross the border?

"Abdullah is ready," said Razi Gul. "We will have to walk about three hours in the mountains. We will take food and water, because the walk is hard and we will have to break our fast." During Ramadan, the very young, the sick, pregnant women, and travelers are allowed to break the fast. "We will go for a few days. Another time we can go on a longer trip."

I looked at him, and at Sami. I was filled with energy. "Let's go," I said. I was excited about climbing into the mountains, going where no Westerner had gone alone in years, of going deep into the heart of the Taliban. I wondered how long I could go without food and water. I would push it. It would be like running a long, hard race.

Sami looked straight at me. His eyes were cold. "No," he said, shaking his head. Something was up. "You can do it. You can do anything, but I am too fat. I don't want to walk during Ramadan. I won't go."

He was angry. His comment that I could do anything showed it. I lost my energy. I couldn't force him. I could never ask anyone to do something dangerous if he didn't want to.

"We are ready to go at any time," said Razi Gul. "We are doing this in friendship. You are Mullah Malang's friend. We will take you across the mountains and protect you."

We shook hands and he left. I watched him, with a sense of fear, as he walked down the path through the trees. That was five months ago.

But now it was comforting to see him in our guesthouse. Razi Gul and I shook hands, a bit like old friends. His were rough, a farmer's hands. Mine were soft and urban.

I asked where he had just come from. He said Landi Khotal, the end of the rail line, the last town before the border. It was also where Pakistan said its ambassador had been kidnapped. I asked if the Pakistani army was all around there, or if he had any trouble crossing the border.

Razi Gul brought his hand up and flicked his wrist as Pashtuns do when they want to dismiss a thought. "There are always soldiers around," he said. "There are no more than usual. It is all a game. So is the election. If there was a real election, there would be no Musharraf. It is all in the hands of the army."

Malang was misinformed. There was no problem. Or was he warning me against something else? He couldn't talk on the phone.

Daoud said he had to go out. An hour later someone knocked at the door. A rough bulky man, with short hair and a round face, looked at me closely and asked for Daoud. Razi Gul talked to him. I called Daoud and told him to get back here. He returned five minutes later. The man at the door was the driver for Hajji Din Mohammed's son. He had come to see us about going to Tora Bora. A man tied to Abdullah and a man tied to Hajji Din Mohammed were in my room. It was dangerous and wrong. My allegiance was to Hajji Din Mohammed, not Abdullah. I had to make a decision. Where was I going to go: Tora Bora or Pakistan? I turned to Razi Gul. How long would we be gone?

"Three to five days, at the most," he told Daoud. I could go to Tora Bora when I returned.

"Okay," I said. "Let's go." I shook hands with the driver and told him I'd see him soon. He left. Shortly thereafter Ahmed returned, and that night we all—Ahmed, Razi Gul, Daoud, and I—drank tea, ate oranges, and watched a television drama. A young couple married and had a child. They farmed a small plot of land. The man's older brother coveted the land. He poisoned his younger brother and told his wife that he wanted to marry his brother's wife. She was angry, but there was nothing that she could do. This was Pashtun society.

The killer went to his brother's widow, but she pushed him away. He threatened her with a knife while her baby cried in a cradle next to them. He tried to force himself on her. She broke away and ran down to a riverbank. She talked to her child and to her dead husband and waded out into the water. Her shawl lay floating on the surface.

"That is Pashtunwali," said Ahmed. I felt darkness in the room.

I first came in contact with Pashtunwali in 1973 when I went to visit a Kuchi camp near Kabul. A man invited me into his tent, his home, and his wife, unveiled like all nomad women, walked barefoot, gracefully, in a dress, to the back to get glasses and sugar for tea. I sat with them and their children in the late afternoon. I was their guest.

To be a good host is a form of *milmastia*, or hospitality, one of the main tenets of Pashtunwali, a detailed and demanding code that goes back thousands of years, governing law and order in a hard, warrior society. *Wali* means "the code," or "the way," in Pashto. It can also mean "ism," in English, as in Pashtunism. *Pashtunwali* means "the way of the Pashtuns." It applies no matter where Pashtuns live in the world, but it is especially sacred among the isolated men of the tribal areas, men who have never been conquered or taxed.

Since December 2001, when Osama bin Laden supposedly fled Tora Bora for the tribal areas, virtually all the terrorism experts, intelligence analysts, commentators, journalists, politicians, government officials, newspaper pundits, and editorial page writers around the world always refer to the tribal areas as a "lawless" region. Either they know little or they are lying. Pashtunwali is as strict a code as any.

In brief, the main tenet of Pashtunwali is honor. All other tenets—hospitality, revenge, right of refuge, inheritance, marriage, divorce, and all forms of punishment—stem from honor. It goes to the heart of what it means to be a Pashtun. A man has no tolerance for anyone who attacks his personal, family, or tribal honor.

All men must tell the truth, for to lie is a form of cowardice. A man must protect to the death someone seeking refuge with him. Pashtunwali demands blood vengeance, contradicting the Koran, which states that a man must not kill another Muslim. A man must never let an insult go unpunished. Sharia, or Islamic law, on the other hand, is interested in arbitration, settling a dispute, paying blood money for murder rather than killing the murderer, and restoring stolen property rather than punishing the thief.

All men are equal under Pashtunwali, and noble, but if a man looks at a woman with the slightest slant, demeaning her honor, it is grounds for murder. Rarely is a woman ever disgraced or molested, nor is she considered equal to a man. Courtship and romantic love are forbidden. A man marries his father's brother's daughter. A man and woman who elope lose respect. The family can retrieve its honor and status only if they kill the elopers. The woman must die first. Nowhere in the world are they safe. Male and female are stoned or buried alive. Under Sharia, adultery must be witnessed by four people. Under Pashtunwali, a rumor can end a woman's life.

Razi Gul found a television station with music and dancing. I was surprised that he watched it. Daoud had told me that Razi Gul didn't get a chance to listen to music or watch dancing where he lived. He was our guest and could do what he wanted. I asked Razi Gul if he trusted the men who were going to take us. "All the men are trustworthy," he said. "Will they betray us? I don't know.

If they do, our heads go first and then yours." He played with a toothpick in his mouth. "Abdullah is upset that he had to ask for money," he said. "We could have done this for free during Ramadan, but now it costs money. These things should be done in friendship."

I had sent three thousand dollars, over a period of weeks, to Abdullah to "pave the way," and I was still upset about it. "Abdullah has become greedy. Do not give him any more," Mullah Malang said when I told him about the payments. In the 1980s, the mujahideen were happy to have a journalist come with them. They were waging a noble religious war, against the invasion of the Russian infidels. They wanted the world to know of their struggle. Things were different now. After 9/11, the United States poured billions of dollars into Afghanistan and Pakistan to defeat al-Qaeda and the Taliban. Every Afghan, even children, seeing so many become so wealthy, now wanted money, too.

"Mullah Malang and Abdullah know the weight of the other," said Razi Gul. "Abdullah wants to come back to Afghanistan and needs Malang. Malang told him to help Mr. Jere." This was his incentive to protect me. It wasn't just my money.

Daoud took my hand and traced the numbers 81 and 18, in Arabic, in the lines in my palm. There were ninety-nine names of God in Islam. He was the omnipotent, the merciful, the kind, and ninety-six other names. It made me uncomfortable that Daoud was acting so religious.

I laid out on my cot what I would take with me the next day: a digital camera, a film camera, a small video camera, two notebooks, a few pens, reading glasses, a sweater, an extra jamay and pair of socks, the Koran, prayer beads, called *tesbah,* and my *maswok,* a small branch, the size of a thick pencil, used by pious Muslims as a toothbrush. Muhammad is said to have used maswok. I gave the rest of my clothes to Daoud. He would take them and my pack to his family in Jalalabad. He said he would bring his father over to breakfast tomorrow. "I want him to see this man"—he nodded toward Razi Gul—"in case I disappear," he said.

Razi Gul asked what I thought of death. "We believe that after you die there is a Day of Judgment," he said. "What do you think?" I was silent. I didn't want to discuss this, not now, but I didn't want to alienate Razi Gul. "We believe that if a U.S. or other soldier comes here, we must kill him," he went on. "But Mr. Jere comes with a notebook. We believe, according to the Koran, that we must not harm even a piece of paper." It appeared that Razi Gul was indeed a member of the Taliban.

I said I understood that Abdullah was involved in some way in the death of Hajji Qadir. Razi Gul didn't blink. "It is true," he said. "I will explain it later." I wasn't worried what he thought. He would know that Mullah Malang told me. He wanted to talk about other things. "The Prophet," he said, meaning Muhammad, "saw a funeral procession one day and cried. 'Why are you crying?' someone asked. 'Someone has died, and we have not preached to him and brought him to Islam,' he said. You, Mr. Jere, are here to study the Pashtuns. There are a lot of bad things about the Pashtuns, bad traditions and bad habits. But, as Muslims, this world for us is useless. This building is nothing. For us the only thing that counts is the hereafter and Judgment Day.

"Bush is powerful. He is the head of a superpower, but he cannot run away from death. When the time comes he will have to face it. Everything we do now is for the hereafter. If we do not have enough food in this life, we will have sufficient food in the hereafter. I invite you to have these blessings." I thanked him and told him I would think about what he said. I didn't dare tell him to be quiet. I didn't like this talk and felt trapped, but there was nowhere to go.

He continued: "God said we need fire on Earth. He told an angel to ask an angel from Hell to bring a date made of fire. The angel said this date would destroy the whole world. The pit would do the same. So would a grain of wheat. It is greater than all the nuclear power in the world and all the arms. That is what Hell is like. It is my duty as a Muslim to warn you of the Day of Judgment."

I said I understood. I did.

Many older men had preached to me in my youth about the Day of Judgment, about the eternal fire of Hell, that the only thing that counted was what I did for God, and how I must prepare for eternity. I understood that Razi Gul had to preach to me, out of duty, but I still wanted the conversation to end. I hated it. Razi Gul said the heap of a body—the grave—was a house of Heaven or Hell. I nodded. He had listened to music and watched women dancing on television, but this was his other side. I knew it well. "You need help to cross the border," he said, "but after death you will be alone. You will have no mother, brother, sister, or father to help you. You will be alone."

Saturday, February 16

I went one last time to the Internet café, on the second floor of a concrete building, entered the room, took off my shoes, and a young man pointed me to number six. I sat on a plastic chair in a narrow wood cubicle, in my bare feet, like the other men around me, started the computer and waited, listening to the other men around me talking. I was happy here normally, communicating with the outside world, but today I was on edge.

I waded through the e-mails, and then I saw one from my niece Sarah, asking if she and two friends could stay in my apartment in New York in June. "We're going to Spain," she wrote. "It's a coming-of-age thing." I felt warmth spread through me. Already she was graduating from high school. I wrote back and told her that someone was renting it, but I would work something out.

I rushed back to the hotel for breakfast. It was 9:00 a.m. Razi Gul was there, drinking green tea. Daoud's father, heavyset, hunched over, with white hair and a small, trimmed white beard, was eating a plate of kababs, with bread and salad. Daoud said his father was about fifty-two years old. He looked eighty. He nodded and looked at me now and then as he ate. He didn't smile. He was sizing me up. I tried to be upbeat so that he wouldn't be afraid. I would take care of his son.

I felt sorry for him. He was poor and no longer working. When I gave money to Daoud he said that he sent it to his family. I realized that I was helping to support his father. I thought again of what Daoud had said: "My father is living in darkness. He beat me for studying English. My life has been hard. My father thinks I should only study the Koran."

Ahmed came in and gave me a solid hug. His arms and shoulders were hard. We exchanged greetings, smiling. It was good to see him. "*Andawal*," he called me again, as he sat down, "a true friend." We sat drinking tea, talking quietly. I looked casually around the room, wondering who we knew in the restaurant and who might be watching us. Bearded, turbaned men sat at tables or cross-legged on the meez, eating kababs or rice pilaf, or drinking tea, talking, laughing, smoking cigarettes, and chewing tobacco. One man sat with a girl of about ten or twelve. She ate quickly, shyly stuffing rice in her mouth. Her face was dirty, and her fingernails were painted. I hoped it was his daughter or granddaughter and not his wife.

It was getting close to ten o'clock, late in the day to begin a trip. It was strange. Almost every other time I had gone on a trip in Afghanistan, we left early in the morning to get where we were going before dark. Now the men ordered kababs, bread, and salad for the trip, so we wouldn't have to stop in a village. There were no places to eat in the mountains. As the waiters wrapped the food in newspapers, a waiter asked if we were going to Kunar. We didn't answer him.

Daoud wanted to take his father to a taxi and told me to give him my cell phone and charger. He would take care of them for me. I put them on the table and immediately felt naked without them. I could no longer communicate with the world. The father came around and shook my hand. I was responsible now for his son. I was taking him deep into the tribal areas.

They left, I paid the bill, and Razi Gul, Ahmed, and I walked outside and up a flight of steps to the top floor and unlocked the padlock to our room. Fifteen minutes later Daoud returned. He had bought a new shirt, which he took out from its wrapper, and then he took out a pair of elastic braces for his arms and ankles.

I tried not to laugh as Daoud sat on the floor, slid the braces on, and patted his ankles. He smiled. He was ready to go. For months I had been trying to get him to do some exercise, and now these things. We shared the last of our oranges, and Ahmed left to get the car. Daoud took out two plastic bags that he had bought in the bazaar, and we put our gear in them. I threw my patoo around me. We were ready. We took separate flights of stairs to the street to find Ahmed standing by his car. The street was crowded. It was warm out. I glanced around, wondered if anyone was watching or following us, climbed in quickly, and we drove away. This was it. We were going. I was scared and excited.

We drove west for a hundred yards, made a quick U-turn, and headed east on the main, paved, two-lane road toward Pakistan, a road I had taken many times. We passed the large U.S. military base, at the airport. Osama bin Laden had landed here when he returned from Sudan in 1996 and stayed near Yunus Khalis. I barely glanced at it.

We drove for close to an hour, past villages, with rows of low baked-mud buildings and men in turbans, walking or sitting, sharing tea. We came to a check post where men in black T-shirts, fatigue pants, and black boots, holding black M-4 U.S. rifles, were stopping cars. It was the Afghan antidrug Criminal Justice Task Force. The men waved us on. We went slowly over speed bumps and through police check posts. The men wore the same baggy, gray wool uniforms as the police wore thirty-five years ago. We kept going. There were palm trees, eucalyptus trees, and more villages, and then the land opened up and it was rocky and treeless. We were approaching the border. Ahmed turned onto a bumpy dirt track northeast, through a small village and onward past people walking toward us.

We passed an Afghan border post. It looked like a crumbling stone fortress. A policeman, standing on a turret, was throwing rocks at two other policemen and laughing. They didn't pay any attention to us. An Afghan flag fluttered in the breeze. We drove for a few miles and stopped in a grassy cove. High rocks rose in front of us. The land was silent. There was a baked-mud house nearby. We were near a small village. We got out, and I walked to a tree, the only one nearby. I could hear a bird sing. I took a deep breath. *Let's go,* I said to myself. I turned and came back and gave Ahmed my passport and other identification, as we agreed I would do.

Daoud told me to give him one thousand rupees for gas. I took out a blue and white Pakistani note from my pocket and gave Ahmed the money. His eyes were watery. He gave me a gentle, embracing hug, which he had never done before, said something I didn't understand, and kissed me on the cheek. No Afghan had ever kissed me before. I realized that what I was about to do was very dangerous.

We left Ahmed and walked north. Razi Gul was in the lead, carrying one of our plastic sacks. I was in the middle. Daoud, carrying the other sack, was behind me. I was filled with energy; we were on our way. I wore Afghan clothes. My beard was long. I had nothing on me that identified me as an American except an old pair of Timberland shoes. It was sunny, warm, and quiet. The air was clean. I breathed deeply. I was happy to walk after having been cooped up in Jalalabad for four days.

We turned east and kept walking on dirt and grass, gradually upward, climbing now. We hiked up a hill and came to a mud compound. A tall, hefty, bearded man, wearing a white skullcap and heavy patoo, stood in the doorway holding a rifle. He hugged me. "Welcome," he said, in English. His name was Abdul Samad. He looked to be about forty years old.

We entered a courtyard, where a young man sitting on a cot stuck out his hand. "Pashto only," said Samad, under his breath. We entered a *hujra*, a communal guest room, a part of every Pashtun village, dark and with carpets and a few cots on the dirt floor. A man was praying. Samad handed me a pan of water. I took a drink. The man finished praying, and we walked back outside and out another door, where a small white car was waiting, its engine running. It was sitting on a paved road. Now I knew we were in Pakistan because there are no isolated paved roads in Afghanistan. Daoud, Abdul Samad, and I got in the backseat. Razi Gul sat in front, on the left side, with the driver on the right, in the British style, as they did in Pakistan. Razi Gul held a rifle and wore a bandolier and an ammunition belt. Someone must have handed them to him when I wasn't looking. He talked casually with the driver. We drove for a few miles and stopped. Samad got out and asked me to join him. We walked away from the automobile.

"Never speak English in the car," he said. I saw power lines overhead. We were definitely in Pakistan. I wondered why we stopped here. "We are now in Pakistan," he said, as if reading my thoughts. I asked who was in charge here. "The Pakistani army patrols in the mountains sometimes," Samad replied.

I asked if the Pakistanis were friends or enemies. He said, "They are Pakistanis. We are Afghans." Then why did he live here? He said they had animosities with people in Afghanistan. He would explain it later. They were in exile, and they weren't. It was complicated. He told me to take pictures, but not to let the driver see me. Samad pointed to a village across the Kabul River, which flowed by on our left. It was in Afghanistan. This side was Pakistan.

"There are four heroin factories in the village," he said. "U.S. soldiers come down there sometimes. Once they came to disarm the village. They took everyone's rifle away. One twelve-year-old boy refused to give up his rifle. He pointed it at a U.S. soldier. 'Your father cannot take this from me,' he said. The soldier was nervous." Samad smiled. He liked telling this story. The boy was Pashtun. He was a warrior. It was in his blood. Later, village elders got the boy to give up his rifle.

We drove a few more miles and stopped again. It was strange; I wasn't a tourist. The land was rocky and barren, like the American Southwest in summer. Samad pointed across the river. The Americans were going to build a base there, but Pakistan was planning to bring in the Taliban to destroy it.

"What do you mean?" I asked.

There were good Taliban and destructive Taliban, he said. This area was where Emil Khan Mohammad and Dar Khan Afridi defeated the British in the nineteenth century. They were prominent warriors. Their names were in history books. I asked why this tradition was so strong to fight outsiders. "Pashtunwali," he said. "They were Pashtuns." He too was proud. The Pashtuns were a warrior race; they had been living for thousands of years in this hot, rocky expanse; for only a brief span of a hundred years had the infidel British been here. The British were rough. "Butcher and Bolt" they called their policy here. Even today, Pashtun mothers say to their children, "Be good, or the British will get you."

We turned off the road and took a bumpy, dusty track up into the mountains and stopped again. The land was empty and silent. There were no villages, no electric lines, no roads—only rocky, jagged mountains, plains, and valleys in the hot, dry heat. The wind came up and dust swirled around. This was Mohmand Agency, created by Pakistan in 1947, named for the Mohmand tribe, half of whom lived in Afghanistan. The Mohmands believe that they are the descendants of the followers of Muhammad. Afghan kings ruled them from Kabul, until the British drew the Durand Line.

I asked if there were any Taliban here. Samad said yes, but not right here. What did he think of the Taliban? He said he liked them.

I stared out at the land, feeling the hot, dry wind in my face. Heat waves hovered in the distance. British soldiers were tough to cross this desert on horseback. We drove down and came again to the Kabul River and stopped at a village. Samad went into a house for a minute, and then we walked through farmland and high brush near the water. A man in his twenties sat in a rowboat, hidden in a cove. He pulled on a cord and an outboard motor sputtered softly. As we crossed, Samad told me to take his picture. I was trying to blend in and he kept asking me to take pictures. It was strange. I thought it was dangerous here. He would make me stand out. No, he said, he was helping me with my story. I was grateful. He was my guide; he would protect me. He was Pashtun.

We disembarked on the other side of the river, which at this point was wholly within Pakistan. We walked through a poppy field. The plants, only a few inches high, were in perfect rows, each plant a foot apart. Small boats came down the river, riding low in the water, like canoes laden with goods in the Amazon. They were smuggling wheat into Afghanistan. Samad told me to take their pictures.

For a great many years smuggling has been one of the main sources of income here: guns, cars, drugs, and now wheat. There is little land to cultivate. This is one reason why tribes fight with one another. They know, within feet, where their land ends. We walked along a sandy beach and then Samad, in the lead, stopped, and Razi Gul told him which way to go. I didn't like this. Samad clearly wasn't from here. Where were the twenty men Abdullah had promised? I had to trust Samad. I was Abdullah's guest, and he was Abdullah's representative.

Samad found the path, and we climbed north up into the desolate, rocky mountains. I liked the exercise and that we were walking in the tribal areas. My body, like a car engine, had been idling too long. For three hours we hiked. We passed three boys, with two donkeys, carrying bags of wheat toward the river, a few men now and then traveling south, but otherwise nobody. There were no trees, no streams, no villages.

Around midafternoon, we reached a trickling stream in a gully and stopped. My bodyguards and Daoud performed their ablutions, spread out their patoos, and prayed. I washed my face and hands and waited. We ate our salad, kababs, bread, and chutney. It was a picnic. *It is a warm Mediterranean afternoon*, I wrote in my notebook. I had never stopped like this before with Afghans. It was strange to go so slowly. Two boys came up the path. We said hello. They responded and rushed forward, almost running.

"You are very brave to come here," said Razi Gul. "No outsiders come here. You are also *spin gier*"—a gray beard. It was a sign of respect.

"No," I said, smiling. "*Nim spin gier.*" I was "half gray beard." I was only half old. Razi Gul smiled. "*Nim spin gier.*" He liked that.

The four of us sat in a circle, eating. The food was delicious; it always was outside, and especially here. They had come this way to protect me, Razi Gul said. There was no Pakistani army here, only thieves and Taliban.

We set out again, Samad taking the lead. Razi Gul and I followed. Daoud, tiring now, lagged behind.

"All we need is for you to become Muslim, and we will get you a wife and there will be no need for you to ever return to America," said Razi Gul.

I smiled as we walked. I said we'll see.

"*Inshallah*," he said, God willing.

We descended through rolling, dusty hills. Three old men walked toward us. A skinny old man with a wide smile wanted to talk. "Once I had a donkey, once we had food, but now I don't have enough to eat," he said. I wanted to give him money, but that would start a conversation. Samad told me to take his picture. I did, reluctantly. I said thank you and good-bye to the old man, hoping he wouldn't notice my accent. We came down into a valley, and a village appeared in front of us. A group of boys and men sat in a dirt circle by the path talking, a teapot beside them. We greeted them and kept going. I was afraid they might notice me.

We walked through the village, called Tatra. It was like entering the Stone Age. There was no electricity and no running water. Some houses were made of baked mud, others of branches. I discreetly took a few pictures. I didn't see anyone, but I knew people were watching. Each man would have a rifle. There was a canyon wall to the south with a row of caves thirty or forty feet high, smaller versions of those in Bamiyan where the giant Buddhas once stood. The caves went back only a few yards. There was no one living in them.

We continued north, the sun on my left, climbing back up into the mountains. Two women approached us in blue chadaries, thrown back showing their faces. They carried loads of branches on their heads, each one holding her load in place with one hand. They stopped and turned away. We passed silently. I looked back, a dangerous thing to do. If any man saw me looking at his women, he could shoot me. The women were watching us. They had noted something different about us. I walked on, nervously.

We climbed upward. The mountain was covered with a herd

of about a hundred black goats, searching for what grass they could find, blending in, like natural camouflage, with the black rocks, like volcanic ash that had hardened all around us. I asked how much a goat cost. Razi Gul thought for a minute. He said about three thousand rupees, sixty dollars. We walked in single file. For a few minutes I took the lead, but we were going too slowly. Daoud was now almost a hundred yards back. Samad sat down on a rock and waited. I had never seen an Afghan wait like this before. He was so casual. I thought this was a dangerous area. I wanted to get to our destination before nightfall.

The boys with the donkeys, who had been going the other way, had unloaded their sacks and now caught up with us coming back. One boy, about fourteen, wearing a skullcap, said we could put our sacks on their donkeys. "How about one of us?" asked Samad.

We waited, and Daoud finally caught up with us and collapsed on the ground. We waited a few minutes longer for him to recover and walked on, the boys and their donkeys bringing up the rear. We came to a plateau and waited again, as the boys caught up with us and Daoud followed slowly behind. At Samad's urging, Daoud climbed on a donkey. It quickly trotted forward. Laughing, Samad told me to take Daoud's picture. Daoud fell off and we all laughed. I put my camera away. "Come on, let's go," I said. I didn't feel comfortable playing. I took the lead again, and we began to climb higher up into the mountains. Samad took over. It wasn't right for me to lead. I was the oldest, and their guest, the one whom they were charged to protect. "*Nim spin gier,*" said Razi Gul behind me, smiling. He made me relax.

I asked Samad who the Taliban leader was in this area. He said his name was Shah Sahib and that the Pakistani government supported his training center. Other training centers were supported by donations from people like him, the poor, and anyone else they could force to pay. He sounded now like he wasn't a member of the Taliban.

We passed a tall, strong young man, about seventeen years old, leading a donkey, holding a baby goat gently in one hand. "It was just born," the young man said. We kept climbing. It was getting harder now. Daoud kept stopping. We hiked for about a half hour, and Samad sat down again, his rifle on his lap, watching the sun move close to the mountains in the west. Twice he stopped to rest, yet he didn't seem tired. We had been walking for five or maybe six hours.

I looked at the land and the canyons around us. Everything was rugged, rust-colored in the fading sun, starkly beautiful, jagged, and empty. Behind us, down below, we could hear one of the boys calling to someone. His voice echoed through the canyons. It was warm and pleasant and again silent, deathly silent. The boy called again, his voice like a plaintive cry for help. It was eerie. I looked around and there was no one.

Samad said that one of the boys and his donkey were far behind somewhere. I filmed the mountains, watching the sun move closer to the horizon. I was getting worried. Daoud struggled up the path far below us. We had to wait for him. Time moved differently here than in the West. We couldn't rush. I thought of Abdullah and his compound, dinner, and safety.

I asked Samad how many children he had. He said he had one wife and six children. He also said that he was about twenty-eight. I had never met an Afghan who knew his exact age. His father, Mohammed Nabi, had four wives. He went with a different one each night. Samad loved his one wife. That was enough. Razi Gul reached us and sat down. "*Nim spin gier,*" he said, smiling broadly. Already I liked him. I was strong and could still push it. I loved climbing in the mountains. "*Nim spin gier,*" he said again. Down below the boys were calling and whistling. The echo bounced off the rocks. Then it was silent.

Daoud caught up with us and fell on the ground again. I told him to take off the elastic braces and put them in the sacks, both of which Razi Gul was now carrying. We sat for a while talking quietly, waiting for Daoud to recover, and then we were silent. The sun was sinking and about to touch the mountains. We continued climbing.

The land leveled off a half hour later. We followed the dirt path around a bend and walked along a grassy, sloping hill. Razi Gul was in front now, then Samad, then me, with Daoud at the rear. We were ten yards apart. The sun was behind us, almost gone now. We were walking easily. I looked ahead. We were in a valley. There was grass, and it was comforting. I wasn't tired. We walked on.

I looked up and saw a black turban appear from behind a rock on the hill in front of us. I froze. *Oh, my God. Oh no. It's not possible.* I stared in disbelief. A tall, lanky man came up running, shouting, jumping over another rock, holding a rocket-propelled grenade launcher, and other men followed behind him. It was the Taliban.

They came swarming down the mountain, spreading out, shouting, *"Kenna, kenna!"*—Get down, get down!—holding their rifles and rocket launchers high, like Indians attacking in an old Western movie. *I'm dead*, I said to myself. *I'm dead.*

A small man was in the lead, holding a walkie-talkie and coming toward me. All my energy and strength disappeared. They stood around us, at least a dozen men, mostly in black turbans, like Muhammad wore, supposedly, when he went into battle, with rifles and grenade launchers, all pointed at us. I didn't move. I was about to die. I felt weak, hopeless, frustrated, and trapped. I couldn't run. I couldn't do anything. I was dead. I was going to die.

A man in white with a wide black turban stood a few feet away from me, pointing a rocket-propelled grenade launcher at my head. His eyes were black and filled with hate. I couldn't look at him. Razi Gul was up front sitting on the ground twenty yards away, facing me. A man grabbed his rifle with one hand and threatened to beat him with a rifle that he held in his other. Razi Gul's eyes were afraid. He looked old, weak, and scared.

I saw on my right, slightly up the hill and ahead of me, Abdul Samad crouched down beside a rock. I assumed he had taken cover there to fight. No one had fired. A man stood over him, threatening to beat him with his rifle butt. Behind me, below the path, the leader, about five foot seven, was interrogating Daoud. I stood there, feeling naked and scared. I was trembling. I took off my patoo and vest, in which I had my notebook and cameras. I wanted to hide them. Then I sat on the ground, waiting. A gray-haired man, with a rifle on his back, knelt down and went through one of our bags. He took out a roll of film. I said it was for my camera. I felt relaxed. I was still alive. He nodded and put the film back. It was strange, this acknowledgment between him and me. He didn't seem to hate me.

Daoud was standing, looking down. His face was dark. I couldn't tell if he was afraid or distraught or what. The leader came toward me. This was it. I saw, behind me, on the path, two of the boys, with their donkey. Their eyes were wide with fear. The leader was angry. He put up his hand to them and they stopped. One of the boys started crying. "*Za*," said the leader, flicking his hand. "Go." A boy pushed the donkey forward. I envied them. They were free. They would tell their mother what had happened. People would know. They would alert Abdullah.

The leader came up to me. I stood up. I felt skinny, naked, and alone. He asked, in Pashto, where I came from. I told him Kabul and then Jalalabad. He asked where I was going. I said I was going to Peshawar. My mouth was dry. I had cottonmouth. I spoke slowly. When I said "Peshawar" I pronounced it *Pesh-hour*, as I had always heard it pronounced. That is the English pronunciation. No one had ever corrected me. I learned later that here it is pronounced *Peck-a-waar*.

"You are not Pashtun," the leader said softly. He frisked me and found the American money I had in one of my pockets. He counted slowly in halting English, peeling the notes back, as if he were peeling a banana. "Eight hundred dollars," he said.

I answered in Pashto. I couldn't let him find out I was American. He clicked his teeth, gave me a disgusted look, and put the money back in my shirt pocket. He didn't keep it. Maybe he was a decent man. I was grasping. Samad said I was from Nuristan, a nearby region of Afghanistan where the people are light skinned and speak a different dialect. (Legend has it that the Nuristanis are the descendants of Alexander the Great's legions.) I didn't speak Pashto, he said. All my language study meant nothing. I had failed.

Two men took my wrists and marched me forward up the path. There were men all around us. I heard a man up on the hill say something. I looked up pretending that I understood him. I knew he was talking in Nuristani. He was in white, wore a black turban, and carried a rocket launcher. It was he who had pointed it at my head. I was in shock. I didn't know what to do.

We walked higher into the mountains, and Daoud collapsed on the ground. "Get up, or we will kill you," said a man. He got up. A minute later, Razi Gul said he wanted to rest and tried to sit down. "If you stop, your head will be over the hill and your body here," said another man. I dreaded what lay ahead. We came to a ridge. They sat me down facing west. I sat cross-legged looking at the light fading. *So this is where I die, on this mountain, in Pakistan.* I thought of my family, especially my father. I kept my head up, waiting for the knife. I could feel myself breathing, waiting for the end. The sun had set, but I could still see light, growing dark, and then someone slowly began to blindfold me. Two men took my patoo and tied my arms. It was quiet. I felt a soft breeze flow over me. Men whispered, and then they were quiet. A man on my left fingered his rifle. It would be any second now. I was facing west, toward my home, my head was still up. They would behead me, or perhaps they would shoot me. I was calm. I kept my back straight. I waited for the knife. The breeze was soothing. It was pleasant, a perfect balmy evening. I felt sad and lonely dying so far away from home. I waited. It was silent.

Two men took my arms, pulled me up, and led me down the mountain. I stumbled forward, walking fast. I fell once, and they pulled me up as we walked quickly downhill. They were strong. A man took my hand. It was strange, a man holding my hand. His hand was strong and callused, but it was comforting. Would they hold my hand and then kill me? I wondered. We kept walking down, and then we stopped and they pushed me down so that I was sitting on flat ground. I heard a car engine running and doors opening and closing.

They pushed me into the backseat of a car. A big man sat on my left. A smaller man—the leader?—got in on my right and put his arm around me. "No problem," he said in English. What did that mean? We drove on a paved road, a dirt road, gravel road, paved road, back and forth, on and on. The car was small, and we were crunched together. The man on my right drew me toward him a bit, and then he took his arm away. The man on my left took my left hand, opened my palm, and wrote "OK?"

I wrote back "OK" and held his wrist briefly. I was fine. I was alive. He took my palm again and wrote "Abdullah" and held my hand tightly. Abdullah would rescue us. I held his hand briefly to signify that I understood. It gave me hope. He wrote something else, which I couldn't understand. He wrote it again. I still couldn't understand. We kept driving. My right leg went to sleep. I struggled to free it but not so much that they would think I was trying to escape. My mind was in a void. It was blank.

We must have driven for an hour and a half. If we were going north, which I felt we were, we would soon be in Bajaur Agency, the next tribal area north in Pakistan. Abdullah would never find us there. We stopped, and I thought someone said *"Teshnab,"* which means "toilet." They pulled me from the car and sat me on the ground. I tried to untie my pants. I heard two men whispering. I retied the cord. They frisked me all over. Were they going to rape me? What were they going to do to me? What kind of torture? They found the eight hundred dollars and the five hundred dollars in Afghan and Pakistani bills that I had in another pocket, and this time they took it. I felt naked. I waited for someone to kill me. I kept waiting.

Men talked all around me. A man whispered in my ear, "Mosulmaan?" Was I Muslim? I began to recite softly the opening sentence of the Kalima, the profession of faith that Daoud and Ahmed had taught me: *La illaha illalaha Muhammad urrasullalah.* There is no god but God, and Muhammad is his messenger. I was nervous and stumbled. I had no right to say this, but I was trying to stay alive. The man joined me, and we recited it together softly. He patted me gently on the shoulder. I felt hope, but I wasn't Muslim. When they found out, they would kill me.

I silently thanked Nazaneen. I was still alive. I heard another car engine and other doors opening and closing. There were two cars now. I was certain of it. Someone pushed me into the backseat of a car. This time I was alone. The hope I had just felt disappeared. We began to climb a mountain. They were taking me to a place to kill me alone. I wondered if they would do it quickly. I wondered how they would kill me.

We were on a dirt and rocky road. The car stopped, and they got out, and the wheels started spinning. We moved forward, spinning again. I smelled oil burning, or was it rubber? Men jumped back in, and again we climbed. Again they got out, got in, and got out again. We were climbing higher. Each time men got out, and it was just the driver and me, it seemed. How could I escape? I could run and disappear into the dark, but where would I go? We kept climbing over dirt and rocks. We stopped, and they pulled me from the car. It was cold, and dogs were barking.

Two men held my arms on either side and led me up a road or pathway and along a wall. I put one hand out and used the wall to guide me. A dog barked viciously a few feet away. A man brought my wrists together, and slowly we climbed a few steps and went through a door and kept walking. I sensed that I was in a compound. We walked along the wall and into a room, and they sat me down on what felt like a cot. A man gently but firmly pushed me down and half covered me with a quilt.

Now what? I closed my eyes. I waited. I almost fell asleep, a form of escape and protection. A half hour or so later a man pulled back the quilt, took my arm, and pulled me, firmly but not too roughly, up into a sitting position. It gave me a feeling of hope. I couldn't see, but I was sensitive to my captors' slightest touch, trying to figure out if it meant that they hated me or if I had a chance to survive.

This was it. He slowly untied my blindfold. I was in a small baked-mud room filled with light from lanterns and flashlights. I was sitting on a rope cot. I saw Daoud, Razi Gul, and Abdul Samad, blindfolded, sitting on cots each against a wall. I sighed gratefully. I was not alone. I looked behind me to see if there was any blood on the wall. Was this a torture chamber? I saw black marks and wasn't sure. I saw chains on the dirt floor on my right. They were tied to a steel stake. It was a prison. I was far away up in the mountains in a Taliban prison in Pakistan.

The leader, now wearing a white pakool instead of a turban, sat next to me. He held a small notebook and pen. The room was filled with riflemen. "Who are you?" the leader asked. "Where do you come from? What is your name?"

I hesitated, and then it came out. "*Za man num* Wilmer Gerald Van Dyk, Junior, *dey*," I said. It was strange that I would say my full name. I almost never did that. I didn't like my name. People laughed at it. A cousin said it sounded rural.

The leader grimaced, trying to pronounce my name and write

it down. "What is your father's name?" another man asked, standing next to me.

For a split second I smiled to myself. My father's name? These men were really isolated. This was deep Pashtun culture, where it was necessary to know a man's father's name, and his grandfather's name, to know who he was, where he fit in society, and what kind of family he came from. These were Taliban. They wanted to create a new world where the equality of Islam overruled rigid, tribal hierarchy, but they were still Pashtuns.

"My father's name is Wilmer Gerald Van Dyk, Senior," I said. I was my father's son. It never dawned on me like this before. I said I was a writer and a journalist. The leader struggled to write this down.

Daoud began to talk, explaining who we were. A man started to hit him. Abdul Samad began to talk. A man stood over him and slapped him around. Samad put up his hands to defend himself.

The leader looked at me hard. Men held their rifles. I couldn't keep up this pretense any more. "I am American," I said. It was out. I said it. A burden lifted. I felt lighter, free, and strong. The leader put down his pen. I sat calmly. They would kill me now. I was dead. But I no longer had to pretend. I felt good.

Daoud tried to talk again. The leader realized that he needed him and said to take his blindfold off. I waited. Would they take me out now and kill me? For a second, it didn't matter. The leader said to take off the others' blindfolds, too. The leader went over and sat next to Daoud. He asked him his name, his father's name, where he was from, and other questions I couldn't understand. Then he sat with Razi Gul and asked similar questions. Then he sat with Samad, who said we had come to see Abdullah. We were going to travel with him. He had arranged our trip and got permission from Shah Sahib, the Taliban commander of Mohmand Agency, to bring a foreigner in.

The leader asked, "Who is this Abdullah?" Samad, Razi Gul, and Daoud explained who he was and my ties to him. The leader took notes, and then he and his men left. We sat on a kilim, a rough carpet without a pile, on the floor. They left a lantern for light. I looked around. There was a rope tied to the chains. There were six cots in our cell. It was about twelve feet by twelve feet. There were rough wood beams across the ceiling and four pillars holding them up. The pillars were beveled. The ceiling was made of branches.

I looked again for dried blood on the walls. There didn't seem to be any. There were two *mogays*, wood pegs, what Daoud called tree nails, on each wall, pieces of round wood, an inch thick, sticking out about eight inches. Men hung their rifles from them. Next to my cot there was a shallow wash pit, about two feet across, against the wall, with a hole, an inch or so wide, that led outside. It was surrounded by a dirt wall a few inches high.

A man I hadn't seen before entered the room, carrying a folding metal-stock Kalashnikov, and told Razi Gul to come with him. Razi Gul put on his sandals and walked outside. My stomach tightened. We waited. We heard a moan. Samad brought his arms up and down as if he was beating someone with a rifle. He shook his head sadly. I looked at the floor. We listened for shouts, cries, or the sound of a man screaming. There was nothing. Twenty minutes later, the door opened and Razi Gul walked through. I was never so happy to see a man. He was alive. He was still alive. He took off his sandals and sat down.

"Did they torture you?" we asked. "Did they beat you? What did they do?" He kept his head down. "They hit me a little," he said. "They said I was working with a foreigner, an infidel. He is a spy. They asked, 'How long have you been working with this man? How long have you been working with this man Abdullah? How much money does the infidel pay you? Who brought you here?'"

They thought I was a spy. I closed my eyes.

The man came back in and told Samad to come with him. Samad stepped into his shoes and went outside. We waited. Razi Gul didn't look at me. I looked closer at the kilim. It was light beige with brown stripes. I looked at the dirt floor underneath the cots, wondering what residue lay under them. Samad returned, and the same man then took Daoud with him. Razi Gul and Samad talked with each other. Samad said they asked him the same questions as they asked Razi Gul. They had hit him at the start, but not much. They asked about Abdullah and how he knew Shah Sahib.

Twenty minutes later Daoud returned. His eyes looked far away. They beat him, too, he said, a little, but he told them that he had done nothing wrong. They asked him the same questions: How long had we been working together? How did we meet? How much did I pay him? "I said you paid me fifty dollars an interview," he said. "This is what you must tell them." Again, he had lied. How many times had I told him not to lie? I wondered what other lies he had told them. I waited, staring at the floor. They didn't call me.

The leader and a half dozen riflemen came back into our cell. We returned to our cots. The men stood in the center. A few held flashlights, giving off an even glow. One man put our two plastic sacks in the center. The leader took out my gear and two cell phones.

"All your things are here," he said. "We are going to investigate you. We will contact Shah Sahib and Abdullah. If you have been invited by Shah Sahib, you will be free to go on your way and to write what you want. If you haven't been invited, we will judge you under Sharia." I all but shuddered. The message was clear. They would judge us as spies and kill us. They took our bags and left, taking the lantern with them.

The room was dark. I sat on my cot waiting for my eyes to adjust. A few minutes later, two men, with short-stock Kalashnikovs, came into the room and stood by the door. One man carried a lantern. "You must wait for the investigation to be completed," he said. "Go to sleep now."

They shut the door and bolted it. I sat on my cot staring in the dark. I was still alive. I would be alive at least until tomorrow. I wondered about the last prisoner who used this cot. Did they torture him? Did they kill him? Where was he now? How long was he here? The room was black. I heard the other men whispering.

"They are all in the room next to us," said Samad. We were quiet. We could hear voices through the walls on my right. If they decided to torture or kill us, Samad said, we had to try to kill them. We first had to kill the two men who had just walked in, take their rifles, go next door, and kill as many as we could. "I can take the first one," said Razi Gul.

I realized that my life had just changed. I would have to help them overpower the two men; the first one was wiry, about Samad's height; the other man was Razi Gul's height, but very solid, a bit hunched over, with thick, dark hair that half covered his ears and an unkempt beard. He wore a dark pakool, dark jamay, and old sandals. Samad would take him.

I would have to help silence them and kill them. Samad and Razi Gul would then burst into the room next door and fire on the others sitting, eating dinner maybe, killing as many as they could. I would stand behind them, pick up a rifle from a dead man, and kill the rest. It was kill or be killed. We would have to kill everyone and then run. We had no choice. I had never thought like this before. My old life had just ended. I closed my eyes. I imagined myself in the next room, grabbing a Kalashnikov on the floor and firing into the men. Where was the safety? I couldn't remember.

My father had taught me how to shoot and clean a rifle. I thought back to when I was in the army in 1969. I was in basic training. We stood holding our rifles above our heads while the drill instructor, standing on a platform in the center, shouted, "Kill, kill,

kill!" I lowered my rifle. I didn't want to kill anyone. It was all different now. I felt cold. America was far away. No one would ever find us here. How could Abdullah find us? I felt lonely. I got under the quilt. I lay there thinking and fell asleep.

Sunday, February 17

I woke up. Someone was coming into the room. It was dark. I had been dreaming and realized where I was. I felt afraid, frustrated, and trapped. I couldn't believe it. I was in a prison in the mountains in Pakistan. How did this happen? I thought I knew what I was doing. How could this be?

I heard a rooster crow. The stocky man from last night, a folding-stock Kalashnikov over his shoulder, brought in two large plastic cans and put them by the door. He went outside, locked the door, and soon returned, carrying two other cans. It was too dark to see clearly. It was morning. I was happy. I was alive. I was still alive. I hadn't woken up happy in years.

The man, now carrying a lantern, woke up Razi Gul, sleeping in a cot against a wall to my left, and talked softly with him. The man put the lantern on the floor and left. It gave off a low orange glow. Razi Gul got up and took a bucket of water and went over to the pit, crouched down, and began to perform his ablutions. It was time for morning prayers.

He finished washing, unfolded a jahnamaz that was lying by a pillar, and began to pray by my cot. Abdul Samad got up, washed, and prayed. They finished and went back to bed. An hour or so later, the same man brought in a small metal teapot and small cups without handles and placed them on the kilim. "*Sheen chai*," he said. Green tea. He took the lantern and left, bolting the door behind him.

Razi Gul, Abdul Samad, and I got up and sat on the floor.

Daoud was still asleep. It was cold, and we huddled together as Razi Gul poured the tea. There was also a cup with small chunks of *goura*, or brown sugar, in it. I took a piece and put it in my mouth and sucked on it, according to custom, and drank the tea. It was delicious, life itself. I hadn't drunk anything since yesterday afternoon. They brought water for ablutions and now tea. We were prisoners—and guests. They were required, as Pashtuns, to treat us well, after which they could take us out and kill us.

"Where is Abdullah?" I asked. "We didn't arrive at his compound last night. He would know by now that something had happened to us. He would come looking for us, wouldn't he?" But how would he know where to look? We were so far away. I felt despair sweep over me. We agreed that we had driven for at least two hours. We were somewhere in the mountains. "*Inshallah*, he will come," said Samad. Yes, God willing. Who were these people who had captured us? They were the Taliban. That was all I knew. What were they going to do with us? We drank our tea silently.

Daoud woke up an hour or so later and joined us. He had a terrible toothache, he said, as he bent over holding the side of his face. I asked how he got this. He wasn't sick last night. He said it had come in the night. He started to moan softly. Samad said that he could fix it for him. He asked for a pen and paper. Daoud took a pen from his vest pocket and tore off a piece of paper from a larger piece he had with him. My pockets were empty. The Taliban had taken everything. I had only the clothes I wore and my maswok.

Samad wrote a verse from the Koran on the paper and folded it up. He told Daoud to put it between his teeth that were painful. Daoud stuck the piece of paper in his teeth.

We went back to our cots and climbed beneath our quilts. They were about a half inch thick. I had slept under similar quilts in other villages. It was winter. An hour or so later the man returned and took the pot and cups. We talked in the dark and slept again.

Toward midday, I guessed, the door opened again, and the same man entered. I could see daylight outside for a second before he shut the door. He carried two small, pounded metal bowls and a cloth under his arm. He was one of the men who had told us to go to sleep. He looked strong. He would be hard to kill. But he had brought us water and tea. He told Samad to take the cloth. Samad opened it and spread it out on the kilim. Inside, there were four round loaves, like large pancakes. Razi Gul took the bread and placed each loaf on the cloth, like place mats. The jailer put the bowls down and left. There were chopped, boiled potatoes in one and lentils in the other.

I asked Daoud about his toothache. He said it was gone. "So the verse from the Koran worked," I said. He and Samad nodded. We each tore off a piece of bread and dipped it in a bowl and used it like a spoon. The food was hot and tasted nutritious.

A half hour later the jailer returned. He stacked the remaining pieces of bread in the center, folded the cloth, took it and the bowls, and left. Razi Gul went to the buckets by the door, poured some water out into a small metal bowl, took a drink, and brought it to us. The water tasted good and refreshing.

"Why did you insist on coming?" Daoud asked me. "Mullah Malang told you not to." He was angry. I too felt the anger rising in me. Yes, I said, I did choose to come here, but it was Daoud's job to protect me. He had told me that it was all arranged. I had put my life in his hands, and he, as a Pashtun, was supposed to protect me.

But I didn't trust anyone. I felt that everyone was trying to take advantage of me. Daoud had listened to me talk on the phone with the woman, Nazaneen. He didn't want to come but, after listening to me, he decided to. He wanted to show me that not all Pashtuns were bad. I had pushed this.

He was right. I had told Nazaneen that I didn't trust anybody. I was living in a world of darkness and intrigue. I was calm, but I was also nervous and scared. Now here we were. I was looking at a possible death sentence. I asked Daoud what good it was to be angry at me. I knew what I'd done. I knew what he was supposed to have done, and didn't do. "You can blame me all you want," I said, "but it doesn't change the fact that we're here."

We spent the afternoon on our cots, our quilts around us, thinking, staring, and occasionally talking. I kept surveying the room. There was a hollowed-out shelf, like a half-finished window cut out from the wall, behind my bed. Two Korans, wrapped in green and black fabric, sat on the lower ledge of the shelf.

Above the shelf was a wood plank, resting on mogays, the wood pegs men hung their rifles from, and on it a black pot, a cloth sack, and an old thermos, all covered with dirt. A pile of branches by the door was next to Razi Gul's cot. There were old quilts rolled up and tied on the two empty cots. Next to Samad's cot was a frosted glass window, covered with dirt, with bars, part of which was broken and covered with wood. It was too dark for us to see one another clearly. Samad took down one of the Korans. He sat cross-legged on his cot, opened it, and began to recite his holy book, a mixture of chanting and singing. He rocked back and forth.

I asked if he was a Qarie, one who had memorized the Koran. He said yes. He would teach me about Islam. He continued chanting. His voice was like a tenor's voice, even higher. That evening the jailer returned with dinner. He brought a lantern so we could see what we were eating. He put the food down and left, and Razi Gul cried. I put my hand on his shoulder. He too was scared.

After we finished eating, again potatoes and lentils, the jailer returned. Daoud asked his name. He said it was Gulob. He picked up our bowls. I said the water was good and asked where it came from. He said from a spring in the mountains; a pipe brought it down to here. Again, I said it was good. He smiled slightly and left. Razi Gul, Samad, and Daoud had used the water to perform their ablutions, sitting on their haunches in front of the pit. Now they prayed again. For Razi Gul and Samad it was their fourth prayer of the day. I sat on my cot, the outsider, to give them room.

Daoud said he thought I should pray. Razi Gul and Samad nodded. They would teach me how. I would be going to school. I would learn all about Islam, to finally understand it. I was in the heart of it now. Razi Gul finished his prayers and returned to his cot. I slowly tried to remember the first words of the Kalima. He corrected my pronunciation, repeating the words until I got them right. *La illaha illalaha . . .* and on and on. He came over and sat on the floor with me. Samad joined him. Slowly, carefully, I nervously went through the motions. I felt that I was leaving myself and the West, and my past, and entering another world.

They showed me how to pray. I had to begin by being pure in thought before God. I then had to clean myself to be pure in body as well. I had to wash, to perform my ablutions, my *wadu*. I was to crouch down on my haunches and, as I did, to say "*Bismillah*" ("In the name of God") and pour water onto my left hand, which I would use to wash my right hand up to my wrist and between each finger. I was to do this three times. Then I was to wash my left hand in the same way, and then my mouth, my nose (cleaning each nostril), my face, my beard, my arms up to my elbows, my head, my ears, my feet up to my ankles, my toes, and finally my private parts.

I stood before the jahnamaz, feeling clean, naked, exposed, and vulnerable. I was facing Mecca. They taught me how to pray as a Wahhabi, a follower of the teachings of Abdul Wahhab Najdi (1703–92), a preacher from the desert of Najd, in today's Saudi Arabia. He preached that his fellow Arabs had become weak and worldly and that they had to return to the true Islam. I opened my hands and placed them between my ears and my shoulders and softly called "*Allah-o-Akbar*" twice, and then I placed my hands on my chest. I also had to bring my pants up so that they were higher above my ankles than other men would wear theirs. I had to know the true ritual, they said, in order to follow the true path.

Almost all Pashtuns are Sunni Muslims. The vast majority belong to the Deobandi sect, which began in a small madrassa called Dar-ul-Uloom, House of Islamic Learning, in Deoband, India, which Muslims started after the Indian mutiny of 1857 against the British. The Muslims of the time wanted to give young men strength and self-esteem to stand up against British colonialism. Dar-ul-Uloom is now one of the most important universities in the Muslim world. I had gone there one year ago, in 2007, when writing a monograph on Islamic fundamentalism for the U.S. Army War College. An official there told me that a graduate of Dar-ul-Uloom went to Afghanistan in 1915, where he preached against British colonialism and won many followers.

The Deobandis in the 1920s began to work with Mahatma Gandhi to free India from British rule, but they wanted to remain separate from Western influence and to seek the right way to live through their own faith. When Pakistan was formed in 1947, they opposed its neocolonialist, pro-British elite. They sought equality, as the Prophet Muhammad did, and a return to Muslim rule. They spread from India along the frontier and into Afghanistan. They preached from mosques to their Pashtun followers. The Taliban trace their lineage to the Deobandis.

The Wahhabis, on the other hand, came from the harsh deserts of Arabia, the fountainhead of Islam, and brought a desert simplicity, a Puritanism, and a conquering warrior spirit to the world. The Wahhabis were true fundamentalists and opposed any deviation from the strictest interpretation of the Koran. They opposed the idea of miracles and shrines at cemeteries, for fear that they were the first step back to idol worship. As Saudi Arabia became rich, Wahhabis began to reach out and spread their version of Islam. There are now Wahhabi preachers in madrassas in Pakistan. There are also small groups of Wahhabis in the border region, mainly in

Bajaur Agency in Pakistan and across the border in Afghanistan's Kunar Province. They teach in madrassas there, too.

Wahhabis are the fiercest of Muslim warriors. The 9/11 hijackers from Saudi Arabia were Wahhabis. Osama bin Laden is a Wahhabi. In the nineteenth century, the British called them Hindustani fanatics; they were fewer in number then, but they led the fight against the British along the border. They came in greater numbers in the 1980s, as Saudi fighters sought martyrdom in the struggle against the Soviet Union. In the 1990s, when the Taliban rose, the Wahhabis fought in the front lines, more fiercely (it was said) than the Pashtuns.

Wahhabi Afghan fighters are tied closest to al-Qaeda, and it seemed clear from their instructions to me that Razi Gul and Abdul Samad were themselves Wahhabis. They taught me how to do a *rukat*, the act of bowing, and where to put my hands, then my knees and my forehead as I touched it to the ground. I was a traveler. I was not at home. Therefore I was only required to do three rakats each time; otherwise, the number varied with each prayer. I was intrigued. For years I had wanted to know how this was all done. Now I knew. I was being slowly initiated into a brotherhood.

Gulob returned an hour later carrying a small dim flashlight. I was sitting against a pillar reciting the Kalima, and as much as I could of the Salat, the whole Muslim prayer. It was hard, but I enjoyed the memorization, making my mind work in a way that it hadn't in years.

"I advise you to come close to Islam," said Gulob, as he watched me. "It is the best way, maybe the only way, for you to survive. If you don't, we will hurt you." It was a knife in my gut. My joy disappeared. I couldn't simply go through the motions. I would have to convert or die. How was I going to do this? I couldn't. What was I going to do? I had to walk a fine line. I would have to recite the whole Salat. "We will teach you," said Samad.

Gulob stood by the door. He said there was a toilet for us

outside. We would have a few minutes. We were to cough when we were finished. He gave Razi Gul a roll of rough, pink toilet paper of the type that existed throughout Afghanistan and Pakistan. It was comforting. Someone cared. Razi Gul went outside with Gulob, who bolted the door behind him. A few minutes later he returned. Samad went next, and then it was my turn.

I was nervous. I would be alone with Gulob. He stood at the door holding a flashlight. I kept my head down. I did not look at him, and he did not look at me. He shut the door and pointed the flashlight to the left. I walked past another door and came to a wall. Our toilet was a few rocks on the ground. Gulob shut off the light and stood back in the dark. I was in a compound. A sea of stars covered the sky. It was comforting to see them. I was still in the world. I shivered. There was snow on a mountain in front of us. I heard a dog barking far away. I calculated that I would have to overpower Gulob before I could get over the wall. But he carried a rifle. I was afraid to stay outside more than a few minutes. I coughed and he turned the flashlight on. I kept my head down, showing humility as I followed the light back to the cell. Later, in bed, I heard Daoud crying softly.

Monday, February 18

Gulob came in again before dawn, bringing water. Razi Gul and Samad prayed, and I followed. Daoud slept for most of the morning. The room was freezing, and I walked back and forth trying to keep warm, reciting the Kalima and the beginning of the Salat. When I wasn't walking, I huddled in my patoo. I was cold. I wanted my sweater. I also wanted a pen and paper. I just couldn't sit there all day with nothing to do. I would go mad. That afternoon, Gulob brought us tea and sugar. I gathered my courage.

I asked for my sweater. I didn't care if he thought I was weak.

He stood by the door. He was not authorized, he said, but he would see. He left, bolting the door behind him. He returned an hour later to pick up the cups. I thought about the tea. It was a kind gesture. I took a chance. Could I have a pen and a notebook, too? I asked. They were with my sweater.

"I am not authorized to give you these things," Gulob said sternly and left.

Samad walked around our cell trying to keep warm and to burn off energy. Razi Gul was lying under his quilt, trying to keep warm. Samad laughed and called him a snake. And yes, Razi Gul looked like one under his quilt. Samad sat on Razi Gul's cot, pulled the quilt back, and gave him a massage on his back and legs. Razi Gul told him to stop, but then let him continue.

Samad then came over to my cot, smiling, being friendly and started to rub my legs. "You must be tired from hiking in the mountains," he said. "You need a massage." I politely but firmly told him to stop. I didn't want him to think that he was in charge, and I didn't want to be physically close to him. I didn't want him on my cot. I still didn't know why we had started so late and stopped twice to rest in the mountains. I didn't like it that he had so easily jumped on Razi Gul's cot, a young man treating an older man like he was a boy. I couldn't understand a Pashtun acting like that.

That night Gulob brought us bread, a platter of rice with pieces of chicken, and a bowl of spinach. It was milmastia. Gulob was being a good host, a good Pashtun. We were prisoners, but guests, and not yet guilty. The Taliban were investigating us. We sat in a circle, and Razi Gul raised his hands, palms up, and said quietly, the others joining, "*Bismallah ir rahman ir rahim . . .*" In the name of God, the most gracious, the most merciful . . .

They were thanking God for our food. I wondered if this meal was for another reason, if it was like in prison in the United States, where a condemned man got to order a special meal before he was executed. Samad took a piece of chicken, broke it in two, and gave the bigger piece to me. I was the guest. I would receive the most and the best parts. The food was delicious but I wasn't hungry.

That night Daoud again cried in bed. I was unsure what to do, so I decided I would just let him be. He kept moaning. I asked if he was okay. "I am thinking of my mother," he said. "She is sick and has high blood pressure. When she finds out about this, I don't know what will happen." I asked if he didn't worry about his children. "I don't care about them as much as my mother," he said. I turned away from him and tried to sleep.

Tuesday, February 19

Gulob came again before dawn, bringing water. Razi Gul rose first, washed, and prayed. Samad followed him. Gulob returned with tea and later came in to collect our cups. "They wanted to transfer the three of you to the *markez*," he said, "but I told the Maulavi that because he"—he nodded at me—"can't speak Pashto, he would be unhappy here alone."

We were sitting on the floor, our patoos around us, in the cold. We stared at one another. I cringed. *Markez* meant "center." It could be a training camp but probably meant their headquarters. It was much worse there than here, Gulob said. We would not survive one day there alive. I sat with my head down, shivering. He was protecting me. I was scared. He walked back outside.

Gulob returned at what we calculated was about noon, bring-ing two metal bowls, each the size of a small cereal bowl at home, of potatoes and lentils. Again, I gathered my courage. My whole body was tight. I couldn't stand not having a pen and notebook. I took a deep breath and asked again if I could have them. There, I had done it. He stood by the door. "I will talk with the Maulavi," he said and left. He returned late that afternoon and laid a small spiral notebook and pen on the kilim. I was filled with joy. *"Mira-bane, mirabane."* Thank you, thank you, I said, smiling, trying not to grovel. Now I knew I could survive this. The notebook said "Made in China." I took the pen and began to write, trying to remember everything that had happened in the last few days. I last wrote in my notebook when we were having our picnic. I could barely see in the dark, and my head hurt without my glasses. I wrote for about a half hour before I had to stop. I was exhausted.

Gulob came in again and stood by the door. He was checking on us. I was sitting on the kilim, reciting a new sentence of the Salat. Razi Gul was prompting me. Again, I gathered my courage, and, pressing my luck, I asked if I could have my reading glasses. I couldn't see without them. "The Maulavi said I couldn't give them to you, but I will see," he said. "The Maulavi will come tonight, and I will ask him."

"And my sweater? It's cold in here." I was really pushing it, but I sensed that I could get away with it. Gulob did bring us tea, after all. He nodded. "Thank you, thank you very much," I said. I smiled and put my head down. He left.

"I think they are going to release us," I wrote in my notebook. "The Maulavi will come tonight." The Maulavi was the leader, the short but commanding man who had frisked me and counted the money in English. He had interrogated us briefly the first night. A maulavi in my experience was someone who was graduated from a madrassa.

We were all nervous. The Maulavi was coming, this man who held the power of life or death over us. Gulob returned an hour later and put my sweater on the kilim. "Thank you, thank you," I said. I was so grateful and happy. I put it on. I had bought it for twenty afghani, about forty cents, off a cart in the bazaar in Kabul a couple months ago. *I feel warmer now*, I wrote in my notebook after I put it on. *I don't think I will be killed, God willing.* Gulob walked back outside and bolted the door.

Late that afternoon, he came again, again bringing a pot of tea. He sat on a small stool, six inches high, with a rope seat, like our cots. It was called a *kotgai*, or little cot. He didn't bring his rifle. Razi Gul poured tea for all of us. Gulob joined us, sipping from his small cup without a handle. "They are not going to contact Shah Sahib or Abdullah," he said, looking over the cup at us. I looked down. What were they going to do with us? "Afghans are not good people," Gulob said. "Whatever we do, we do for this man." He nodded at me. "We respect you."

I sat on the kilim, cross-legged. I looked at him and down again. I didn't know what to think. He was giving me hope, but at the same time if they weren't going to contact Shah Sahib or Abdullah that meant we were stuck here. They had lied. It was one of the worst sins in Islam. What were they going to do to us? I didn't trust him.

"I have given you pen and paper without permission of the Maulavi," Gulob said. We were in Pakistan, but I realized that he had used the word *Afghan* to describe himself and the men with him. Razi Gul and Samad had also called themselves Afghan. Once, this land was all Afghanistan. He was giving me an opening. Who was in charge here now, I asked—the government of Pakistan or the Taliban? "The Koran is the constitution now," Gulob replied. "Before, people went to the government. That has all changed in the last fifteen years, because we believe in Allah and the Holy Koran."

We sat in the dark, with a soft shade of light coming in through the window. I couldn't see Gulob clearly, but I could understand his facial expressions. He spoke in Pashto to Daoud, who translated for me. I looked at Gulob briefly and at the floor. In Pashtun culture, a man must never look at another man straight in the eye for too long. He must show respect.

"There was a poor man who lived in the mountains," Gulob said. "A rich man took part of his land from him. He went to the

Taliban and complained. They investigated his story and made the rich man give the land back. They said, 'If you open your mouth, we will kill you.' You don't want to go against the Taliban. They will kill your whole family."

He rose and left. Samad and Razi Gul went back to their cots. Daoud stayed on the floor and whispered to me to give him my notebook and pen. I took them from my cot and handed them to him. He wrote *conspiracy*, using an *e* instead of an *i*, and then he wrote a capital *C* next to it. "Do you understand?" he asked. I did. He would use the letter *C* to stand for *conspiracy*. Daoud had developed a number of code words over the past few months, which we used when others were around. *Rasul Amin* was our code for the Taliban, *Zarmina*, his assistant, meant the ISI, Pakistan's intelligence agency. *Rahman* meant al-Qaeda. The code for my name was *Hilal*, which he said meant the one who brings light. This was an addition to our lexicon.

"I think there may be a *C* involving our companions," he said. "Why did we go so slowly? Why did we stop so much? Why didn't we start at dawn, instead of so late?"

I got angry. He was as responsible, if not more so, for our slow pace. I had told him in Kabul months ago to start exercising. He had laughed at me. I was still put off at how he had once raised his hand in a sign of dismissal and smirked one day when I told him to get in shape. I was a foolish old man, a foreigner.

I could feel the anger growing in me. I was on edge, scared, and felt trapped in this cold, crowded dark cell. I had been sitting down, but now I moved away from Daoud. I didn't want to be close to him. I didn't trust him, but I needed him too desperately not to. "I want to know everything, every small detail of what you know that I don't," I told him. Earlier, we had been discussing our capture. "You said that Samad was behind the rock ready to shoot, and you told him not to fire. Isn't that what you said?" I asked. I didn't believe him. I didn't hear him say anything, but he could have. I didn't hear or see anything except men shouting and swarming down the mountain, their rifles and rocket launchers high, coming to kill us.

Daoud nodded. "Yes, I told Samad not to fire."

"If Samad had fired," I responded quietly, "we'd all be dead. There were at least twelve of them." Maybe he had helped save my life, at least for a while. I didn't know what to think. I got up and walked back and forth in my bare feet, a few steps each way, on the kilim. We always took our shoes or sandals off when we were on the kilim, our dining room and our living room. I didn't believe his talk about a conspiracy. I was angry at him, at the world.

I gestured toward Razi Gul. "And what about our other friend? He cried yesterday. Was he pretending?"

"I miss Amina," Razi Gul kept saying. He mentioned her name ten times a day. He had eight boys and one daughter, Amina, whose name meant "the trusted one," or "the friendly one." She was four or five years old. His eyes were bright and sad at the same time when he talked about her. He never talked about his sons.

"Amina is engaged," said Daoud. I didn't like this. I imagined a cute little girl with dark hair and earrings running around the house, and her father doting on her. I asked Razi Gul if this was true. "She is engaged to my cousin's son," he said, "although she will decide when the time comes who she wants." He had sold her, but if she rejected her cousin, he had the right to buy her back. He sold her, he said, because he was poor.

"Our friends," said Daoud, meaning Razi Gul and Samad, "said that Abdullah said that no man should ever have his rifle taken from him. He should fight to the death. Otherwise, he is not Pashtun."

"Some Pashtun you are," I said. "You couldn't even walk through the mountains without falling down to rest all the time." Daoud smiled. He wasn't bothered by my anger. He knew it would pass and that I needed him. But I was angry now. It was different.

If he hadn't walked so slowly, we would have made it to Abdullah's before being attacked.

Razi Gul came and sat on my cot next to me. He watched me write. I stopped. "Write, write," he said. I told him to write in Pashto, and I would write in English. I gave him my pen. He waved his hand. He couldn't write. "Write about Amina," he told me. "*De Amina Kee Saw*. Your book will be *The Story of Amina*."

I smiled. Yes, *De Amina Kee Saw*. We laughed and shook hands. It was a moment of release. We were alive. We were in prison but we were alive.

Evening came, and what little light we saw outside the window faded. The door opened and Gulob entered, carrying his faded dark red cloth bundle of bread and this time a platter of rice, formed perfectly in a mound. How did the women, who surely cooked over nothing but an open fire, do that? There was meat in the rice. Gulob went back outside and returned with a small bowl of spinach and a bowl of watery yogurt. Razi Gul, Samad, and Daoud took out the meat. Razi Gul tore off a piece and handed it to me. It was goose. We had heard squawking that afternoon. Gulob had killed the bird for us.

"I never eat such food," said Gulob. "The Maulavi is coming tonight. Mamur Sahib, when this is over, give me your telephone number, and we will discuss everything." Mamur Sahib meant Sir Clerk. He had chosen a name for me. I was a writer and therefore a clerk. He pronounced my name Mamur Sab, shortening Sahib, as Samad and Razi Gul did for Shah Sahib, the Taliban leader who had given us permission to come here.

"You can tell me about the Taliban," I said. I felt good. We would possibly be released soon. The Maulavi was coming tonight. We were eating so well, and now I had a nickname. I could ask him about the Taliban.

"You can never discuss such things," Gulob said. He looked at me hard. I had been lulled into thinking that all would be well.

He was serving me the best food he could offer, and he had given me my sweater and a notebook and pen, not because he liked me, but because he was Pashtun and was required under Pashtunwali to treat a guest with honor. Gulob walked back outside.

Razi Gul and Abdul Samad gave me the best pieces of meat, brought me water, and poured my tea after dinner. It was not just Pashtunwali. I was their ticket to survival. Daoud ate little. He put his hand to his forehead. He had a fever. I put my hand on his forehead and on mine. I could not tell the difference.

Gulob returned, bringing the lantern for us, and left. We sat by the soft, warm light, nervously drinking tea. If the Taliban asked for money, how would I get it to them? Daoud asked. Did they want money? I didn't know what they wanted. Maybe they would just kill us, me for being a spy and him for working with me. But what if they asked for money? he asked. He wouldn't let go of the topic.

I said I didn't know. I would have them contact Rahimullah Yousafzai, a journalist based in Peshawar. I'd known him for years. He was the only man who had interviewed Osama bin Laden, Ayman al-Zawahiri, and Mullah Omar. He would be a good conduit. I didn't want to talk about money. I was thinking of the Maulavi. We all were. I wondered if the goose was our final dinner, the condemned man's steak. We could hear children's voices and the sound of someone chopping wood, or was that someone building a gallows from which to hang us before a crowd that would shout, "God is great"?

My cell mates washed and recited their final prayer of the day. In the dark, with their patoos around them and over their heads for warmth, bending over, kneeling, sitting on their knees, mouthing their prayers, their voices deep, they looked and sounded like monks in medieval Europe. Gulob returned and brought a bright battery-powered light with him. He put it on the floor. That, and the lantern, gave us light. I still couldn't see anyone's face clearly, but it was better. The men finished praying, and I felt awkward and nervous, the outsider, the infidel. We sat together on the floor.

"You will sit there and not do anything," Gulob said to me. "You will not be unhappy." He sat on the kotgai, keeping himself higher than us, and turned to the others. "You have been investigated," he said, giving no other details. He then looked at Daoud and said simply, "They have returned from Kunar." They had gone there to investigate, but what? What would they do? I felt cold. What was going to happen?

"His mouth circles on money," whispered Razi Gul, referring to Gulob. "He says many things, always different stories. 'I love this man, I will save him, I will protect him.'"

Gulob left, bolting the door behind him. We had to wait.

I asked Abdul Samad about his family. He said that his father died of brain cancer when he was fifty-two. "I have thirteen sisters and seven brothers," he said. "Four others, I think, died. I have five older sisters, but I am the first boy. I run the family." We were quiet. Had they decided I was a spy, or would they release us? Under Sharia, you could kill a spy. "I miss my mother and my children," said Samad. "I love my wife more than my mother, but I miss my mother more than my wife. I have two boys and three girls." This was an unusual response; most rural Pashtun men, when asked how many children they had, counted only their boys. A man's sons and grandsons formed a militia. Girls they had to give up before they were teenagers. It hurt too much to be close to them and then lose them so quickly.

"I miss myself," Daoud interrupted. "I think of myself first, nobody else." I stared at him, only half trying not to show my disgust at his narcissism.

I asked Samad at what age did his daughters begin to stay at home. I had seen in so many villages over the years cute young girls working in the fields or playing with their friends. On religious holidays they wore frilly dresses, with ribbons in their hair. Once, I saw a girl of about eleven with her hair streaked blond, in a dress, wearing high heels, standing in the dirt buying candy at a small wood shack shop. Like most Afghan girls, she would disappear into her village when she reached puberty and never appear with her face uncovered to the outside world again.

"Ten years old," said Daoud.

"Eleven," said Samad.

"You don't care about your children in the West," said Daoud. I asked why he said that. "Because," he said, "you let them go outside." Here life was brutal. Men settled disputes with rifles, not lawyers. The pegs in the walls attested to this. Samad said he wanted to have four wives, like his father. Before he had said that he was happy with one.

Another man, the one who had been with Gulob the first night, entered the room, bringing a teapot and cups. He sat on his haunches while Razi Gul poured our tea. Daoud asked his name. "Abdul Rahman," he said. His face was gaunt, and his dark eyes piercing in the eerie half light, like those of a hawk. He had dark hair and a dark beard.

"It's very cold in here," said Daoud. Rahman took some branches from the pile by the door and put them on the floor, took a book of matches from his vest pocket, and lit the wood. A fire started to crackle. Smoke rose to a small round hole in the ceiling. Warmth and smoke filled the room.

I asked how old this house was. "This hujra?" he responded. It was forty years old. If the roof did not get soaked clear through, it would last another sixty years. There was a hujra in almost every village in Afghanistan. A traveler could eat and sleep for a night in one, like in a monastery in medieval Europe. The walls were made of mud and straw; the beams and columns were fir. The roof was made of branches, mud, and straw, on top of which was a plastic sheet and then more mud and straw. It took three months to build.

This was not a hujra, said Daoud, it was a prison. Rahman took out a piece of paper from one of his vest pockets and showed it to us. It was a doctor's report from a hospital in Islamabad. He had asthma. He had gone for an X-ray. He had to give himself injections. He took out a small bottle of medicine and asked for my advice. I wanted to help him. I felt sorry for him. He was vulnerable asking my advice. I asked if he knew how to give himself a shot or if I could help him. He was my jailer, but if I could get close to him, maybe he wouldn't hurt me. Maybe he would even help me. I asked if the doctor gave him something to breathe through. He said yes. He was already giving himself shots. He didn't need me.

"I read the date on the doctor's report," whispered Daoud, adding that we could go to the hospital and find out his ID number and with that find out where he lived. We could capture him. "I am interested in revenge," he said softly.

Gulob came in, his patoo over his head, covering his pakool and part of his face, and took the light. Rahman left with him. We waited in silence as the fire went out. It was dark.

A half hour later, Gulob returned and told Daoud to come with him. Daoud rose, stepped into his shoes, wrapped his patoo around him, and left. I wondered if I would ever see him again.

Razi Gul sat on his cot, his patoo—his comfort, his shelter against the cold and the world—wrapped around him. I was fortunate. I had a sweater. Samad got up and sat on the bed with Razi Gul. They whispered. "Daoud has been investigated," said Samad. I wondered what they would find out about me. Or were they negotiating the price for our release? I had to be calm. I stared at the kilim.

"*Moshqil assan Allah*," said Razi Gul, pointing upward. God solves all problems. I wondered if he truly believed this. I didn't and wished I did.

Daoud had been gone a half hour when Gulob came in. "Who

is Zarmina?" he asked me. I shivered inside. They were going deep. I told him that she was the assistant to a professor I knew in Kabul and she had introduced Daoud to me. He shook his head. "This is not good," he said and left. My stomach knotted. Was it because she was a woman, an Afghan, and I knew her, or was there something else? Did Daoud tell them that *Zarmina* was also our code word for the ISI? A half hour later a hard-looking man, in a white jamay, a black turban, an ammunition vest filled with Kalashnikov banana clips, and carrying a rifle, brought Daoud back. He looked familiar. Daoud sat down, keeping his head down. The man now told Razi Gul to come with him. They returned a half hour later. The Talib then motioned to Samad. He stood up, his face blank, put his bare feet in his shoes, and walked out. Razi Gul, Daoud, and I sat on the floor.

"They went to my village and investigated my family," said Daoud. He kept his head down as Razi Gul stared at the floor. The Taliban had done their research. Gulob then brought Samad back. He sat with us, and Gulob sat on his cot. He had brought the lantern. We waited. The light burned low. It was silent. I was next.

The door opened. The Maulavi walked in, his back straight, a group of gunmen behind him, like a king leading a procession. He had come to me. This was it. I had to give the speech of my life right now. I sat on the kilim with my head down, waiting.

The Maulavi told everyone to move out of the way. He sat down on the kilim in front of me. I leaned forward. Some men carried flashlights. The room was bright and crowded now. Some men stood, while others sat on the ground and on cots. This was the main event. The Maulavi wore a white jamay with blue tinge and a black turban crisscrossed tightly in front. He motioned for Daoud to sit on his left and translate. The room was silent. He took out a small, thin black notebook and a pen and placed the notebook in front of him. His eyes were gleaming. We sat cross-legged, two feet apart. He sat straight. I looked him in the eye and then looked down. I was the prisoner, fighting for my life.

"I have a few questions I want to ask you," he said in Pashto. His voice was strong. I knew instinctively he was smart. He leaned forward, his pen in his right hand. "What is your name?" he asked. "What is your father's name?" I could feel everyone watching me but saw no one. Everyone disappeared. It was just the Maulavi and me. "Where are you from?"

I said that I lived in New York. Who sent me here? My publisher, I said. I was a writer and a journalist. Why did I come here? I had come to write a book. I had come here many years ago during jihad. I had been with the mujahideen. I had come this time to write about the Pashtuns. The West did not understand them. I came to write about the Taliban, to give you an opportunity to explain your views to the world. I had been with the mujahideen, and now I want to learn from you. I had already been with the Taliban in Afghanistan.

He asked what I meant when I said I had been with the mujahideen. I told them about meeting the mujahideen leader Yunus Khalis in Peshawar in 1981 and that he had sent me to Jalaladin Haqqani. I lived with him and his men in Paktia Province. I had to let these men know that I was different from other journalists. I had a background here. Haqqani was a legend among the Taliban. I didn't really know him, but I felt that I did.

I told the Maulavi that I had seen Khalis twice in Jalalabad in the past few years. I was the only Western journalist, to my knowledge, to see him. I wrote an article about our meeting in the *Baltimore Sun*, an American newspaper. He could read it on the Internet. An Afghan journalist I knew had shown the article to Khalis's son. The Maulavi showed no emotion. A part of me wished I hadn't mentioned the article because in it I wrote that I had changed and no longer believed in God.

I didn't say any more about Khalis, nor did I say that Haqqani had once worked with the CIA. "Abdullah said he would try to take me to meet Jalaladin," I told the Maulavi. "He knows Sirajuddin. That is one reason why I came here."

I didn't want to talk about Sirajuddin, Haqqani's son. I didn't care that he was said to be in charge now and one of the Taliban leaders along the border. I didn't come here to see him. But I had to convince the Maulavi that I wasn't a spy.

Once again I told him that he could read everything I had written on the Internet. He was part of the Pakistani Taliban, more sophisticated (I assumed) in using modern technology than the Taliban in Afghanistan. I leaned forward as he leaned toward me. I looked at him briefly and put my eyes down, acknowledging his authority. I glanced at Gulob, to his left, leaning forward stroking his beard, his eyes bright with interest. He seemed friendly. I had to save my life and the lives of my cell mates.

The Maulavi asked me to explain who my publisher was. I told him and tried to explain, as I understood it, the structure of the company. I didn't understand why I was going into such detail. The Maulavi tried to write the names down. I explained again my background with the mujahideen and my interest in the Pashtuns; I had come to explain the Taliban to the world, from their point of view, as I had once tried to explain the mujahideen. I felt that this was the only thing that would save me.

He asked how much money the publisher gave me. I told him how much my advance was and that it was divided into three parts: a third to do the research and write the book, a third came when I turned in the manuscript, the final third when it was published. I needed the money to live on and to hire people to work for me. I didn't have much money left. This time I knew why I was going into such detail. I was afraid and wanted to show him, by telling him everything, that I was not hiding anything. I wasn't lying. I wasn't a spy.

He asked how long it took to write a book. I said a year. He asked how many books had I written. I told him four. Two had been published. Again this was too much information. It was like being on television, with lights all around me, and millions watching, and yet there were just the two of us, the interviewer and me, and it had become a confessional. I should have written more books by now. I hadn't tried hard enough. Why did I berate myself?

"Why did you bring the video camera if you are writing a book?" he asked. It was a good question. I explained that I was a consultant to CBS News, an American radio and television company, on Afghanistan and Pakistan. He asked how much money I made there. I told him exactly how much. I explained my job in detail. It was as if he had injected me with truth serum. I assumed too that some of his people could find everything on the Internet. He kept asking questions, quickly, strongly, kept listening intently, occasionally taking notes. His eyes were shining, like a cat's eyes. He put his pen in his mouth as he listened. He asked who else I worked for.

I told him I was also a senior fellow at the Carnegie Council for Ethics in International Affairs, a public-policy organization in New York. I had an office there but I didn't receive a salary. I tried to explain what a think tank was and how it worked. I told him to check the Internet. I wanted his men to do this. I wanted them to read what I had written. I forgot that there was information on there about my past ties to the U.S. government. I thought of Friends of Afghanistan, the nonprofit organization I had directed in the 1980s, established by the National Security Council and the State Department. A former CIA agent I knew said, years later, "It sounds like something we would have created." I had worked in the U.S. Senate. I had been in the U.S. Army. If any of this showed up on the Internet, I was dead.

The Maulavi asked how much Carnegie paid me. He hadn't understood me. He was thinking too much about money. I wondered where and how I was going to get the money to free myself, or if I was going to have that chance. "He is also a professor," said Daoud. I silently thanked him for this. I hoped it would take the Maulavi's mind off of money.

He asked how long I had been a professor. I knew this gave me some stature, in the same way that Gulob and Rahman were impressed that I could read and write. The Maulavi was considered a scholar. It was his knowledge of Islam, and his diploma, that gave him power over the other men. Muhammad, who could not read or write, had said, "Seek knowledge, even if you have to go to China."

I said I had taught only one semester at New York University, but that would suffice. I wondered if I should tell him that I had taught a class titled "The Politics of Islam." Who was I, a non-Muslim, to teach such a class? There was a chance the information might help. I told him. I said I had a deep interest in Islam. It was true.

I said that my companions were teaching me about Islam—and here I gestured to Samad sitting cross-legged on a cot on my left, Razi Gul sitting somewhere behind the lights, Daoud in front of me. I would help them; I would save their lives; I had brought them here; it was my responsibility. They were teaching me how to pray, I said.

The Maulavi's eyes sparkled. "You have made me very happy," he said. He spoke loudly, his voice filling the room. "If you become Muslim, you will know the true faith. You will come to know God as you never have before. You will be part of a worldwide brotherhood. You will know love and kindness and happiness." I shook my head yes. I understood. "You will not go to Hell but will know the joys of Paradise. If you become Muslim, you can join our movement. We will find you a wife. If you choose to return to America, you can tell the world about Islam. Islam gives you dignity. It gives you strength. It gives you peace." He looked at another man and smiled, said something I didn't understand. The man was sitting on the kotgai, his rifle on his knees, leaning forward, relaxed. "If you become Muslim," said the Maulavi, "you will know happiness that you cannot describe."

I said I was trying to learn to pray. I began the Kalima, "*La illaha illalaha Muhammad . . .*" He cut me off, laughing at my pronunciation. I said I made mistakes.

He smiled, speaking loudly. "God rewards us when we make mistakes in prayer," he said. He wanted to help me now. He wanted to convert me. It was his duty as a Muslim. "I will teach you about Islam," he said. I said I would learn from him. "I will find English books for you," he said.

Was he telling the truth? Did I have a chance to survive? I felt alive. There seemed, now, a possibility. I would read the books, I said.

"You will go back to America and tell them all about Islam and that the Taliban treated you kindly," he said. "We will be proud of you if you become Muslim."

I thanked him. I said that if I returned to America, I would say that they had treated me with kindness. I would talk about Islam. I wondered if I would ever return. I didn't know if I believed him, but he gave me hope. I was trying to win him over, without lying or betraying myself. If I did, I knew that I would pay in some way.

"I invite you to come to Islam," he said. I bowed my head. I had to be careful. I couldn't say that I wanted to convert. I had to be honest, but I couldn't alienate him. I was scared. "*Mirabane,*" I said. Thank you. If he felt I was using this to get released, I would be in trouble. The Maulavi spoke like a preacher. "Islam is a brotherhood. It is a religion of brotherhood, fraternity, and freedom. There is no adultery in Islam. Everyone's property is protected. There is dignity. You will go to Paradise. Why do men become suicide bombers? It is not for the money for their families. It is to go to Paradise, where virgins await them."

I listened. There was nothing I could say. "There is no compulsion in religion," he said. He was quoting from the Koran. I saw an opening. I said the best way to preach was by example. The Maulavi's eyes grew warm. He nodded, looked at his companions, and said something I didn't understand.

Then I made a mistake. "I remember when you took my money," I said, "counted it, and gave it back to me. I said to myself, *He's an honorable man.*" The Maulavi looked at me blankly. I had embarrassed him. In the end, he wasn't honorable, because his men had taken the money from me. I had been impressed when he put my money back in my pocket, but now I knew I would never get the money back.

He asked what I thought of the American invasion of Afghanistan. "I opposed it," I said. "I said so on American television. You can look it up on the Internet." I was one of the few Americans who opposed the U.S. invasion following the 9/11 attacks. Most Americans would consider me a traitor, but they only wanted revenge. They didn't understand Afghanistan, or the fact that we had once used the Afghans to fight our war in the 1980s, and then we left. We didn't care about them. We didn't help them recover afterward. I knew for certain that al-Qaeda was still in Afghanistan. I had seen one of their soldiers when I was with the Taliban in Kunar a few weeks earlier. I felt that bin Laden was the one responsible for 9/11, not the Afghans, those poor desolate people who lived in small isolated villages, cut off from the world, who once again would suffer.

I sensed that only the top leadership of the Taliban knew about the plans for 9/11, if they even knew, and that once again thousands of innocent Afghans would die. The United States had to destroy the al-Qaeda leadership, but I knew that the Taliban would take off their turbans and wait and watch and that war would return.

The Maulavi asked where I had gone in Afghanistan. I said I

had been in Kunar, Nangarhar, Khost, and Paktia provinces. I had twice been with the Taliban in Kunar and once with them south of Tora Bora. He asked who I had been with, and when I mentioned particular names he raised his eyes and cocked his head to one side, looking at me quizzically. "It is dangerous being with the Taliban, and you are lucky to be alive," he said. I nodded. I had been playing with fire. Listening to him, I realized that I didn't know how lucky I was. I knew not to say certain names to him; that some leaders were at war with one another; that some of the Taliban I had been with were trying to find me.

He asked why I had carried prayer beads and maswok with me. I had had them in my vest pocket when we were captured. They were part of my disguise, but there was another reason, too. I said that when I lived with Haqqani and his men and observed the mujahideen and their closeness to God, I began to develop a deep interest in Islam. I was impressed that men with nothing but old British rifles would have the strength and courage to fight the Russians. They shouted *"Allah-o-Akbar"* and went up against the Red Army. I admired that. I had watched rough men place their rifles in front of them and bow their heads in the dirt. I liked this simplicity and their humility before God. I had wanted to join them but never did. I wasn't Muslim, nor was I Afghan. But I was a seeker. I wanted their strength, their courage, their closeness to God.

I addressed the Maulavi, not the men around him. We were two men, facing each other, worlds apart, but something had brought us together, what Gulob later called "the book of life." I talked as I could not talk to other men. "I've been very kind to you," he said. His message was that he could torture or kill me at any time. "You torture us in Cuba and at Bagram and at your other bases in Afghanistan. You humiliate us by desecrating the Holy Koran. You mock us with cartoons of the Prophet. But we will not hurt you. This is not Islam."

I lowered my head. I felt ashamed, grateful, and weak. He could do anything he wanted to me. I had once met an Afghan who had been in Guantanamo and had written a book about his experiences there. He put photographs in the book, taken by U.S. soldiers, that had been on the Internet. One soldier, holding a rifle, was kicking a naked inmate, making him run. A retired FBI agent had told me he had been to Guantanamo and that some of the inmates "looked pretty messed up." He said they had been tortured. America had changed, or maybe I didn't know America.

I said I was opposed to Guantanamo. The Maulavi leaned forward, his face close to mine. "We want to use you to exchange prisoners from Cuba or Bagram," he said. I felt cold. I felt a pit in my stomach. My hope disappeared. The United States did not negotiate with terrorists. I had to tell him.

"I am not important," I said. "I am only one small, insignificant man. America doesn't care about me. I am only important to myself."

"You are important for us," said the Maulavi. "If you are small to America, you are important to us for release of our comrades in prison."

I would be here for months, and then they would kill me. I had to stop this. "The United States will not negotiate," I said. I was taking a chance. I was pushing it. I had no choice. I didn't dare call them terrorists. They were a brotherhood fighting to kill the invader, as their ancestors had fought countless invaders. They were young men anxious to create a more equal and perfect world. "That is America's policy," I said. "It will never exchange prisoners for me. I am important to you, but not to America. I don't work for the government. I am by myself." *I am dead*, I said to myself.

The Maulavi motioned to one of his men, who placed two plastic sacks in front of him. He opened one and took out three toothbrushes, two bars of soap, a bottle of shampoo, toilet paper, petroleum jelly, and two towels and put all of this in front of him.

"Thank you. Thank you very much," I said. It was for us. They weren't going to kill me. He opened the second bag and took out Daoud's and my change of clothes and felt them to make sure there was nothing hidden in them. He looked at me blankly, shook my hand perfunctorily, stood up, using his legs only, not his hands—he was fit—and walked out. His bodyguards followed him.

It was over. I looked at the others. No one showed any emotion. Their faces were blank. He wouldn't have brought all this for us if he was going to kill us immediately. I sat there.

A few minutes passed, and the Maulavi walked back in. He was holding my video camera. Behind him came two riflemen wearing fatigue jackets, black turbans, ammunition vests filled with clips of bullets, and sunglasses. They stood behind me. Another gunman, wearing a white jamay and with a piece of straw in his mouth, stood on the side, his face dark and cocky, looking at me.

The Maulavi was silent. He stood five feet away. He motioned to the gunmen to stand closer. They came forward. I could see their rifle barrels out of the corner of my eyes. This was it. It had all been a show. He had made his decision. He was going to kill me now. Me, of all people. I couldn't believe it. The irony of it all. They were going to kill me. I sat there, a pit in my stomach, as everyone stared at me. They would watch me die.

The Maulavi tried to turn on the camera. He gave it to Daoud, who tried and gave it back to him. The Maulavi came forward and gave me the camera. "How do I turn this on?" he asked. His face was angry. I fumbled with it and reluctantly, nervously turned the camera on. *I am helping you film my own execution*, I said to myself. I hung my head in fear, disbelief, and utter despair. The Maulavi gave the camera to Daoud. He said he didn't know how to use it.

Two months before, I had tried to show him how to use the camera. He flicked his wrist. "That camera is no good," he had said. "It's a cheap one." I was angry at his arrogance. Daoud fumbled now with the same camera. He had to learn now, or maybe they would kill him, too.

The Maulavi started to film me. I didn't know what to do. He motioned for the men behind me to come closer. I turned to my right and saw a Kalashnikov, with its barrel cut at an angle, a few inches from my head. The man moved closer. I felt the barrel against my temple. The Maulavi gave the camera to Daoud and told him to film me. He held the camera against his eye. I stared at it for a second, and then I looked down.

The Maulavi motioned, and a man behind me took my pakool off and threw it on the cot next to me. I felt more naked. It would make it easier for him to cut off my head, or was it so they could see me better in the video, or both? I had to be strong. I put my head down. I didn't want to die a coward. I couldn't keep my head up. I put my hand on my forehead, my elbow on my knee, and kept looking down. *I am going to die now,* I said to myself. I felt my heart pounding. I was looking down to protect my throat. I kept looking down. I was trembling inside. I had to die with dignity. I had to be strong for my father, my brother, and my sister, and for my nephews and nieces. I said their names silently.

I told myself to sit up straight and to hold my head up. It was so hard. I kept trying and trying. It was like lifting lead. I forced myself and finally held my head up. My neck was exposed, but I was strong. I was not a coward. I knew my eyes showed fear. I looked straight into the camera. *I'm about to die. Oh, God.* I thought of men standing before firing squads. I thought of Nicholas Berg and Daniel Pearl. It takes courage to look your killers in the eye. I had to be strong. I thought of my family, especially my father, watching me on television. *Be strong . . . be strong. I am about to die.*

I heard a rustle behind me. *Oh my God, they are going to pull out a knife and cut off my head right now.* I looked around and saw the man right behind me put his hand in his jacket as I had seen men do in videos on television. *He is pulling out the knife.* I knew how long it would be. I had once seen a man use it to cut the throat of a sheep and a water buffalo. I turned and raised my hand to protect myself. *He is going to come down on me and try to cut my throat, and I am going to fight him, holding his wrists. The other man will grab my arms, and as we struggle the first man will cut my throat, or another man, on orders from the Maulavi, will empty his clip of bullets into me.*

I turned around. I was shaking inside. Daoud kept filming. The room was silent. I stared ahead. I kept staring, waiting to die. *It will be any second now. Be strong. Be strong.*

The Maulavi took the camera from Daoud. He stopped it and walked out. The men behind me, and others, with their rifles, walked out with him. Someone said in English, "No problem." Daoud fell forward on the floor, his face down, shaking.

I looked down, staring at nothing. They weren't going to kill me tonight. Or were they? I sat there, in my sweater, my patoo down by my waist, lying on the floor. I put my head in my hand. I could feel the lights all around me and everyone staring at me. *I am dead*, I said to myself again. The United States did not negotiate. What kind of life did I lead? Did I achieve my potential? Was this it? I was sixty-two years old. That is not young to most people, but I felt young. I didn't want to die, not now, not here in the mountains of Pakistan. It wasn't possible. *Nim spin gier*—half gray beard. I didn't want to die.

The door opened. The Maulavi and his men returned. *Oh no. They are going to do it all over again. This is the real thing. Oh no.* They lined up behind me again, and the room was silent. Daoud filmed me. The Maulavi, like a director, told the men behind me to come closer. They did. He didn't like what they did the first time. That was the rehearsal. I stared at the camera. At least my head was up as I waited for the knife or for the bullet to my head. The minutes passed. I waited, and I waited. My body was trembling inside. I couldn't talk. I couldn't swallow. No one moved. I felt the rifle against my head. I waited. This was it.

The Maulavi took the camera and walked out. The men went with him. No one said anything. I slumped forward. A few minutes later the Maulavi returned again with the two gunmen who stood by the door watching me. He sat down in front of me. "I could see you were nervous," he said. "That is why I have come back. No harm is going to come to you. We are going to negotiate a prisoner exchange. If that doesn't work, we are going to ask you to make a donation to the mujahideen."

I looked right at him. I was beyond fear. I didn't know what to believe. Finally, remembering my position, I looked down, and up at him again. I nodded. I would pay him whatever he wanted. I would sell my apartment, borrow money from others, and go live in one room somewhere. I didn't care. I would be happy there.

"We called the other three men into a room and interrogated them there," he said, "but I came here to see you. It was out of respect. No harm will come to you. Do you understand? You are important to us. We want you to go back to America and preach Islam and tell the world that the Taliban were kind to you."

"Thank you," I said. I took a deep breath. I felt good. There was hope. He wasn't going to kill me. Not now, or was he? I didn't know anything. I was exhausted. I chose to believe him. Warmth spread through me. I looked at him cautiously and then down.

"We are the political committee," he said. "You still have to meet with the military commission. They will decide what to do with you."

I looked at him and at the floor. Military commission? What was that? All the joy I had allowed myself to feel disappeared. All this didn't matter. I now had to face a military commission. I imagined older men, in their forties or fifties, with long black beards and hard, stern faces, men hardened by war and hatred of America. I would have to do this all over again. They would sit there, in judgment. I would plead my case. They would kill me. Maybe they would torture me first.

"I have told the warden to chain these other men to their beds, but not you," he said. "You won't know where to go if you escape, and you won't be able to talk to people."

His eyes were now warm. He shook my hand. His handshake was firm. "When I saw you I said, 'This man is from Nuristan.' You look completely Afghan. But when you opened your mouth, you couldn't speak Pashto." He laughed. I was hurt. I did speak some Pashto. It was my accent. He was talking as if we were friends recounting an old experience together, not about the time when his men came running down the mountain, with rifles and grenade launchers, pointed them at us, and I thought I was dead.

The man in the white jamay, now sitting on a kotgai, leaned forward, smiling warmly, his rifle across his lap. "I'm the one who talked to you in Nuristani," he said.

I remembered. He was also the same man who stood next to me pointing a rocket-propelled grenade launcher at my head. "I turned around so you would think I understood," I replied. I smiled. I didn't know what to think. I was alive. The gunman smiled back, his face lined with creases. His swagger and his dark sinister look of a few hours earlier were gone. For now.

The Maulavi stood up, and as he walked out he stopped, turned, and shook my hand again. He pointed to my cot. "Now put your sorrows underneath your bed and go to sleep," he said. He and the others walked out, but the gunman who had talked to me in Nuristani, and who had had the piece of straw in his mouth, stayed behind. He put out his hand and smiled. We shook hands and he left.

I sat there for a long time. I was dazed. The room was dark now. There was only a lantern burning low. I stood up and walked slowly over to my bed. Gulob came in carrying a load of bright, thick, iron chains. Daoud, Samad, and Razi Gul were in their cots. Gulob leaned over Samad's cot, put his flashlight in his mouth to give himself light and to free his hands. He wrapped a chain around part of the frame of Samad's cot, then wrapped it around Samad's left leg, took out a key and lock, and locked the chain.

He did the same to Razi Gul and to Daoud. I lay in my cot watching them. He took the lantern and left, bolting the door behind him. It was dark and silent. No one talked. I put my head down and pulled my quilt over my head. I wanted to be alone. I thought of my family. I thought of the e-mail I had sent to my niece Sarah. She was growing up. She was going to Europe. "It's a coming-of-age thing," she had said.

I cried softly for a few seconds. I hadn't cried in years. I felt better, and I felt sad. I lay there thinking. *How do I want to die, by beheading or with bullets across my chest?* I imagined the bullets ripping into me, being thrown back, the burning sensation, wondering how long the pain would last, a few seconds, maybe longer. I thought of my neck. I couldn't bring myself to touch it. How long would it take, once they started to cut, before I died? I didn't know how I wanted to die. I stared in the dark.

The door opened, and a group of men, with rifles and flashlights, came in. *Oh my God, here they come. This is it.* They went to Daoud's cot. He sat up and they gave him a cell phone. He put in a phone number. They walked out and shut the door and bolted it. "They wanted my brother's number," he said. I fell asleep.

PART TWO

The God of My Youth

Wednesday, February 20

I woke up a few hours later and saw the darkness. It took a second, and then I realized where I was. I was sad but grateful. I was alive.

The rooster crowed, and a few minutes later Gulob entered, carrying four large plastic five-gallon containers of water. He set the containers down and went to Razi Gul's bed and, talking quietly, unlocked his chains. He did the same for the others.

Gulob went out and soon returned with two other, smaller plastic containers, called *coolers* in Pashto, and left, bolting the door. Razi Gul wrapped his thin dark patoo around his shoulders and over his head to keep warm and stepped into his old sandals. He then poured water into a small metal bucket with a curved spout and walked to the pit, where he sat on his haunches and began to wash. He sounded like a horse as he cleaned his nostrils and mouth.

I pulled the quilt over my head. I didn't want to hear him wash, and I didn't want to be around Islam. I sat up and watched Razi Gul take off his sandals, spread out the jahnamaz, put his hands behind his ears, and begin. After he finished the Salat, he prayed on his own, on his knees, for another five minutes. I didn't like it that he prayed so long. Samad got up, washed, and prayed beside him, quickly, using another jahnamaz, and went back to bed.

Now it was my turn. It was the only way that I was going to

save my life. I got up, shivering in the cold, and crouched down as best I could—on my haunches, like an Afghan. I poured water from the small bucket into my hands. The water was warm. The women in the house must have risen very early, built a fire, and heated the water. I washed as Razi Gul and Samad had shown me. It was a complicated ritual, and I knew I was making mistakes.

Afterward, I stood on the jahnamaz, my mind blank and dizzy. I was nervous, knowing that the other men were watching me. I faced in the direction of Mecca and rolled the top of my baggy pants over my cotton belt, shortening the legs to come up above my ankles, Wahhabi style. I then placed my hands between my shoulders and my ears, my palms outward, and slowly, haltingly, softly said *"Allah-o-Akbar"* three times. I knew what I was saying; I felt like a hypocrite. This was not practice. This was not pretending. This was real. Where was I going with this? Where would this end? I didn't know.

I stood there, my mind still blank and sluggish. I looked forward, my eyes slightly down, as I had been told to do. Nothing happened. I took a deep breath. Finally the words began to come to me: *"La illaha illalaha, Muhammad urrasullalah."* There is no god but God, and Muhammad is his messenger. I couldn't remember any more of what I had learned. I was nervous. Behind me I heard Razi Gul speaking the rest of the prayer. I repeated each word after him, softly, like a schoolboy. It was blasphemous what I was doing. I could be killed for this, couldn't I? I wasn't Muslim. I couldn't do any more.

"Shabash, shabash," said Razi Gul, his voice low and encouraging. Well done, well done. There was much more to the prayer, but that was enough for now.

I had entered another world. Twenty-five years ago, a part of me had wanted to join the mujahideen, these men who put their rifles on the ground and bowed down behind their weapons, touch-

ing their foreheads and their turbans in the dirt. How I admired
the simplicity of their worship and the humility of these very tough
men before God. Now here I was. It was different now. I didn't
want to join these new holy warriors. I was doing this to survive so
that they wouldn't kill me. I had to be careful. The Maulavi had
invited me to Islam. He would be rewarded in Paradise for con-
verting me. I had told him I was praying, but I felt nothing. I was
sad and afraid. As I sat there Gulob walked in, put down a pot
of tea and cups, and left. I sighed. It was good. He had seen me
praying.

I sat on my knees and whispered, *"Asalaam alaikum,"* peace be
unto you. Following Razi Gul's example, I remained on my knees
and bowed my head and prayed on my own. But now I prayed to
the God of my youth, as I had as a boy. I wanted comfort. I wanted
home. I wanted to stay alive. No one would know what I was saying. I sat there enjoying the comfort, the warmth, and the security.
The Taliban wouldn't take me away while I was praying.

After I finished, Razi Gul joined me and sat on the kilim,
drinking tea. It was peaceful. Samad was now awake. I said, to no
one in particular, that I would have to sell my house, if I lived that
long. It was only an apartment, after all. The door opened, and the
Maulavi walked in, in the dark, with his riflemen behind him. My
body tightened. Had he come to take us out and shoot us or cut off
our heads? Was last night all a show? Why was he here? I kept my
head down, waiting.

He walked to Samad's bed. Samad sat up. "We are taking you
to the markez," said the Maulavi. Gulob stood behind him, holding another set of chains, which he proceeded to wrap around
Samad's wrists. Then he wrapped the other set, from Samad's bed,
around each leg. Gulob controlled Samad now, like a dog. Another
man blindfolded him. Samad said something, but I didn't understand.

The Maulavi came over to me. I rose, but only halfway, to show respect. I was taller than he was. I had to give him power and show humility.

He asked if I had slept well. I said I had and thanked him. He said that when he came back he would ask each time about my health. I lowered my head, thanking him. They stood Samad up, and he stood straight, facing me in the dark. "Good-bye, sir," he said. I said good-bye. I looked at him. He wasn't coming back. They were going to kill him. *Oh my God.* Gulob led him away, his chains clanging in the darkness. I wondered who was next.

Daoud said that Samad had said "Take him," meaning Razi Gul, instead of himself. I hated Samad for saying that, but I couldn't judge him. He was scared. So would I be. We sat there in the morning cold, sharing tea. An hour or so later Gulob returned to take away the teapot. "His tongue took him away," Gulob said. "I would like to take you to the markez. There are Wazaris and Punjabis and all kinds of people there. There are training centers all over this area. You could learn many things, but there are other Taliban groups that would grab you."

The Wazaris, from Waziristan, just south of where we were, had a long history of fighting outsiders. The Punjabis, from the Punjab, the most populated province in Pakistan, ran Jaish-e-Muhammad (Muhammad's Army) and Lashkar-e-Taiba (Militia of the Pure), two militant groups that had been created, it was said, by the ISI. They were tied to al-Qaeda. "Pakistan defeated the Soviet Union in Afghanistan," said Gulob, "and it will now defeat America. Musharraf is smart, and Bush is stupid."

That evening, he brought a small bowl of lentils and potatoes in thin gravy. There were three of us now. I missed Samad and was afraid that we were next. Razi Gul raised his hands; "*Bismillah ir rahman ir rahim . . . ,*" he repeated. We raised our hands with him. I broke off a piece of bread and ate it slowly, grateful for the food and to be where I was. Gulob sat on the kotgai, took off his sandals, and rubbed his right ankle. It was swollen. He had fallen from a tree a few days ago. "I love this man," he said, nodding at me. "I will protect him."

"Thank you," I said, looking down. I didn't believe him. He got up and left, bolting the door behind him. He returned a few minutes later carrying an oval-shaped metal box with three holes on top and an open bottom. It was about ten inches deep. Gulob said that he would normally let the rain come in through the hole in the roof and wouldn't care about the cold, but he had gone today for us to Bajaur City and bought this *bokhari,* a small stove, to give us heat. He went outside and returned with a handful of mud and later came back with more mud and an aluminum chimney, ten feet long and five inches in diameter, which he put through the hole in the roof. Razi Gul held the chimney while Gulob put the bokhari on the floor and inserted the chimney in one of the stove's three holes. Gulob then plastered the mud against the bokhari and the floor. We were his guests, he said. The Maulavi had wanted to take us to the markez, but he said no.

The Maulavi could not take us from here, Daoud explained. It was part of Pashtunwali. This was Gulob's house. We were his guests. I didn't know if it was milmastia or panah. Milmastia was over now, said Gulob. He had given us chicken two nights in a row, and goose. We would now eat simpler food. Under panah, if someone tried to take us away, Gulob had to protect us to the death. I asked him to give me an example of panah.

"Mullah Muhammad Omar destroyed his government and allowed Afghanistan to be invaded, in order to protect Osama, his guest," Gulob said. He finished plastering. The mud would dry overnight. He chained Daoud and Razi Gul to their beds and left. We heard jet fighters roaring in the distance. I wondered if they were American or Pakistani planes bombing the Taliban.

Thursday, February 21

Gulob came again in the afternoon with a small pot of green tea. He sat on the kotgai, scratching his leg, which was now swollen. He took out a small cellophane packet of *naswar*, chewing tobacco, and put some beneath his lower lip. "They want $100,000 for the translator, $80,000 for Razi Gul, and $90,000 for Abdul Samad," he said. He looked at me. "Don't think about selling your house."

What did that mean? My stomach tightened. Were they going to ask a lot of money for me? Were they going to try to exchange me for prisoners from Guantanamo? Or something else? Maybe they hadn't decided. Maybe they had. I thought again, as I did often, whether I preferred to be beheaded or shot by an automatic rifle in the chest.

Gulob spit out a piece of snuff on the floor. I was not to be sad, he said. He would try to resolve this in a few days. I looked down again. My hopes rose. Was he in charge? Did he have this power? He left without offering any further information or explanation. All afternoon we listened for the sound of an engine from a car or a motorcycle, waiting for the Taliban. We heard children playing and a cow lowing. Soon the sun would set.

"We didn't hear a car all day," said Daoud. "I think Abdul Samad is still here. They took him to another room." We were sitting on the floor, where we could see one another in the dark and be closer. Daoud ran his hand over his beard. This was all *C*, a conspiracy. He had listened to the voice on the other end of the walkie-talkie when they captured us. It was Abdullah's voice. Daoud had met Abdullah two months ago, when I sent him across the border to Peshawar to make the initial arrangements. I had sent him again a month later, to deliver two letters that Abdullah had asked me to write, which he promised to deliver to Jalaladin Haqqani and

Gulbadeen Hekmatyar. Abdullah's face looked like Samad's face, Daoud said.

Was it possible that Abdullah was my enemy? In my daydreams he was my savior; he and his men would burst into the compound, guns blazing, and rescue all of us.

I asked Razi Gul how close we had been to Abdullah's compound when we were captured. He thought for a second. "About twenty minutes," he said.

My mind was racing. If Daoud hadn't kept stopping to rest; if we had only started earlier; if Samad hadn't stopped to rest; if, if, if . . . We were that close to safety. And how would Gulob even know that I would consider selling my house if I hadn't discussed it in this room? Someone must have told him. Who? Were they real Taliban or thieves? Maybe they would decide to simply kill us and not even demand money. I walked to the door and back to the pit, our washbasin and urinal. I walked slowly back and forth, back and forth, like an animal in a cage.

Where was the military commission? How could I get money here? I stared at the double doors, about a half inch thick, each about eighteen inches wide. There was a steel bolt across them. The wood was old. If I broke it, I would be in a courtyard, with women and children. Outside the compound were Gulob's Kuchi dogs. They would be big, lean, and vicious. If I got outside, and if the dogs were chained, and if I got past them, then what would I do? Was there a village? Everyone would know everyone else. I would have to run into the mountains and make my way west, to Afghanistan. How could I do this?

I kept pacing. How did I know there weren't Taliban in the next room? They were here all the time, Gulob said. How much money did they want? Maybe they would kill me. Back and forth I went, back and forth. "*Ne fiquer*," said Razi Gul, shaking his head. Quit thinking. "*Moshqil assan Allah.*" He pointed his finger upward.

"Yes, *moshqil assan Allah.*" I envied his simple faith. I wondered if he really believed that. "No dollars, no talibs, no mullah. Don't think," he said. "The money will come from God."

I raised my hands in frustration and kept walking, looking at the door. I was afraid of it. Every time it opened I didn't know who might walk in. I sat on the kilim. It was three feet by three feet, now also our prayer room. Razi Gul took my pakool, looked at it closely, and put it back on my head. He asked where I had bought it. I told him Kabul. "Do you wear it in America?" he asked. I said I wore it sometimes in the winter. It was warm, but people looked at me strangely. I felt they thought that I sympathized with the enemy. Razi Gul said he would come to see me in America.

"I won't have a home for you to stay in," I said. "I may have to sell it to get out of here."

Razi Gul tilted his pakool forward over his forehead, looking now more like a mujahid or a Talib, rather than the kindly father of Amina. "Pashtuns don't think of Islam or Pashtunwali—only money," he said. He put his hand on my knee. "Do not be sad."

Evening came and with it a joyful sound, as if someone were clapping, hitting their palms, and creating a hollow sound. Women were making bread. Food was coming.

Gulob brought in our bread and two metal pans. Razi Gul picked up the small bucket of water and a small round metal pan, about a foot wide, with a strainer on top. It was called a *chillum chee,* or little sink. He held it in one hand and poured water from the bucket over my hands into the chillum chee. I used one of our towels to dry my hands. There was a chillum chee in every hujra in Afghanistan.

We sat down and Razi Gul raised his hands and prayed, "*Bis-millah ir rahman ir rahim.*" We broke off pieces of bread and ate. Gulob sat on the kotgai, watching. I asked him if he worked with the Pakistani army. "There would not be a bullet fired in Afghan-istan if Pakistan didn't give its permission," he said. He then asked who I thought was behind the attacks in New York and Washington. I said al-Qaeda. I had seen the video where bin Laden talked with a mullah from Saudi Arabia about his involvement. Gulob shook his head. "The U.S. and Pakistan were behind it so the U.S. could invade to keep Russia, Iran, and China out of Afghanistan," said Gulob. He walked out angrily.

After dinner, Gulob returned to collect the bowls and the remaining bread, and we prayed. I was nervous praying in front of him. He would notice my mistakes or, worse, determine that I did not want to become a Muslim. I was afraid of him, especially that he was part of some larger conspiracy. After prayers were over, Gulob built a fire in the new bokhari. Smoke filled the room and dissipated. For the first time it was warm and comfortable. I took out my maswok and brushed my teeth, to show Gulob.

He watched me brushing. The fibers on the stick were worn and beginning to look like a shaving brush. "There are seventy benefits of maswok for us," he said. "There are seventy benefits of Pakistan for the Taliban." They all laughed. Maswok was said to be good for your back, for an upset stomach, and for many other ailments.

I sensed that it was a good time to talk. I said that Pakistan claimed it had ninety thousand soldiers along the border hunting for al-Qaeda and the Taliban, but I had never seen any soldiers. Gulob laughed. "And you won't," he said. "The Taliban patrol the border for the Pakistani army."

How could I prove that? I asked. "Look what happened to you," he said. Unfortunately, I was a prisoner, or Gulob would show me. Abdul Wali and Mohammad Fakhir had camps around here, he said. They were Taliban leaders in Bajaur and Mohmand agencies. "They brought an Afghan soldier here, who was innocent, but who had a tractor," he said. He shook his head, laughing. "The Maulavi said we will compel him to sell it. I felt sorry for the soldier."

He said that a British female journalist and a Turkish journalist had been captured, too. They were demanding $600,000 for the Turk.

Behind these kidnappings, Gulob explained, were the Frontier Scouts, a Pashtun paramilitary organization that operated only in the Northwest Frontier Province of Pakistan. The Frontier Scouts are a vestige of British colonial times, having been founded in 1846 to gather intelligence and provide security in this border region. When Pakistan became independent of British rule a century later, the new government retained the Scouts along with the onerous Frontier Crimes Regulations, which were designed to keep the Pashtun tribes in line. Pakistan also retained the Political Agent, the government representative who ruled each agency. Even today he can punish a tribe for the crimes of an individual; if a suspect remains at large, the government can put his family in jail. There are no courts in the tribal areas, but under the Frontier Crimes Regulations the Pakistani government can raze a man's house and can prevent anyone from the frontier tribal areas from entering the "settled districts." Pakistan treated the tribal areas as a colony, just as the British had done. Many Pashtun tribal leaders had told me that they feel they are being squeezed by the United States (in Afghanistan) and Pakistan (in the tribal areas).

Daoud said that it was forbidden in Islam to receive even a grain of wheat in an evil way, and that God would make everyone involved in our kidnapping pay.

Gulob responded firmly. "I am doing all I can to help this man. I will end up either in Guantanamo or in my village."

Later that night, I didn't feel well and wasn't hungry. "You make me unhappy, Mamur Sahib," said Gulob, staring at me. I was afraid to upset him. It was important that he be a good host. It went to the core of what it meant to be a Pashtun. There were chains on the floor and dark marks on the wall, but this was his home.

Razi Gul brought some small branches from the woodpile and made a fire in the bokhari. I sat close, trying to get warm. I was starting to shiver. I was getting worried. I wore a sweater, a vest, my wool patoo, and my pakool, and still I shivered. I now had a new worry. I was afraid I would die here of pneumonia.

Friday, February 22

I woke up feeling weak and thirsty. I prayed, feeling dizzy, going through the motions. I slept all morning. It was Friday, when men went to the mosque, and the imam preached a sermon. A boy, about ten, brought in our bowls of lentils and potatoes. I sat on my cot, in the dark, feeling better, but I didn't want him to see me wearing glasses and writing. He would tell his friends. They would tell their parents. He put our bowls down and quickly left, bolting the door behind him.

I went over and stood on Samad's cot. I found a slit between two pieces of wood over the window. I pulled one slat back and pushed the other forward. I saw an older woman, with her pale blue chadari back over her head, sitting, cooking over a fire. "Do not do that. It's very dangerous," said Daoud. I quickly backed away. Rahman came in and sat on the kotgai, watching us. His beard could not hide his thin, lined face, and there was something cold and ruthless in his eyes.

I looked at our prayer mats. They faced toward Mecca. Saudi Arabia was southwest from here. That meant that if I got out the door and through the compound I would have to turn right, the direction we prayed. That was toward Afghanistan.

I wondered out loud if I could get by Rahman and how far I could get. The women here knew how to fire weapons, said Daoud. They trained their women. They knew how to use walkie-talkies. Daoud once told me that his sister could fire a rifle.

That night, Rahman brought us our dinner, a bowl of *masta* curry, pieces of bread soaked in chicken broth, and pilaf, a platter of rice with a few pieces of chicken in it. It was a feast. We gave thanks and ate. I asked how long it took to prepare the pilaf. Rahman said about two hours. I told him the food was good, hoping he would tell the women, who worked so hard.

"How are you tonight?" he asked. "How is *de zarou cherg*?"

I felt cold. He had just called me what sounded like "the Golden Goose."

"You use that expression?" I asked. "You say 'Golden Goose'?"

Razi Gul and Daoud smiled. "He thinks you are worth billions of dollars to them," said Daoud. "Yes, we say 'Golden Goose.'" Daoud was translating loosely; in truth what Rahman had called me was "the golden rooster," a common phrase for someone worth a lot of money.

Razi Gul put his hand on my knee, laughing gently. "*De zarou cherg*," he said.

I said that we had a story, too, where a married couple killed their Golden Goose. I was thinking of Aesop's fable. But if they killed me, they wouldn't get any money. Now I didn't want to eat, but Razi Gul broke up a piece of chicken and gave me the biggest piece. "*Ne fiquer, ne fiquer*," he said. "*Moshqil assan Allah.*" He pointed upward. I sighed.

The door opened, and Gulob walked in, wearing a cream-colored jamay. He had dressed up for Friday prayers. We smiled. We were happy and relieved to see him, our jailer and protector. He had been to Bajaur City to go to the mosque. I asked if we were in Bajaur. "You are where the Americans shot a rocket killing a number of our children two years ago," he said. "We found their body parts and had to bury them in a mass grave. If anyone knew you were here, they would drag you out and kill you immediately." The look in his eyes had changed. He was not my protector.

We were, if he was telling the truth, in Damadola, the site of a U.S. missile attack by unmanned Predator drones in January 2006. When the attack took place, I was in lower Swat, staying with a Pakistani journalist friend and his family. We returned to Peshawar, where I read the Pakistani newspapers. They listed the names and ages of the many children who were killed. The CIA believed that Ayman al-Zawahiri, the number-two man in al-Qaeda, was visiting the village. It was Eid al-Adha, the festival at the end of Hajj, the annual pilgrimage to Mecca, and it was said that al-Zawahiri was in Damadola to celebrate. There were rumors that he had a wife there whom he sometimes came to visit. Rahimullah Yousafzai, the Pakistani journalist, later went to Damadola and told me that intelligence agencies were controlling all the information. I asked the U.S. consul in Peshawar about al-Zawahiri. He didn't know. In October 2007, I asked a local tribal chief about Damadola. He had heard that other chiefs were preparing dinners for al-Zawahiri but that he never came that night. He had heard about the children who were killed.

I was afraid now of Gulob's eyes and wanted him to know that I too was angry that the United States had killed so many children; and that U.S. officials said they would do it again, in order to try to kill al-Zawahiri. I needed to change the subject. I asked which was stronger here, the Taliban or the tribes? He said the Taliban were stronger. I asked why. "Because of Islam," he said. "For the tribes Pashtunwali is stronger; for the Taliban, Islam."

"Do you fight in America?" asked Rahman, sitting on the kotgai. I nodded. Mostly with lawyers, I said, but people did sometimes shoot and kill one another. "Here, if a cow comes on our land, we at first warn a man," Rahman said. "The same goes if a man slaps another man's child. If he does it again, we fight."

What about women? I asked. "It is forbidden to look at a woman or to sit at a gate where there are women in the house," Rahman said. "It is forbidden in Islam." The Koran says no such thing, but I kept quiet. I asked: What if there is a big dispute? Do you have a *jirga* or a *shura*? (A jirga is a meeting of tribal leaders; a shura is a council of religious leaders and tribal representatives.)

"Before," Rahman said, "we had a jirga, now a shura. It is better under the Taliban." A shura would be more equal, he felt. It was Islam over Pashtunwali. "Most of the people support it."

Rahman, who always seemed to be more interested in cultural matters rather than war, spoke up again. "Under Pashtunwali, if a boy and a girl like each other, and I refuse to give my daughter to the boy, he and his father can come to my house and fire a rifle in the air. This announces that my daughter is now their daughter-in-law. If I oppose this, they will kill me. In revenge, I or my relatives will kill them, and the animosity begins."

"That is Afghanistan," said Gulob. "This doesn't happen among the Pashtuns in Pakistan. It is not Islam. Under Islam there is an agreement." By "Pakistan," he meant the tribal areas, which, at other times, he had called "Afghanistan." He told a story that he had heard in the mosque about a wedding. "In Swat today, a bomb went off beneath where the bride was sitting, killing many people. This is not in Pashtunwali, Islam, or in paganism. She may have loved someone else once. He lost out and killed her. In Pashtunwali, we kill only the man, never women and children. The consensus is that the father of her first love killed her."

"I engaged Amina to the family of one of my sons," said Razi Gul again. "I am poor and needed the money, but if my daughter doesn't like any of the boys I can buy her back." He said he cried at night thinking of his children, especially Amina.

"How could you bear to lose her so young?" I asked.

He spoke softly. "I will die in fifteen years or so. It won't matter. *Allah-o-Akbar.*" He was now forty-nine or fifty. He accepted death easily. He would go to Paradise.

Gulob spit on the floor and put his elbows on his knees. "The Maulavi will not come tonight," he said softly. "He will go to Kabul with others to resolve this." Why? To take my video to the U.S. Embassy or to a television station or to CBS and ask for money? Or is Abdullah involved, and are they going to see Mullah Malang? If in fact they were going at all.

But now was time for prayers, after which Gulob took us outside, one by one. I walked slowly, afraid of Gulob or that other Taliban would see me and kill me. I looked at the sky. I took a deep breath. The fresh air felt good. I imagined overpowering Gulob, getting past the dogs, and running down the road. I would have to travel through the night and hide in the mountains during the day.

There was a roof over me. I couldn't climb over a wall here. We were on the top floor of a house. The courtyard was ten feet below us, dug into the ground, like an open basement. There was a fence between us and the courtyard and beyond that the compound walls. I coughed. Gulob switched on his flashlight and guided me back to our cell and its warmth and safety.

Sunday, February 24

I waited for the rooster to crow, my sign to get up. I had to pray. I wanted the respect of the others. Rahman brought in our water and I washed. Razi Gul finished praying and sat on the floor. I prayed out loud, and he softly, gently helped me remember the words.

Rahman brought in *dood-patee* (hot milk, black tea, and sugar) and a plate of *parata* (yesterday's bread fried in oil). We didn't eat or drink but sat talking as best we could. I asked Razi Gul how he slept. He held his thumb and forefinger a half an inch apart. "*Legga, legga*," he said. Only a little. The chains kept him awake. I was getting off easy. I should suffer like him. He went back to bed. I was starting to get depressed. My body would soon go. I needed to keep fit. It would help me mentally, and I needed to be strong, to fight and run through the mountains without food and water.

I folded up the two jahnamaz and put the cups and teapot to one side of the kilim. I began to warm up in the same way I did when I ran track as a boy. I felt warm and at home. I thought of my father telling me to stretch and to always try to win. I thought of warming up this way before a race. I wasn't afraid. I finished and slowly I did a set of deep knee bends and sat on the kilim breathing deeply. I had to be careful. Go slowly. I knew how to train. I had been doing it all my life.

I did a set of finger push-ups as I did them at home, but I was barely able to finish, and I sat on the kilim for longer than normal breathing deeply, waiting for my heart to stop pounding. I did another set of push-ups and deep knee bends and rested. I stretched for a long time. It was enough for today. It was a beginning. I sat there, relaxed and tired. I had accomplished my goal. A few thin rays of dim light came through the dirt on the window. It was like a church. It was silent. I drank some water from our communal pan and felt the warmth of the sweat sweep over me. I felt at peace. I sat for a long time, grateful to be alive.

Afternoon came. Daoud and Razi Gul sat on the kilim, looking at each other. Daoud grinned. "Gulob said that you were skinny and looked poor and would probably only bring forty lakh," he said to the older man. "Samad was healthier and younger and would bring maybe fifty. 'Daoud,' he said, 'you are a translator and have already made money off of Mamur Sahib and are worth one hundred lakh. For him, well, he is the Golden Goose.'"

We were slaves in a dungeon. Maybe they would sell us. A lakh was one hundred thousand. Forty lakh meant four million rupees, roughly $65,000.

Late that afternoon we heard a motor. Was it a car, a motorcycle? Twice I thought I heard a helicopter. When would the Maulavi return? We were afraid of him, but we needed him if we were to be released. We waited, listening. I could hear birds singing and children playing.

I asked Razi Gul about his life. He said that he lived in Landi Khotal. He had lived in Pakistan for thirty years. It was easier for his children to go to school in Pakistan. There was electricity. There was work. "Our scholars tell us it is prohibited in Islam to work with the Americans, with pagans," he said. "We should only go to pagan countries for medical care or to preach."

"The Prophet, peace be unto him, said we should seek knowledge even if it be in China," said Daoud.

Razi Gul shook his head. "We should go to China only to get Islamic learning," he said. "It is easy to say '*La illaha*' but hard to live a Muslim life. These people who have imprisoned us are not good Muslims. We have heard that where there are Americans there are problems. I am a poor shopkeeper. I have not worked for five years. I have animosities, and Abdullah is helping me in that."

I asked what he meant by *animosities*. "A poor man, a cousin on my mother's side, had a quarrel with a man," he replied. "The other man was beating him, so I went to help him. Two relatives of the man who was beating him killed my cousin. We didn't have any weapons, not even a pistol. We didn't kill anyone. It started when some children were playing and started fighting, and the father of one of the children beat my cousin's child. My cousin was twenty-five. We are seeking revenge. The family lives in the village we passed where there are heroin factories. Abdullah, too, because of his own animosities, has become friends with the Taliban."

Gulob came in with a small radio and sat where Samad used to sleep. I asked him to explain the Taliban to me. "A Talib means a student in a madrassa," he said. "They are not supposed to fight, but do and are backed by the government. The definition of the Taliban would be someone created by and supported by Pakistan to fight against the Americans and NATO. There are different bands of Taliban. Abdul Wali fought against the government, and so the Pakistani army bombarded him. Some groups are backed by the government, and some fight it. It is confusing. The interior minister said the Lal Masjid must be destroyed, and the Taliban said we will destroy you."

Twice the interior minister had escaped suicide bombers. Back in 2006, I had gone to see Abdul Rashid Ghazi, the co-imam with his brother of the Lal Masjid, or Red Mosque, named for the color of its bricks, in Islamabad. It was built on government land, near the ISI headquarters. ISI officers worshipped there. "Musharraf and I have an understanding," he said. "We both have to say certain things in public. The minister of religious affairs said nothing would ever happen to me."

In March 2007, I went to see Ghazi again. He was the same—soft-spoken, articulate, and smiling. I observed the students from his madrassa. They were no different from students in other madrassas. They walked down the street in front of the guesthouse where I was staying in Islamabad, quiet, serious young men. His female madrassa, Jamia Hafsa, next to the mosque, was said to be the largest of its kind in the world. Most of the students, male and female, were Pashtuns from the Northwest Frontier Province. In April, the students began to demonstrate in the streets against prostitution and indecent films. The demonstrations grew violent. I was told that many of the female students shouted from inside their madrassa, "*Zindabad Osama!*" (Long live Osama!) In July, the Pakistani army and its elite Special Services Group commandos, in black T-shirts with rifles, finally moved in and surrounded the mosque. The siege lasted almost a week. Ghazi remained inside, holed up in the basement, it was said, with women and children. The army attacked, and many students and some soldiers were killed. No one knew how many. There were rumors of mass graves. Ghazi became a martyr, ironic because his name, *ghazi*, means "one who has waged jihad and returned."

For at least two months after the attack on the Lal Masjid, a wave of suicide bombings directed against the army swept across the Northwest Frontier Province and even into Pakistan proper.

On September 13, an eighteen-year-old man, whose sister was said to have been martyred at the Lal Masjid, walked into the mess hall at Tarbela Ghazi, a Special Services Group base south of Islamabad, and blew himself up, killing twenty-two elite commandos. Overall, hundreds of soldiers and civilians were killed and injured. There were reports that militants in Waziristan had kidnapped more than a hundred soldiers; other reports stated that the soldiers, many of them Pashtuns, had refused to fight their fellow Pashtuns, their fellow Muslims, their fellow countrymen, and had surrendered voluntarily. It was confusing, as so much was in Pakistan.

"I don't want to say anymore," said Gulob. "I am afraid someone will read your notes. Wait until, *inshallah*, we are in Kabul."

He found a radio station where a young man was reciting the Koran in a beautiful, lilting singsong chant. The sound filled the room. "This is like the Prophet lived centuries ago," Gulob said, looking around. Our cell was dark, dank, and cold. Daoud sat on an empty cot, near the dark window, reading the Koran; Razi Gul had just finished praying, while I, with my beard, long hair, and glasses, like an aging, ancient Muslim cleric, sat on the floor writing.

Gulob left, and Razi Gul found another station. A woman called Naghma, whom I had seen on television, her face uncovered, holding a microphone, dancing gently, a band behind her, was singing. She was from Kandahar and lived in California. I asked if he liked listening to her. "Oh, yes," said this devout Muslim, who had switched the station from the Qarie singing the Koran to one where he could listen to music banned by the Taliban.

Gulob opened the door. Razi Gul turned off the radio. "Who killed Saddam?" he asked. He was looking to argue. I said quickly, the Shiites. I didn't want to argue. "America killed him," he said. He snickered. He liked defeating me. I lowered my head. Saddam was hanged on Eid al-Adha, one of the holiest days in Islam.

It was like executing an American on the Fourth of July. Gulob left.

We waited nervously all afternoon for the Maulavi. Now I was waiting for a man to come and decide my fate. Razi Gul prayed again. I joined him in prayer. *The more you pray,* I wrote in my notebook, *the more you listen to a Qarie, the more God takes over your life, the more you are repulsed by and drawn to the West.*

Gulob returned late that afternoon. There had been a big Taliban meeting today, he said, with people from all over the border region. He wouldn't elaborate. I asked Daoud to press him. He said it was not a good time. "They talked about how to present themselves in a unified way: showing brotherhood, treating people well, wearing prayer caps, having a joint policy toward spies and women," said Gulob. We had heard a motorcycle come and go. Did he go to the meeting? He wouldn't say.

He told us that he had heard on the radio that Vice President Dick Cheney was in Kunar Province. I didn't believe him, but it gave me a chance to ask a question. When Cheney visited Bagram, the U.S. air base in Afghanistan, the year before, after visiting Pakistan, there had been a suicide bombing at the main gate. How did the suicide bomber know he was there? The public didn't know beforehand. Gulob said that Pakistan knew in advance that Cheney was going to be there—the Pakistanis were responsible. Someone had caused a boy to waste his life.

Now the radio announced an attack in Kunar. An Afghan army officer was killed along with soldiers and road workers. "The men from here were responsible for that operation," said Gulob. That's where the Maulavi was, killing fellow Muslims.

"*Peecheda mamala interzar hausala,*" said Razi Gul. Complicated problems require patience. "*Peecheda moshqil assan Allah.*" All complicated problems are easy for God. I sighed.

Gulob turned to me. "When I walk in you are not practicing your prayers like you were when you first came here," he said. "I am disappointed. If you do not practice, it will be harder for you to leave. My advice is to learn more. It will be better for you." Again, he was threatening me. *There shall be no compulsion in religion*, I said to myself, quoting Muhammad.

"The Maulavi said we must teach him the prayer," said Daoud. "If not, he will beat us." I began repeating that part of the prayer that I had learned. I sat on the floor, against a wood pillar, making my brain memorize, going to the next phrase. Razi Gul again corrected and encouraged me and taught me more. "*Shabash, shabash*," he said. Well done, well done. I was grateful for his encouragement. In a world where most men are illiterate, the spoken word was powerful. Gulob listened and left. I was no longer depressed.

Razi Gul turned the radio back on.

"You are listening to music," I said. "It is sinful."

He smiled. "I am human," he said. "I need relaxation. In my home I do not have a radio or a television." But in the hotel in Jalalabad he had watched music videos. He put up his hand in resignation. "Yes, I did. I admit I make mistakes. I am human." We shook hands. "*Peecheda*," he said. Life is complicated.

We sat near the bokhari, and Daoud sang an off key version of "The Yellow Rose of Texas," a song he had learned while studying at Peshawar University. He asked me to sing an American song. I sang "Clementine" and "Home on the Range," songs I last sang when the mujahideen asked me to sing twenty-five years earlier.

"Tell us proverbs," said Daoud. I thought of those I learned as a boy. "Judge not that you are not judged . . . You reap what you sow . . . Pride goes before a fall." He smiled. They had the same ones. If you pointed one finger at someone, three were pointing back at you. I smiled. We had the same expression.

We stopped for prayers. I prayed the Muslim prayer, but afterward I prayed to the God I knew as a boy. I was afraid. I was not the same man I was a week ago.

"Please ask the Maulavi to give us a few minutes of sunlight," asked Razi Gul. I said I would. I wondered if I had the courage to ask him.

Night came, and Gulob brought dinner: turnips, potatoes, and lentils. The radio announced that the Taliban had killed seven men in Kunar in another attack. "We did that," said Gulob. The Maulavi and his men had killed these men, each with a family, as they built a road to better the lives of fellow Pashtuns. How could they do this? "Infidels were paying for the road," said Gulob, and they would bring Christianity and democracy.

After dinner we sat, straining our ears for the sound of a motor. Where was the Maulavi? Razi Gul prayed. I joined him. I missed one prayer earlier. Four was enough for today.

Rahman brought in tea. I asked how he was doing. He smiled brightly. He said he was fine. I would exchange greetings, but I refused to banter. I was afraid of him, but I had to grit my teeth and not be too friendly. I didn't want to hate myself. I wouldn't grovel. I asked about his health. He was fine. He smiled again.

He had God, a family, land, and was reasonably healthy. I admired him for saying that life was good. "*Sehat zar dee.* Health is wealth," said Daoud. I asked Rahman about his asthma. He was fine. I told him to be careful of infection when he gave himself injections. He nodded. Daoud asked if he had any news. He shook his head. I gathered my courage. I said I would like to see the sun sometime. He was silent. He didn't smile. I changed the subject. I asked if he had a car.

He said no, but he had seven acres of land. It had belonged to his family for generations. I was certain that his children would know the exact boundaries, in case he died. I had met a chief in Mohmand Agency five months before whose sons were fighting another tribe over a few feet of land. Rahman smiled, showing in the shadows deep creases in his thin, lined face. "We are going to take the money from the Golden Goose and build a marble castle," he said.

No wonder he was fine. I was going to make him wealthy. He would ruin me, but I shouldn't take it personally. We sat silently. I heard a steady droning sound overhead. It was a Predator. Maybe it was hunting for the Maulavi and his men on their way back from Kunar. Hopefully, they won't use a phone when they're here. The Americans would track it and kill us with a missile.

Gulob returned with his locks and keys. "The Maulavi asked me why I didn't come in here with my rifle," he said. "I am supposed to bring it and with a bullet in the chamber. I said I didn't need it." I lay in bed wondering what the Maulavi's plans for us really were.

Monday, February 25

At dawn I heard the Predator still overhead. I wondered, daydreaming, if it was looking for us. If only I could go outside and wave my hands in the air. I prayed and went back to sleep.

At around ten or so, Gulob came in. "I called the Maulavi," he said. "He asked, 'What can I do there? I am trying to secure their release.' He will not come today." Then he left.

"They may be trying to sell us," said Razi Gul. Fear swept over me. If they sold us, the next group could torture us or kill us outright. Daoud came over to my cot, his dark, sad eyes six inches from mine. "There is a camera on a Predator?" he asked. I said yes. Could it see through the roof? I said no. He moved back away and sat on the kilim.

When Gulob returned with our food, at midday, I was nervous and couldn't eat. He sat on the kotgai rubbing his leg. It was a chance for me to engage him in conversation. I told him he had probably sprained it and to stay off it. He said the Maulavi had read from the Koran and spit on it. It would now heal. I asked his advice about our situation. What should we do? "Wait," he said.

"This is a good place for you. I have promised you, as a Muslim and as a Pashtun, to secure your release. I promise you that you will not be removed from here."

I said I trusted him. I didn't know if I did. I was grasping, looking for anything. I had read that the best way to trust a man was to trust him. I had no choice. I tore off a piece of bread, put it in the greasy broth, and ate. "If the Pakistani army starts an operation here, they may destroy my house and my family," said Gulob. "I want to resolve this." I didn't understand. How could this happen if the Taliban were tied to the government? The radio said that the government would mount an operation near Landi Khotal to get the ambassador back. He was still in prison. "Everything is a drama to show the world that Pakistan is fighting the Taliban," said Gulob. "It doesn't mean anything."

What if the army came here? I asked. Gulob replied that it would capture me and hand me over to Afghanistan and say that we were all Taliban. Then it would send people to Kabul to kill us. His eyes were cold. He moved physically away from us. If this was not resolved, he would take us to the border. He got up. As he opened the door, I saw mist above the snow. We were probably less than a few hours from the border. He shut the door, and it was dark again.

"We have to try to escape," I said. "We can cross the mountains and try to reach Afghanistan." There were probably people at the border who would capture us, said Razi Gul, as he made a fire in the bokhari. He found a piece of wire in the corner, by the window, next to boxes of what I had realized before, but tried not to think about, was Russian ammunition. *We could strangle a man*, I thought, *with that wire*.

Rahman came in bringing tea and, I sensed, to watch us. He sat on the floor. I asked how important the Pakistani government was here. It had no influence, he said. They had Sharia. The constitution of Pakistan was Western. He was right. It was based upon English law, not Muslim law. "I am a farmer," he said. "If I buy ten kilos of wheat to plant, I pay it back in about ten months. We never pay interest. It is against Islam. We planted two months ago, no poppies."

The Taliban wanted to create what Muhammad had created in Medina over a thousand years ago, a perfect, isolated Muslim world. It was man's search for purity, for God and for eternal life, and for the best way to live, while here on Earth, in brotherhood. They would kill in order to reach their goal.

Rahman asked what our rites were when we buried someone. I didn't like this question. The room grew quiet. Gulob came in to say that a car had brought the mujahideen. The Maulavi would arrive later. My stomach tightened. Daoud said he was sick and asked to go outside. Dogs barked in the night.

"*Ne fiquer, ne fiquer*," said Razi Gul. I was almost shivering with fear. Razi Gul pointed upward. "*Moshqil assan Allah—Allah malaak*." God owns everything. He smiled.

The door opened and a man with a black turban holding a rifle stood in the shadows. He stared at us and I at him. I shuddered inside. He left, but the door stayed open. Two other men, with black turbans, one wearing large black sunglasses, came in. The military commission had arrived. Who else was waiting outside? The men looked around slowly and left. We sat on the floor, our heads down.

Gulob returned and motioned to Razi Gul. He rose, stepped into his sandals, wrapped his patoo around his shoulders and over his head, and walked out. I wondered if he was going to his death. We waited. There were no cries or gunshots. About a half hour later, he appeared in the doorway, his face blank. He sat down. "What happened? What did they do?" we asked. "They asked about you," he said.

Now Gulob came for Daoud. He stepped into his shoes, the backs of which were broken, like the shoes of most Afghan men who wore shoes, so they could step in and out of them easily. He then wrapped his patoo around himself and went out. Razi Gul shook his head, looking down. He didn't talk. A half hour later Daoud returned. He said they had accused him of being a spy. "They started to beat me," he said, "but Gulob told them to stop. They asked if I had any contacts with the government of Afghanistan, and if I had any ties with intelligence agencies."

I felt weak with fear. I gathered my strength. We waited in the darkness.

Two men walked in, one with the sunglasses, the other with a darker complexion, a thin beard, and cold, hard eyes. The first man wore a vest and looked like a city dweller; the other man wore a heavy rust-colored patoo and looked like a fighter. He looked vaguely familiar. The man with the sunglasses stood rocking on his feet.

I shook his hand, asked how he was, being polite, trying to draw him in. Always I tried to establish some kind of rapport, something, anything to make it harder, I hoped, for them to kill me. "*Teek*," he said. *Teek* was Pakistani Pashto and Urdu for "I'm fine," or in his case, "I'm cool." He wasn't religious. He was a thug. He would kill me and not think twice about it. This was war. How could I win him over?

The other man was brooding and serious. He had probably killed many times. I could feel that he was religious. He would kill me, but he would treat me with respect. They sat on the floor one on either side of me. Other men stood around us, holding rifles. The room was crowded and quiet. The man with the sunglasses held a large, almost blinding flashlight in my eyes. The other man sat on his knees, took out a sheet of white typing paper, unfolded it, and began to read. I saw the numbered questions. "Tell us clearly and at length your ties to the U.S. government," he read. "We have done an investigation." The man brought the flashlight closer. I could no longer see clearly. I wondered how much they knew. They could check the Internet. If they had done so thoroughly, I was dead.

I explained my background with the mujahideen in the 1980s and my tie to Haqqani. I didn't mention Hekmatyar. He was the enemy here, competing with Mullah Omar to be the leader of the war against the Americans. I didn't talk about my work with the U.S. government. I explained my ties to Afghanistan. I was calm, strong, and petrified. I seemed to be beyond fear, beyond comprehension of where I was, yet I knew exactly where I was. My mind was clear, and the words came easily. I talked for a half hour, slowly, carefully choosing my words. Daoud translated. They listened carefully, staring hard at me.

"How do we know you are a journalist?" asked the man in the patoo. I explained my work, in detail. I told them to check the Internet. This was Pakistan. There were Internet cafés everywhere.

What did I think of the U.S. invasion of Afghanistan? I hated this question. It made me more nervous. I repeated what I had told the Maulavi.

The questions kept coming. Time passed. I was worried about the light. It hurt, but I stared at it. I couldn't be weak in front of them. "Why did you come here? Who do you really work for? Who sent you? Why do you have three cameras? What are you looking for?" I felt coldness and hardness all around me. I kept talking, oblivious to time. I felt alone. I told him I wanted to learn about them, and to give them the opportunity to explain their views.

"I don't believe this donkey," said the man holding the large flashlight.

I sighed inside. They were going to kill me. This was it. It was all a show. I gathered my strength and kept talking. I had no choice. I couldn't show too much fear, and I couldn't be too forceful. I had to show humility and strength. They would despise cowardice. I let my instincts guide me. I knew when I had said enough. I waited for the next question. I kept waiting. The room was silent.

"We want to exchange you for three of our brothers in Guantanamo: Hajji Roohullah, Maulavi Fazul, and Noorullah Noori," said the man in the patoo. My heart sank and I breathed deeply. I was elated. They wouldn't kill me now, but I would never get out of here. It didn't matter. I was going to live, for now. I was flattered that they felt I was important enough to exchange, but I knew I wasn't. I said that the U.S. government would not negotiate. I was just one man on my own. I did not work for the government. I told them I had come to write about them as I had once tried to explain the mujahideen.

Again, there was silence.

"We also want to exchange you for one and a half million dollars," he said. I hung my head. Where could I get this money? How would I get it here? I would have to sell my apartment in Manhattan and borrow money. I thought of people in New York and elsewhere I would have to contact to help me. I had to keep my family out of this. It didn't appear that they were going to kill me. Not now, anyway. The longer I could hold on, the greater my chances were of staying alive.

Gulob, sitting behind the man with the flashlight, spoke up to say that I was trying to get close to Islam. He said that he was speaking as a neutral person here. I quietly thanked him. Maybe he was my friend.

The men filed outside. I stared at the kilim, exhausted, but I had said everything. I had given it my best. I felt relieved and even free. What would they do now? Would they take me out and behead me? I waited. Twenty minutes later they all filed in and surrounded me. Their faces were hard. Men held their rifles in both hands. The room was crowded. I rose, trembling inside. The leader told me to sit down. I sat, lowering my head. Again, there was silence. I waited.

The leader said they had decided to demand only one million dollars. They would not go any lower.

I said okay, as if I had any choice. I was elated. They were not going to kill me, not tonight. There was no death sentence. I would be here for months. I didn't care. I was alive. I was so happy I was almost giddy. I felt light and free. It would take months to get a million dollars, but I would live. The man in the patoo brought out two sheets of clean white paper from his vest. I must write a letter to my wife and tell her to get the money. "Do it now," he said.

My wife? I had told Daoud and the others that I was married and had children. I had lied. I couldn't retract it now. I had constantly admonished Daoud always to tell the truth because our work was too dangerous and I had to trust him completely. I was no better.

Men routinely asked how many children I had. A man was not a man if he didn't have ten or more. He had to have sons. They could fight and carry on your name. Every man was married. I had to fit in. How could I explain that I had never been married, that in my life as a journalist I had always traveled, from one assignment to another, and had never settled down to a conventional life? Was I homosexual? Islamists hated homosexuals.

I thought of Ellen, an old friend from Switzerland who was subletting my apartment. I didn't want to write the letter. The man with the sunglasses brought the light up close to my eyes. "Write the letter now. We only have a few days," said the leader. Ellen would be my wife. Long ago I wondered if I could marry her. I sat on my knees. Riflemen leaned over me. I took my pen and the paper and began to write. "If you write anything in there that leads people here, you will be at risk," said the leader. "Tell your wife that you have been kidnapped by the Taliban. Tell her you have not been harmed. Tell her that if she contacts the U.S. government we will smash your head." The man with the patoo spoke, looking at me hard, but his voice was softer now. "Write something in there that only you two know, so that she knows the letter is from you."

Ellen was separated from her husband, but they remained close. He came from a wealthy family and worked in finance. She might be able to get some money for me. I would sell my apartment to pay her back. I would borrow the rest, somehow. In the letter I gave Ellen the name of the deputy foreign editor at CBS, who would know to contact the people at the Carnegie Council, who would contact my editor. I wrote down the name of an investment banker. I hadn't seen him in years. He had once said to me, "I am your banker." I trusted him.

How could I get a million dollars here in a few days? It was impossible. I wrote the letter quickly. I read it to Daoud, who translated it. The leader and I sat a few inches apart. I accidentally touched his hand. It was strange to touch someone who could kill you in a second. "Write that if they contact *any* government we will kill you," he said. I added this to the letter.

Now write a letter, he said, to someone I trusted in Kabul. The only man was Fazul Rahim, the CBS manager. Fazul would do everything he could to help me, but he was a Tajik and I was with the Pashtuns. I wondered if he had any ties to NDS, the Afghan intelligence agency, or if it was watching him. I was in way over my head, but I wrote the letter to Fazul. He would know what to do.

I had to keep my family out of this. I didn't want my brother and sister to mortgage their homes, borrow money, and take money from their children's education funds. I didn't want them to know what had happened to me. I didn't want them to worry, especially the children. I had got myself into this, and now I had to get myself out.

The leader took out two letter-sized manila envelopes. I was to address one envelope to my wife. I was giving my home address to the Taliban. I was to put my fax number on the envelope. I was definitely in Pakistan. There were no fax machines in Afghanistan.

I was to write the address and the mobile numbers for Fazul. His numbers were in my old diary and address book, which the Taliban had taken. A man brought in the small, black notebook, which had been put in a small plastic bag. It was comforting to see it, but I felt strange as I held it. It was from a more innocent time. I wrote the CBS address in Kabul. I had just exposed Fazul to the Taliban. I wrote his phone numbers on the envelope. I had just put him in danger.

The leader put the envelopes in a pocket in his vest. Now, what were they going to do with me? I looked down. I was filled with shame. They would send one letter to New York, either by mail or by fax, or both. Would someone in the Pakistani post office read it? What would Ellen do when she received a ransom letter? In my mind I saw the phone on my desk. The fax would fall down onto the floor, as faxes always did. Would she see it? Was there paper in the fax machine? Would she pick up the phone when it rang, preventing the fax from going through? Would the Taliban think I was lying and kill me?

Someone would deliver the letter to Fazul. It would be out now. I had been captured. All the trouble I would now cause people. I wanted all this to go away. These men, or those behind them, wanted to exchange me for a million dollars. I didn't feel worthy. I had wanted to cross the border secretly, to do what no one else could do, and to talk with Haqqani and Hekmatyar. I wanted to see them again and perhaps even go to a Taliban and al-Qaeda training camp. I had wanted to find out about bin Laden and where he might be. I understood why they were up in the mountains from the time when I was with them in the 1980s. But I was afraid of them now.

There was activity all around me. Men stood talking. They came and went, holding their rifles. I got up and sat on my cot. The leader came over and sat next to me, as if we were friends. "We are being good to you," he said softly, looking straight at me.

"I know," I said. "I am very grateful." I kept my head down. He stared at me.

"You torture us in Bagram and Guantanamo," he said. "You desecrate our Holy Koran. You mock us with your cartoons. But we will not hurt you. That is not Islam." I nodded. "We can do to you whatever we want." I shuddered inside. I looked at the floor. They could torture me any way they wanted and then kill me slowly, and no one could do anything about it. No one knew where I was. He wanted to torture and to kill me, an American, like those soldiers across the border that were killing his brothers and occupying Afghanistan. He wanted retribution, but someone above him had said no.

They left, and I sat with Razi Gul and Daoud on the floor. I was exhausted. I didn't speak. The door opened, and I froze. Was this it? Gulob walked in, carrying a large shiny silver-colored platter filled with slices of apples and oranges. "This is a gift from the Taliban," he said. I breathed deeply. They weren't going to kill us tonight. They were being good Pashtuns. I ate a few slices. I wasn't hungry, but I wanted to show gratitude, and the fruit would be good for me. "I had never seen the man with the sunglasses before," said Gulob. "There are all kinds of animals in the jungle."

Tuesday, February 26

Morning came. I got up to wash for prayers. I felt dizzy standing. We had finished after 2:00 a.m. When I finished praying, I sat on my knees and prayed to the God of my youth and to the God of Light. I wanted light. I didn't want any more darkness. I went back to bed.

I heard voices, and Gulob came in with our bowls of lentils and potatoes. I wasn't hungry. "I didn't sleep last night, worried about this," he said. "I am trying to get them to lower the amount of money." My hopes rose slightly. Was this a good cop, bad cop routine or was he serious? This roller-coaster was wearing me out.

Gulob sat on the kotgai and was silent for a few minutes; then he came to his main point. "They are trying to capture Abdullah and to find out how much you paid him and what kind of work he was doing for you. Abdullah is trying, through other Taliban, to release you."

I absorbed this. Abdullah, whom we were on our way to see when we were kidnapped, was trying to find me, while they were trying to find him first. They wanted to find out from him if I was a spy. He was trying to rescue me. They were hunting one another. If they killed him, they would kill me. There was no one in charge. Everyone was betraying and fighting one another.

"Gulob is cunning," said Daoud in English. "Do you know cunning?" I had lived in a world of cunning for months now, along the border, confusing me, frightening me, but here, I didn't know what was going on.

Gulob went out and returned with a package, wrapped in a plastic cover, that he placed on the floor. In it were four books on Islam. The Maulavi had kept his word. "Thank you," I said. "This will help me better understand Islam." It was something to read. The Maulavi wasn't going to kill me, at least for the moment. Gulob took out a packet of naswar and put some beneath his lower lip. "The men who were here last night will contact your people within three days," he said, and then he left.

A few hours later, the door opened again, and Abdul Samad stood on the threshold, like a ghost. He was alive. He was blindfolded in a black turban and his wrists were chained together. He walked two steps into the room and stood there. Gulob came behind him, holding the chain, his head down. A man in a black turban stood behind them. Gulob directed Samad to his cot. He took off the chains and the blindfold, and then he and the other man left.

We stood up happily to welcome Samad back. He gave me a long, fierce hug. I looked to see if he had been tortured. "How was it?" we asked. "Where were you? What did they do to you?" I hadn't expected to see him again.

He sat cross-legged on the floor, clasping his hands, his head down. He said that he had been in the markez. He didn't know where it was. He was blindfolded for the whole trip, except when he was in the room. It was a space like this one, but he was the only one there. He didn't see anything. I asked if he heard gunfire. Were they practicing? Did he see men training? How many people were there? How far away was it from here? I sounded like a spy. I had to be careful.

"I don't know how far it is from here," he said. "We drove awhile, that's all I know. I didn't see anything. All I heard when I was there was cars coming and going all the time. I didn't hear anyone firing. Twice they kept me up all night while a man with a rifle kept grilling me about you. How did I know you? How did I know you weren't a spy? Questions like that."

Fear swept over me. Someone there knew I was here. Gulob said they had kept that a secret. They could come here looking for me. I imagined men in black turbans and rifles spread out in a field, coming closer. It was cold. We didn't have a fire. We huddled together under our patoos. I tried to follow the conversation, in Pashto. I still didn't know where the markez was.

Gulob returned. Daoud told him that I had had an operation on my leg and needed sunlight. Gulob said he would take me outside tomorrow. He chained Razi Gul and Daoud but did not chain Samad. Something had happened at the markez. No one said anything.

Wednesday, February 27

I watched Samad closely all day. He didn't seem to have suffered, but it was hard to tell. He lay under his quilt or read the Koran.

I heard children playing outside, shouting and running. They were happy. Gulob came in and put two pens and a notebook on the floor. He sat on the kotgai. I leaned over and shook his hand. I was so grateful. "Mamur Sahib is the one among us wearing a crown," he said. "He is sitting there like a king, the only one who never lies." He asked if I was going to keep my beard when I returned to America.

I told him I kept it the last time I went back. Gulob then addressed Daoud. They were thinking of releasing him to go to Kabul to work with Fazul to get the money. "They have already gone to Kunar and Peshawar and know where your family is," he said. "If you run away with the money, they will destroy your entire family. You don't want to create animosity with the Taliban."

He turned to me and said, "If the larger Taliban find out about you, then they will want to do a prisoner exchange and will kill you one by one as the deadline passes. You are lucky that you fell into the hands of this small group." All the goodwill I felt toward him went away. I saw men coming into our cell and taking Razi Gul one day and Samad a few days later. I imagined what it was like waiting my turn to be taken out and shot or beheaded.

To escape these thoughts, I tried to read one of the books the Maulavi had given me, but it was too hard in the dark and I put the book down. Samad quickly picked it up. I could not put the book on the ground, he said. It had verses from the Holy Koran in it. I put my notebook in the book and put them both on my lap. Daoud told me not to put my notebook in the book. There were verses from the Koran inside. It could not touch these verses. I put the book and my notebook separately on my cot. Samad, the Qarie, had power over the others and was now trying to gain power over me. He had changed. Daoud was trying to impress him.

"My advice is to draw closer to Islam," said Gulob. "If not, I can hurt you."

I hated him. "There is no compulsion in religion," I said softly, in English.

Gulob left, and we were alone, four men in this dungeon. Samad put his patoo over the wire that Razi Gul had tied from one mogay on his wall to one on my wall, creating a small space of privacy over our washing pit. Samad heated water in a black kettle that sat on the bokhari and washed. As he did, Daoud told me quietly that Samad had told him how he and Abdullah, his brother-in-law, had attacked the family of Hajji Din Mohammed. They killed nine and wounded ten.

So Samad was Abdullah's brother-in-law. If Abdullah was my enemy, that meant that Samad was my enemy, too. I was in the same room with a man who very likely had killed relatives of Hajji Din Mohammed, the man I felt so close to. I stared at the ground. I wondered what was going to happen here. I hated Samad, but more than that, I was afraid of him.

Gulob returned with lentils and potatoes for dinner. I had to change his mood, and mine. I asked if he sent his children to school or if they worked for him. "I send my children to the madrassa where they learn the Holy Koran and Hadith," he said. The Hadith are the collected deeds and sayings of Muhammad, compiled by Muslim scholars, in the early centuries after his death.

I asked Gulob if it was free to send his children to a madrassa. He said it cost three hundred rupees a month, about five dollars. "God will not ask if you have a Ph.D. or a master's degree or if you were a journalist or a doctor, but what you did for Him, whether you prayed and whether you learned the Koran and the Hadith," he said.

I asked if the schools were Deobandi or Wahhabi. He said Wahhabi. They were stricter and more rigid. "Here it is obligatory to pray five times a day, to do jihad and preach Islam," Gulob said. "Before, our maulavis said if you even touched a foreigner's clothes you must cut off a piece of that clothing. If you shook hands with a foreigner or ate with him, you were supposed to cut off your hand, but there is nothing in Islam about that. Now it is okay to eat with the non-Muslim." He looked at me. "You look Muslim. If you were to go anywhere and people saw that you were a foreigner, they would behead you."

Gulob was now warming to the subject. "The Taliban have killed many people at checkpoints in Bajaur," he said. "They have taken over the province. There is a tradition here of strong preachers. They've come from Saudi Arabia. Many from here go to universities there. During jihad, Arabs came here and cried, 'We were not acceptable to you, Allah,' if they were not martyred, so great was their desire." (By *jihad*, he meant the war against the Soviets.) Osama bin Laden, a Wahhabi, would find comfort and power in this environment. It was outsiders like him who brought suicide bombing to the Pashtuns.

I asked Gulob where the mullahs came from. He said from here, not Saudi Arabia. They taught, called the people to prayer, performed weddings, funerals, prayed at a child's birth, and called the people to jihad. Traditionally, the mullahs were the poorest in a Pashtun village, taking food in exchange for performing services. In the 1980s, mullahs like Jalaladin Haqqani, nurtured by Pakistan, financed by the United States and Saudi Arabia, led the jihad against the Russians and grew in power. Haqqani had once stood by the road soliciting funds for his small mud-brick mosque near Khost, in Afghanistan, along the border. Now his brand-new mosque was in the center of Khost and dominated the city, with its beautiful twin turquoise minarets, like a cathedral looking over a village in France or Spain.

"The Americans have come to Afghanistan for the precious stones, they say," said Gulob. I said no, the Chinese had just won the biggest contract for minerals so far. They were going to mine copper in Logar, a province southeast of Kabul.

Gulob walked out the door and bolted it. I had made a mistake. My instinct was to protect America. I had to be more humble and more religious. He returned to chain Daoud and Razi Gul to their beds. Samad got up to get a drink of water. He walked confidently around the room. He was equal to me now, free to move about. I didn't like it.

Thursday, February 28

I worked out after morning prayers. I had rested for two days, what I needed for my body to recover. I added another exercise, following a pattern that I had learned in college, gradually doing more. It was a tie to home. I felt strong and calm when I finished. I put my patoo over the wire that Razi Gul had strung up, stood over the pit, and took a small bucket of cold water and soap and washed. The others used warm water. I had to show them I was tougher. I had to show them that I was the strongest in my battle with Samad and if we were going to try to escape. I put my clothes back on and my patoo around my shoulders, like a cape, and sat on the floor. A ray of light shone through the dirty window, like light shining through trees in the forest.

That afternoon Samad removed the mattress from his cot and tightened the rope bottom, pulling on each strand as if he were tightening shoelaces. He grunted like a weight lifter—showing off, I felt. Razi Gul did the same, untying the rope at the foot, pulling on each part, tightening it. His bed was now taut and firm. We did the same to my cot. Samad did not help us. Daoud did nothing.

Gulob came in. "I thought you were trying to escape," he said, "making so much noise." He took my mattress to put out in the sun. I said I wanted to see the sun. He ignored me. He came back and sat with us.

"They gave me a Russian pistol last night and said if you try to escape to kill you," he said. "I said I don't want to use this in my house. The Taliban slaughtered six people in Bajaur last night who didn't agree with them." The sense of peace I felt this morning disappeared. It was not in Islam for him to negotiate money for our release. God would punish him, but he would try to get the Taliban to lower the price. He asked how much I would pay him to do this.

"We will take care of you," said Daoud. "How much do you want?"

"How much is your life worth?" asked Gulob.

I hated him. He would try to get the Taliban to let him negotiate on their behalf. Daoud would negotiate on my behalf. Both of them would swear on the Holy Koran. If either of them betrayed their oath, even their grandchildren would suffer. The penalty would be that great. If Daoud betrayed them, they would kidnap his children.

That afternoon I asked him more about the Red Mosque in Islamabad. What really happened? It was all a drama, he said. The Pakistani government was behind everything to show the world that there was terrorism here, all in order to get money from America. "We are getting stronger all the time," he said. "We have trained 250 suicide bombers to attack a base that the U.S. is going to build on the Kunar border." I asked how he trained a suicide bomber. He leaned forward on the kotgai, his voice low, his face close to mine. "We show videos of Americans in Afghanistan breaking into houses, mistreating women, and desecrating the Holy Koran," he said. "We show them the cartoons of the Prophet, peace be unto him. We read the Holy Koran. I myself tried to become one but decided not to because I have children. Gulbadeen Hekmatyar and Jalaladin Haqqani train suicide bombers, but behind them is the Pakistani army. They do the training. Behind Osama is the Pakistani army."

The room was silent. His voice was firm, his eyes almost gleaming. He frightened me.

He said the Taliban were looking for antiaircraft guns. Iran said it would provide them. If they did, America would be finished. Pakistan would put Iranian markings on them, and Iran and the United States would fight each other. "This fire will continue until the U.S. leaves Afghanistan," he said. "Pakistan will kill all the influential figures, all the leaders and intellectuals."

Gulob went outside and returned with my mattress. It was warm from sitting in the sun. "The Americans eat pigs," he said. He made an ugly face. "We recoil from pigs." He literally shuddered. Pork was forbidden in Islam.

I heard women making bread and was happy. Warmth was coming. Gulob brought our food, and Razi Gul prayed. I watched Samad eating more than the rest of us. Gulob said he had discussed with the Taliban bringing Daoud's father as a hostage and sending Daoud to Kabul to get the money. "The Taliban seem to agree that this might be the best way, but the Maulavi will come in two days," he said. "We can talk about it then."

Daoud's face was somber. His father was an old man. He didn't want to bring him here. I thought of the heavy, white-bearded man, stooped over, living in this dark cell, the fear of death hanging over him.

Gulob thought the price could be negotiated. He was working on it. "They have tried to capture Abdullah," he said, "but each time he's escaped. If they capture him, it will be very bad for you." My stomach tightened. What did he mean? He wouldn't say. I kept hoping that Abdullah would appear with his men and get us out of here. He had to try to rescue us. He was a Pashtun. He had invited us here. We were his guests.

"Don't believe him," Daoud whispered as Gulob talked with Samad. "It is *C*. Our two colleagues keep insisting that he leave the price high."

I put my head in my hands. Razi Gul came to my cot and put his arm around me. After evening prayers, I stayed on my knees, praying for my family and to be kept alive. I knew that it was irrational to pray, that it was impossible there was a great white God, with a long beard, sitting in a chair beyond the clouds, but I didn't care. I wanted comfort. I wanted to live.

"If they bring my father here," whispered Daoud, "it will ruin the brotherhood in my family. This will give my brother power over me. I have had to bring my father here as a hostage, an old man."

We had to get the money from Kabul. It would be too hard to get it here from America. I sat in the dark thinking of people who could possibly help.

Saturday, March 1

After I finished my prayers, while the others were asleep, I sat on the floor, took my notebook, and wrote down a list of names and cell phone numbers. Some I wrote from memory. These were people I knew in Kabul, New York, and elsewhere who might be able to raise a million dollars for me. I would pay them back. I hesitated for a long time, and then I wrote down my brother's and sister's numbers. I wondered if I had put them in danger. I was nervous.

I was taking a chance, a big chance, but I had no choice—I had to get the money. I woke Daoud and made him sit on the kilim with me. I handed him the list. "No one here must see this," I whispered. "If you go to Kabul, take it to Fazul." He looked at it, nodded thoughtfully, put it in his vest pocket, and went back to bed. The two of them would have to call these people. I hoped I could trust Daoud.

The door opened, and Gulob walked in to give us the daily news. The Americans killed forty innocent people yesterday in Afghanistan but were denying it. The Taliban had gone off somewhere, but he had sent Rahman to get permission from them to bring Daoud's father and to send him to Kabul.

It was very hard for me to understand what Gulob was saying. I needed Daoud, but he was spending most of the day now in bed. "I can't sleep at night because of the chains on my legs," he said. "They treat us like animals." I couldn't argue with him. I wasn't chained. I hated it that I had to keep asking him to translate.

Daoud joined us for lunch but kept his head down. Gulob raised his hands and asked God to resolve our problem. I reluctantly raised my hands with my palms up. I felt too close to him, but my heart lifted. Perhaps he did want to save my life. He had prayed for me.

Late that afternoon, Gulob returned, sat on the kotgai, and put snuff in his mouth. His eyes were cold and watery. "If you try to escape, there will be a Talib under every rock waiting for you," he said. "They will see that you are a foreigner and a spy." My happiness disappeared. He had just called me a spy, which meant death. He said it would be very dangerous for me to go to the markez. He was trying to keep me from there. There were many Talibs there whose mothers and fathers had been killed by the Americans. They were filled with Islam. They would spit on me because they had lost their families to U.S. bombings.

I imagined sitting on the ground surrounded by young men holding rifles and staring at me. "It takes the maulavis a long time to make up their minds," he said. "At first they didn't want you to have your reading glasses, but I got them for you." He told a story:

"There was a translator who came from Kunar to Bajaur. He was taken prisoner by the Taliban. Shopkeepers who knew him, and others, pleaded with the Taliban to save him. Within thirty minutes they killed him, put dirt in his mouth, and wrote on his forehead, 'This is what happens to those who work with Americans.'"

He got up and left. He returned that evening, sat on the kotgai, and talked. We sat on the floor, like students, and listened. The mujahideen did not like to take money. It was not in Islam. They slaughtered spies immediately. If other Taliban knew I was here, they would behead me and show the world their intelligence was strong. I was lucky to be in the hands of a small group. Some here were supported by Pakistan, others by people in Saudi Arabia, others by other groups. No one was in charge. Groups operated independently.

I sat there imagining other Taliban, with rifles and black turbans, now slowly surrounding our compound.

"*Ne fiquer. Moshqil assan Allah,*" said Razi Gul, pointing his hand upward.

Daoud handed me a piece of paper. He had been writing while we were talking. Samad's English was getting better, listening to me, he wrote. We had to be extra careful. "It is a *C,*" he wrote. "The Taliban asked for $1.5 million. This is the amount you mentioned the first day when we asked you how much your house was worth." I wasn't sure about the question. I couldn't remember. My apartment wasn't worth that much. Did I actually say that? Daoud put the note in the fire. My thoughts turned to dying. How would I face death when the time came? I thought of being dragged out into the night, my shirt open and my neck exposed. I could do it. I already had.

In my mind I practiced the speech I would give if the Taliban sentenced me to death.

Sunday, March 2

I heard birds this morning, chirping, the sound of life. I wanted to walk in the morning sun through the fields and watch children play. That was all I wanted, that simple pleasure. Rahman had returned from the markez the night before and had brought word from the Maulavi that I must learn the whole Salat. The Maulavi's message gave me hope. He wasn't going to kill me, at least not right now, but I had to show, by my every action, that I was drawing close to Islam.

Gulob came in at midmorning. Daoud was still in his cot, and Gulob called to him to get up. "I reached the Maulavi on the wireless," he said. "He is coming tonight. He sent a car this morning to take all of you to the markez. He said I should send you there if I was bored with you. I said your lives would be at risk. There are young, angry, ambitious men there who want to prove that their intelligence is good and to become famous. They will behead you. I said I wasn't bored. I sent the car back."

I sank back on the floor. I couldn't trust the Maulavi, or was I being manipulated by Gulob? Did the Maulavi want to show the other Taliban whom he had captured? Would this enhance his stature? We hadn't heard a car that morning, but I rarely heard the Taliban arrive. I felt hollow in my stomach, in my whole being.

He said he had talked with the Maulavi about sending Daoud to Kabul, but there was a problem. The Taliban had captured a man who said he worked with widows; in fact he worked for the U.S. Army. But he was poor, and Gulob had pressed the Maulavi to let him go. He went back to his old work with the Americans. The Taliban blamed Gulob. They were now trying to kill the man. Gulob sipped his tea. "Our intelligence is good," he said. "We can always find you." Again, a threat.

He looked at Daoud. He would have to sign a letter saying he had received one million dollars. He said he would try to lower the amount. I felt weak and frustrated. Where could I find that kind of money in Kabul? I scratched my legs gently. I had red welts all over my body. It was either bugs or nerves. The welts had appeared two nights ago.

Daoud began to tell me a Hadith, a saying of Muhammad, in Pashto and English. Razi Gul and Gulob said it wasn't true. Daoud flicked his wrist, dismissing them. "They are illiterate and don't know anything," he said. I told him not to embarrass them, especially Gulob, in front of me. I didn't want to hurt Gulob's pride, his *eftekhar*, his honor. They were stupid, Daoud said. I told him to be quiet. I could feel my anger rising.

"I am going to withdraw my children from the school where they are learning English, because of you," Gulob told Daoud. This confused me, because Gulob had said that his children were going to a madrassa. They would not teach English there. Daoud then said something I didn't understand and wouldn't translate it. I hung my head. He was my bridge and had power over me. I needed him. It was my own fault; my language skills were too poor. We waited for everyone's anger to pass.

I asked Samad about living in Peshawar. What kind of work did he do? He said he was a laborer. He couldn't open a shop because his enemies would destroy it. He said his family owned land in Jalalabad, but he had told the Taliban that he was poor. He said, at another time, that his family owned a fabric shop. I asked where their fabrics came from. He didn't know. His brothers dealt with that. The head of the family didn't know? The Koran said that it was a sin to lie, yet he was lying. He knew I knew it.

I was mad at him and mad at myself for working with him. I thought I understood the Taliban. Now I was their prisoner. I had come to tell their story, and now they were very possibly going to kill me.

Worse, if that was possible, the men who brought me here may have killed the brother of Hajji Din Mohammed, the man to whom I felt closest in Afghanistan. I asked Samad, my voice softer, to tell me the story.

"One of my cousins was a commander during jihad," he said. "He later got a job as commander of a border post." It was a lucrative job. Like a customs agent, he could tax people bringing goods, legally or illegally, across the border. "During this time, Hajji Din Mohammed was governor of Nangarhar Province." It was along the border. Jalalabad was the capital. "Hazrat Ali was head of state security." I didn't tell him that I knew Hajji Din Mohammed or that I had met with Hazrat Ali. He was one of two commanders hired by the United States in 2001 to capture Osama bin Laden at Tora Bora. "Hazrat Ali and Hajji Din Mohammed invited my cousin to one of their houses and killed him. That started the animosities between us. Our family has killed twenty-five people in their families since then."

I asked if he was involved. He said no, waving his hand, he didn't like killing. But Daoud had told me that Samad had killed seventeen people. I was getting angry again.

It was very likely that Samad had been involved in the death of Hajji Qadir, especially since Abdullah, whom I had trusted to be my guide, was married to Samad's sister. I was sick. I said to Samad that I had heard that Abdullah was involved in the death of Hajji Qadir. Was that true? Samad didn't like this question and didn't like that I was the one asking it. He sat across from me in our cell, each of us on his own cot. It was our own territory. It was too dark to see Samad's face clearly, but I could tell by the way he was sitting that he was angry. I didn't care.

"Abdullah was not involved in this," he said. He was lying. "We are trying to kill Hazrat Ali and Hajji Din Mohammed, but we need to wait until they are no longer in power."

I asked how much it would cost to kill them. He wouldn't say.

I wondered if he and Abdullah would get some of my money. Would I, by giving them money to save my life, if that was possible, be giving them money that they would use to try to kill Hajji Din Mohammed? I put my head in my hands.

Thursday, March 6

Rahman came in with the keys this morning. He said the Maulavi had called and that Gulob had gone away. I noticed when he opened the door that the snow on the mountain was gone. It later rained, and the rain turned to hail pounding on the roof.

I asked Rahman if he and Gulob worked together. They lived together, he said, but worked separately. They were a family.

"Like the Taliban are a family?" I asked.

He said yes. He stared at us. "Don't be unhappy," he said. He left.

Gulob came that afternoon, bringing tea and a plate of *cheuhu*, a heady mixture of coconut, walnuts, sugar, and spices. He said they ate it once a year. It was too sweet, and all the sugar made me edgy. For dinner we had chicken, potatoes, spinach, buttermilk, and masta curry. I didn't know if we were being treated as honored guests or if this was my last meal.

Gulob brought in branches for a fire. I asked if women gathered wood. He said they used to but the Taliban put a stop to it. Women had to stay at home. We had to be quiet tonight. His relatives were coming, and he didn't want them to know I was here. I would be at risk. He didn't trust his own family. "I saw a beautiful goat today," he said. "I wanted to buy it and slaughter it for you, but it cost two thousand rupees"—thirty-five dollars. Daoud said we would buy it for him, but we had no money. I didn't believe Gulob.

"I pray that the Maulavi doesn't come tonight," said Gulob. I wondered if he was hiding things from the Maulavi, too. Or was it all a show? They had surely prepared a feast for his relatives, and that was why there was so much food.

Gulob left, and Samad listened to the radio. "Two of our enemies are being interviewed," he said. "*Tarbur.* It's been going on for forty years." Tarbur, or Tarburwali, meant each man fought for power and the honor to lead his clan. It was cousin warfare, over land that Samad's family owned in Jalalabad.

I was upset. The Taliban would take money from me, but not from him. If the Maulavi's men did their research, they would learn that Samad had land. Maybe they were all in this together. I was the Golden Goose, eating every day with a killer.

The fire burned low. It was getting cold. I put my patoo over my pakool to keep warmer. I wondered if they had sent my letters and if people in America now were trying to raise one million dollars. Were they negotiating? Where was the Maulavi? Why didn't they send Daoud to Kabul? I didn't trust Gulob. I didn't trust anybody.

Samad asked if I could tell him the history of Spain. Did I know of Andulus? It was the Arab name for Spain. He wanted to know the Arab names of its cities. I told him that Muslims ruled Spain for eight hundred years and that but for one battle lost would have ruled Europe. They listened. This was how it was for millennia, when men sat around fires telling stories, when conquering tribes came and went, creating civilizations. I liked teaching them. It took the fear out of me.

Gulob came in, wearing a bandolier of bullets and carrying a pistol and a rifle. Had he come to take us away, finally? Would we be shot at night? He sat on Razi Gul's cot.

"I had many guests tonight, but I am happier here with you," he said. "The Taliban said I am supposed to carry a rifle and a pistol and have bullets in the chambers of both of them when I enter this room. I am supposed to give you tea and food and not talk to you. If the Taliban come from the markez, I will give you weapons and we will fight them, or I will give you women's clothes to wear and they won't be able to come in this room. I have many cousins and other relatives at the markez, but when they receive orders they don't care. Blood doesn't matter as much as Islam. I didn't like that Talib who came that night when you wrote the letter, the one with the sunglasses and big mustache. There are a lot of scammers in the Taliban. He is a bad person. There are bad people and good people in the Taliban. I don't trust my relatives. That is why I carry weapons tonight."

It was Tarburwali, cousin warfare. "I promised to protect you," Gulob went on. "You don't know all I'm doing that I don't tell you about. I've done a lot of things to protect you, and I'm doing things now, not for you, but God knows my heart. I am doing these things for God. There are those who take off their suicide vests and run away. Those who really believe in Islam keep the vest on and press the button. The scammer would throw it away. My heartfelt desire is that you will be released, and I will have a rifle and protect you on the way."

Gulob got up to leave but then stopped to tell a story. "An old man in Kunar was sick and came across to Pakistan for medical treatment," he said. "The Taliban captured him and took him to the markez. He's been there four months. 'Why am I here?' he asked. 'Your son is a spy,' they said." He had opened up to us, and now, to counteract that, he was implying that I might be a spy.

Daoud asked for a sleeping pill. Gulob took one from his pocket and then chained Daoud to his bed.

I stared into the darkness. I thought of the prisoners' chorus in Beethoven's opera *Fidelio*. I hadn't thought of it in years. I went to see the opera at the Met in New York some years ago. I bought an expensive ticket and sat up close, just to hear the chorus. I loved the message of this opera, the message of men standing up against tyranny, suffering, telling the truth, just to be free.

Friday, March 7

It rained through the night. Our cell was cold and damp. I had slept poorly and was depressed and afraid. My welts itched. I worked out, to take me away from where I was and to change my mood. Exercise was a form of meditation and made me feel strong and relaxed, a tie to my past and home.

Afterward I poured cold water over myself, shivering but soothing the itching of my welts.

Gulob came in. I was sitting alone, reading one of my books on Islam and fingering my tesbah, my prayer beads. Razi Gul told me to move a bead every time I said a word or phrase of the Salat. It would help me memorize it. Gulob told Daoud to wake up. He was angry that Daoud didn't get up for morning prayers. Samad and Razi Gul joined us on the floor. Gulob wanted to talk. He told us the story of a drug dealer who lived in Khyber Agency. "We took our heroin to him. He said to wait a few days, and he would pay us. We waited and went to see him again. 'Thousands of you come with your heroin and I never pay, so go,' he said. I said to him, 'Do not think we are like these people.'" There were ten people in Gulob's group. They had a quarrel, which turned into a fistfight, and they left. They went to a friend in the Pakistani army. He wrote a letter to the dealer, and they took it to him. He read it and said, "Sit here, you are our special guests." Within two days they got paid.

I asked about the heroin trade. "We make it here," said Gulob. "Those who make heroin have quarrels at home. You don't feel good inside. The rate today for one kilo is 200,000 rupees [$3,500], more in Peshawar and Lahore. In Iran it is 600,000 per kilo. We sell heroin to ISAF and U.S. soldiers. I came in this morning with a rifle and magazines of bullets to check on you. My relatives stayed last night, and I didn't sleep. I was worried."

I asked Gulob to explain Tarburwali. "Tarburwali is the job of the Pashtuns," he said. "If you don't have Tarburwali, you are not Pashtun. Tarburwali is when someone kills your father, and you, in turn, kill his father. It is when someone comes to your hujra, and you receive him and prepare a meal for him. If someone kills your father and he comes to your hujra, and you are proud, and you forgive him, that is Tarburwali. Tarburwali is against Islam."

"Just as we have been captured and are being kept here as prisoners is completely against Islam, we cannot blame Islam," said Daoud.

"True," said Gulob, acknowledging that he was a hypocrite. "Islam accepts only half of Pashtunwali and Tarburwali."

Daoud quoted Sadiqullah Reshteen, an Afghan poet: "Life is too short for loving; I am surprised how people have time for hatred." Gulob said he had a good memory. "I miss my mother so much," said Daoud. "She wanted to have an educated son. I am her favorite. My father beat me for wanting an education. He just wanted me to study Islam. I've had such a hard life."

He looked at me, hoping for sympathy. I gave him none. "A million of your countrymen died during jihad, and millions more were wounded," I said. "This country is filled with people with one leg and one arm. You have a wife, a family, and a good job. We're in trouble now, but you've had an easy life. I understand why your father got angry at you. You sleep all day here; I have to plead with you to translate"—I gave up.

"I'm tired of prison," said Razi Gul. He no longer spoke of his beloved Amina. He spent more and more time under his quilt, coming out only to pray, pace the floor on occasion, or eat.

"This is not a prison, this is a house," said Gulob forcefully. He was providing us with food and tea and a place to sleep. He was a good Pashtun.

Daoud took a piece of paper and wrote that I should pretend I was sick. Gulob could not cope with it. It would make him resolve our problem. I frowned at him. "You don't know Pashtuns," he said, in English. "I do." We drank our tea, all of us watching one another. Daoud had lied to me too often.

"When I come, all I see you doing is sleeping," Gulob said to him. "Prayer and the Holy Koran will help you. Money will not resolve your problem. I pray for you people, and I pray for myself every night. I pray and cry to God all the time that he will resolve this."

The Maulavi wanted me to become Muslim and to take their message to the world. If I could only do that, I wouldn't have to try to find a million dollars. But I couldn't convert. It was impossible. Gulob went outside and returned a few minutes later. He put my old notebook and a pen on the floor. This was the notebook the Taliban had taken from me, along with my diary, when they captured us. I smiled, thanking him, lowering my head. He asked, when this was over, if I would give him my knife. It had different blades, scissors, pliers, a can opener, all in one. He had gone through my things. He could do anything he wanted to me, and he politely asked for my knife. I almost smiled. I said yes, as if I had a choice. If I gave it to him he would feel obligated. I liked the idea of giving it to him. He asked how much it cost. I told him. "Expensive," he said. "But I like it. It's from America."

I opened an old, soiled language primer that Gulob had brought, and with Daoud's help I began to learn to read and write Pashto. It made me think and took me away from where I was. A new world opened up. I was excited and had energy. Razi Gul came and sat next to me. He put his finger on the page, and together we read a few letters of the alphabet. He wasn't completely illiterate. He had begun to use English words, listening to me. We would do this together. "The time to learn is when you're young. I'm an old man," he said.

After dinner, Rahman came in and sat on Razi Gul's cot. We

made a fire, and smoke filled the room. We had a small lantern and a flashlight, but it was still dark and he looked like a hawk staring at us. Gulob told us that Rahman had tied one of his dogs so tight that he killed him. Rahman said that he used to be a heroin dealer. People came here to buy it.

I asked how they made heroin. You added water to the raw opium, stirred, poured it out into bowls, and then added hydrogen chloride and ammonia and dried it and put it in plastic bags. He had done this for three years, but now he forgot. Gulob said that the cost of hydrogen chloride had risen too high and that he no longer made heroin; Rahman was the expert. Rahman explained that the opium mixture had to be cooked and stirred for three hours and transferred to different barrels, using a white wash. Not really understanding, I asked Gulob to explain the process in more detail. "Don't eat my mind," he said. I had pushed too far. I put my head down, afraid. It was quiet.

Gulob picked up his primer and began to read the alphabet, struggling, like a child. Slowly, with Daoud's help, he pronounced the first five or six letters. "Don't be mad at me, Mamur Sahib," he said, "we are classmates."

I felt warm toward him. I had instilled in him a desire to read and write. If I, a foreigner with a half gray beard, was trying to study Pashto, so would he. It was competition. He studied for about fifteen minutes, then put his flashlight in his mouth and chained his teacher and Razi Gul to their cots. "*Shpa pakhair,*" I said. Good night. Always I was trying to stay on his good side, like a child to a parent. I got mad at myself for giving in to him. It was a primal part of me, trying to survive.

"*Zindabad,* Mamur Sahib," he said as he walked out the door. Long life; this, coming from my jailer. I thanked him for letting me use his schoolbook. "I can get anything for you," he said. "You look like a Pashtun." He closed the door.

Saturday, March 8

I lay in the dark waiting for the rooster to crow. There was no call to prayer here, we were so isolated. Where was Abdullah? Were there negotiations going on somewhere? I prayed and afterward stayed on my knees with my patoo around me, like a monk. When I finished, I sat there waiting for my killers. I could face them. It was cold and damp. I got up and walked back and forth from the door to the pit, fingering my tesbah, back and forth, back and forth, five steps each way. Each time I stood up now I felt dizzy and had to put my hand against a wood column for support. My legs ached until I started walking. I had to keep my blood circulating.

Late that morning, Gulob came in and sat on the kotgai. He was quiet and then began to talk. "You made a big mistake by coming here, and I made a big mistake by taking you prisoner," he said. "I am worried about a leak. The Taliban have links with one another from here to Waziristan. There are children here. They talk. If anyone learns that you are here, I and my whole family, all my cousins from here to Peshawar, will be destroyed. But I will die before you. I am Pashtun. This is Pashtunwali. I will protect you. You are my body. My body is your body."

Gulob was starting to get worked up. I wanted him to stop talking. "I am a prisoner here, too," he said. "I am ready to become a suicide bomber. Within two years I will do it. The only thing that counts is Paradise. This life is nothing. Only the hereafter counts." He leaned forward, his knees together, his eyes intense and moist. "I invite you to come to Islam," he said. He repeated this again and again, wearing me down. I told him that a few days earlier he had said he wouldn't become a suicide bomber because he had children. "I don't care about them," he said. "I have Allah.

They have Allah." He looked at me. "Maybe we can get Mamur Sahib to become a suicide bomber at the Pentagon."

I felt sick, thinking of myself wearing a suicide vest, blowing myself up, killing my own people. Why did he bring this up? I was playing with fire, pretending to be what I wasn't and did not want to become. *I am in a land of complete and total darkness,* I wrote in my diary, *as dark as this room at night. I cannot see my hands. Yet I cling to hope that we will make it.*

Gulob said all he wanted to do was resolve this and take me to the border and to safety. He promised me, *inshallah,* we would do this. He wanted to go tomorrow. He hoped within six or seven or twelve days to resolve this. They would take a million, a billion, or half a billion dollars from me, but it would be for the *amarat,* the Taliban rule. *Amarat* means a government ruled by an emir, a Muslim king. The land was now, to them, a Muslim theocracy. "You think about money," he said. "It is nothing against God. You think of your book, of your research, of this life here on Earth. They are nothing. It is only the hereafter that counts."

I was exhausted. If only I had his faith. My book was important, but my life was more important. Gulob's work, his life, was jihad.

"I have put myself at complete risk by bringing you here," he said. "Think of this as being in your brother's house." He put out his hand and asked for mine. We shook hands. His was big and gnarled. I wanted to believe him. I also wanted the conversation to end.

Rahman came in and sat on Razi Gul's cot. He asked how we buried the dead in my country. Did we throw them into rivers? Did we have cemeteries? I said that mostly we buried people, but we cremated them too. I didn't like this conversation. "The Shia open up bodies and clean intestines and put two letters inside, for Paradise, and then they sew the bodies up," said Daoud. "Here we wash the body and put it in a single white cloth and put it in the grave."

Rahman asked if we faced our bodies toward Mecca. I said no. Again, I thought, *I will sell my apartment, live in one room, anything, if only I can get out of here alive.* Gulob was also frightening. I saw ferociousness in him, the ability to attack and rampage and kill in order to cleanse the world of all that stood in the way of Islam.

Late that afternoon, Daoud was giving me a Pashto lesson when Gulob came in and sat on his haunches next to me. I stayed on the ground, to make sure that I was lower than he was. I had to make certain always that he felt secure in his power. I was feeling more and more that Gulob could well be trapped: by the villagers around us who would kill us all if they found out he was harboring an American; by Taliban groups who would do the same; by the Pakistani government, which would take us all into custody—him for kidnapping me, me for crossing the border illegally and going into a region off-limits to foreigners. The others were accomplices. If the ISI found us—I didn't want to think about it. Gulob had said that an ISI officer had come by the other day. Another time he said that four ISI men had come to the village. I cringed each time he said this.

Again Gulob told me that we were classmates and put his finger over the letters and slowly began to pronounce them. I knew more of the alphabet than he did now, but I couldn't let him know that. I pointed to pictures and asked him to tell me what they were in Pashto, and how to pronounce the words. I wanted him to teach me, to give him that power, and to use it to draw us closer together. He told me he had been afraid to stay in school as a boy. He didn't have the confidence and preferred to play in the mountains. He found answers and peace and a home in Islam. He put out his hand. I shook it and looked at him. He looked down, got up, chatted with the others for a minute, and walked outside.

I had gone too far. I shouldn't have looked at him. I had to keep humble. Samad sat on his cot reading and chanting the

Koran. Daoud found solace under his quilt. He whispered that he wanted to talk to Gulob alone about giving money to him to free us. "How do I get the money here?" I asked incredulously. He put his finger to his mouth. Quiet. He didn't trust our cell mates. He told me that I must pull on Gulob's beard. It would draw him to me and make us close. You will see, he said.

That evening, after dinner and prayers, Gulob came in. The Maulavi had arrived, he announced, along with several other Taliban. They were in the other room next to us. We were not to talk. Again, we hadn't heard a car engine. How did the Taliban come here? The Maulavi would come to see us later, after the others were gone.

He left, and we waited in silence. I was scared. He or the other Taliban could take us out and kill us tonight. This must be a Taliban safe house. They came always at night and left the next morning. The Taliban needed Gulob and Rahman to provide sanctuary.

Daoud put his ear to the wall by his cot and listened. They were talking on the "wireless." We waited and waited. It was cold. Gulob finally came in and informed us that the military commission was here. "We don't want to talk with those people while they're here," he said quietly. I was afraid, especially of the man who had called me a donkey. We would talk in the morning. Gulob saw that I was afraid. "Do not be unhappy," he said. "I am your brother." He ran his finger slowly over the first line of the alphabet in his primer. He said not to talk and walked out.

Late that night, long after our last prayer, he took us outside, one by one. I walked slowly, looking at the sky, breathing deeply, gulping in the fresh mountain air. He guided me back, holding his flashlight to the ground. I wanted to return to the cell. I walked in and felt warm. I was returning to what had become my home. The Taliban wouldn't see us here. I was afraid of the outside world.

Sunday, March 9

After morning prayers, Gulob came in, got Abdul Samad out of bed, blindfolded him, and took him away.

I had to be strong, but I was afraid. Samad returned about a half hour later. He was upset. They wanted his home phone number. They were going to demand money from his family. Good. He too would have to pay. He said that the Maulavi and three members of the military commission were in the other room. They asked again how long he had known me and if I was a spy. He said that he didn't have any information about that. They were discussing how to capture Abdullah and how to get a million dollars from me.

So they were negotiating with somebody. Tears came to my eyes, but no one could see me in the dark. Someone was negotiating for my release. I didn't feel worthy. I was ashamed of all the trouble I had caused.

Gulob entered again, blindfolded Razi Gul, and took him away. Ten minutes later, the Maulavi entered. We stood at attention. He shook hands with Daoud. He touched one hand to my shoulder and put his other hand on my chest. I did the same to him. It was *baghal kashee,* a formal yet common Pashtun greeting ritual, a form of hugging, and a sign of respect. The Maulavi's body felt hard; it was as if I was touching steel.

"*Kenna,*" he said. Sit down. We sat cross-legged a few feet apart. He was wearing a black turban, tied crisscross in the front, with its long *lungi,* the end of the turban, hanging down in front. He wore a mustard-colored vest, with thin black checks, and an off-yellow jamay. He wasn't focusing on Judgment Day. He loved his power and dressed beautifully.

His eyes were bright, almost glistening. How was I? How was my health? How had I been treated? How was the food? Was I getting enough to eat? The questions came quickly. He touched his hand to his mustache and his dark beard, and he leaned his head back. Even at this hour his voice was strong and confident. He waited impatiently.

I said I was fine, in good health, and I was being treated well. I spoke carefully. I praised the food and said that Gulob was a good host.

Was I getting any sun? he asked, resting his elbow on his knee, his hand touching his beard, his face cocked slightly to the side. I silently thanked him for this question. I said no.

He thought for a second and realized, I felt, that he couldn't let me outside. Perhaps he worried that someday I would be able to describe the place to others, and he couldn't risk that.

The questions kept coming. Was I washing? Was I getting exercise? Again, a strange question, unless Gulob had told him about my morning workouts. Was I getting warm water for ablutions? I looked at him briefly and then down. Yes, I was washing; I exercised, on the floor here. I hadn't left the darkness of this room but for two or three minutes each night. He asked if I had been praying. How far along was I in the prayer? What word was I up to? I looked at Daoud. Should I recite it? He nodded. I closed my eyes and began to recite the declaration of faith: "*La illaha illalaha Muhammad . . .*"

He cut me off. "If he hasn't learned the whole prayer, the three of you"—he waved his hand at Daoud and the others—"I will harm all of you." He looked back at me. Did I want to ask him about Islam? I hesitated. I wanted to ask about the Taliban and al-Qaeda, but I would start with Islam. I thanked him for the books on Islam and said I had been praying. I'd had many conversations with the others about Islam. They were guiding me. They helped me learn the prayer. I was memorizing more and more each day.

He said the military commission wanted to exchange me for

three men from Guantanamo. "It's terrible what they are doing to Muslims in Guantanamo," he said. He shook his head in sorrow and anger. I was afraid where this would lead. "They are torturing them. Hajji Rashid, one of our leaders, wrote a letter to his children, his wife, and his mother, saying how terrible things were. The Red Cross delivered it. He said he might die but would go to Paradise." The Maulavi shook his head. I put my head down. I felt cold.

Why wouldn't they want to take their revenge out on me? America tortured its prisoners. Why not an eye for an eye? "Gulob said you were not such a man to be treated like this," said the Maulavi. "They are not going to try to exchange you for prisoners. They have decided to exchange you for money. How do we get this money? We are in negotiation with Fazul Rahim, and with your family."

My family. *Oh no, they know.* It was certain. They would be worrying all the time. It would be in the backs of the minds of my nephews and nieces every day in school. I would ruin the fun of their youth. I was not going to be let go, but neither were they going to kill me, yet. "They want to know that you are alive and not being harmed."

There were people who cared for me. They wanted to save me. Fazul was going to try to do all he could. I felt shame again at all the trouble I had caused. This had now become serious. The military commission had delivered my letter to Fazul. They had sent the fax to Ellen. She would contact at least one of the people in the letter. Soon the others would know. She would contact my banker friend. I needed him now.

Maybe they could all put some money together, and Ellen or someone else could bring it over. I would sell my apartment and take money from my father's house. If he found out about me, it might kill him. I would be taking money from my brother and sister, but I would pay them back. I would pay everyone back.

Around and around I went in my mind. It was pointless. I could do nothing from here.

A million dollars is a huge amount of money. I do not have this kind of money. And how do you send this much money from New York to Afghanistan? Since 9/11, governments watch money transfers closely. How do you carry a million dollars through airports?

"It has to be a million dollars," said the Maulavi. He looked at me coldly. All he cared about was the money.

"It all depends upon your people how soon you are released," said the Maulavi. "We want to do this quickly. How can we do this?" Daoud offered to go to Kabul. The Maulavi laughed. They had no confidence in him. They knew everything about him, his village, and his family in Peshawar. If he ran away, his whole family would be at risk. They would kill them.

He opened his hand to reveal my small digital recorder. I would use my own recorder to tell Fazul, my family, and the others who were trying to help me that I was alive. I hadn't used it before. I couldn't make it work right. I got out my reading glasses. "When you become Muslim and recite the Holy Koran, you will not need glasses," the Maulavi exclaimed, raising his voice loudly. His eyes were shining. Humbly, I told him that I was learning to read Arabic so I could read the Koran. (Arabic and Pashto script are almost the same.)

Finally I figured out how to operate the recorder. I showed the Maulavi how to work it. Our hands touched. I felt awkward sitting close to and touching a killer. I pulled my hand away.

But a part of me liked him. He was smart, quick, strong, committed, and he treated me with respect. He could order my death in a second. "This is Jere Van Dyk," I said into the machine. "I am alive. I have been captured by the Taliban. They have not harmed me. Please help me." I spoke softly. I was nervous. I couldn't believe that I was making this statement. Talking into the recorder made my predicament that much more real. I was like those other people I had seen on television. I accidentally erased the message and had to record it again.

The Maulavi stood up without using his hands and left. Again, in spite of everything, I found myself admiring this, a man of action and intellect.

A few minutes later Gulob brought in Razi Gul, his patoo wrapped over his head, like a monk. He stumbled in like an old man. I felt sorry for him. He joined us on the floor. He told us that the Taliban wanted Abdullah's home address; they were still trying to capture him. Daoud asked what else they wanted. They asked only that one question, Razi Gul said. Daoud observed that he was in there a long time, but Razi Gul just looked down, stroking his beard.

The Maulavi came back in. We stood up, but I kept my legs bent. He told us to sit down. He sat next to me and held out the recorder, asking me how to turn up the volume. I showed him.

He looked at me closely. "You must trim your mustache," he said. He ran his finger along his lip. It must not touch my lips. There must be a space between my upper lip and my mustache. He ordered Gulob to get scissors and a mirror for me, and a comb, and oil for my beard. I must look like a real Muslim. "I want to hear through the media that you have become a Muslim," he said. He shook my hand. "And when you return here from America I will find you a wife." He smiled warmly, as if we were the best of friends.

"I will hold you to that," I said.

He hesitated, burst into laughter, shook my hand strongly, and walked toward the door.

I was laughing, shaking hands with a killer, a man who was going to destroy me financially, but he probably wouldn't kill me. I was angry at myself for shaking his hand and for liking him.

He stopped. "Put the tension out of you," he said. He strode out the door and into the sunlight.

Monday, March 10

It was just after dawn. I heard the men in the next room, and then it was silent. They had come last night. Soon after, Gulob had come in to warn us to be quiet. They had six hostages. They were going to behead them in the morning. I watched the shadows now, one by one, pass by the darkened window. There must have been a dozen men. I could feel the lump in my throat. If they stopped at our door, we were dead. They kept going. I wondered which shadows were the Taliban and which were the poor men on their way, like sheep, to the slaughter.

Later, Gulob came in and sat on the kotgai. "The men last night asked me about my children. I didn't realize until this morning that I had grown up with them. They are part of our leader's group. One of the men they kidnapped was one man's brother-in-law. 'You are supposed to help your brother-in-law. How can you do this?' I asked them. They said, 'In Islam there is no blood relation.' They told me a story about two brothers in Waziristan. One was a mujahid, the other a spy. The mujahid beheaded his brother. If you had been kidnapped by these men, you would have gone to your grave twenty days ago."

He unrolled the prayer mat and began to pray. He stopped, sitting on his knees. "I couldn't sleep all night worrying that the Taliban would come in here." He continued praying. I thought of the men walking by our door. I saw the man standing behind me putting his hand into his jacket. I thought of him all the time. I thought about a knife slicing through my neck and cutting deeper. I kept thinking of this.

Tuesday, March 11

It was around midday. We heard a woman shouting downstairs. Maybe she was tired that she had to cook for us, for almost a month now, and the Taliban who kept coming and going. She got up long before sunrise, and when I went outside at night I could hear children crying. Gulob brought in some bread and lentils for lunch. There was some gristle and fat mixed in, but I couldn't eat it. He sat down for a minute. Someone knocked softly on the door. Gulob opened it and went outside, and I saw for two seconds a young woman's hand and bare wrist hand him a bowl. Her wrist was thin and feminine. He took the bowl gently from her. I saw in those two seconds warmth, gentleness, laughter, life outside, far away. Gulob came back in and put down a bowl of yogurt. We shared it happily. Again, Daoud whispered to me to get sick. He knew Pashtuns.

Gulob said that he knew we were all happy to be away from our wives. The older woman—his wife? I didn't dare ask; a man must never ask a Pashtun about his wife or sisters—must have been shouting at him.

Rahman came in late that afternoon, bringing tea. I was sick of all the tea, but we lived for his or Gulob's company. They brought news. Rahman asked what we did in my country when a boy and girl eloped. I said there were over 300 million people in America. Each family was different. "Here we kill them," he said. That's how it was. Next subject. I asked why. They had disobeyed their parents.

"Do you kill, ultimately, because of the importance of the family?" I asked. He said no. It was because of taunting. Others would taunt them. Everything here, all animosities, were the result of taunting. I asked why people taunted. Was it done to punish someone who didn't follow Pashtunwali? So you didn't appear weak? To save family honor? Why? Rahman shook his head. It was because of ignorance. Pashtuns were very rigid. I said there was nothing in Islam about killing people who eloped. He replied that Pashtuns didn't care about Islam when it came to this.

The afternoon passed. I was sitting on my cot, flashlight between my knees, studying. The door opened, and Gulob and the Maulavi walked in. I froze. I could see only everyone's outline in the dark. The Maulavi told Daoud and me to sit on the floor and ordered Gulob to blindfold Razi Gul and Samad and take them outside. The Maulavi took out a sheet of clean white paper, folded it, and tore it into two pieces.

I was to write a letter to Fazul, telling him to transfer the money to Daoud's father and to do this secretly and quickly. If his father communicated in any way with anyone else, our lives would be at risk. The Maulavi took out a pen. I didn't want to touch his, so I took my own and wrote the letter, in the dark, on the floor. He told Daoud to write a letter to his father. He did this. The Maulavi took out my digital recorder from his vest pocket and handed it to me. Again, nervously, I tried to make it work. I read my letter into the recorder. Daoud read his, in Pashto. The Maulavi grabbed the recorder from me. He was quick, a man of no hesitation and no doubts.

"I am doing a lot for you. I am being very kind to you," he said. "I promised you on the first day that no harm would come to you. We have found that you are very important. Even if you were Bush, we would release you because I have promised. If the military commission were to become involved, you would be finished."

He and Gulob walked out, and then the Maulavi immediately came back into the room, alone. He took out another sheet of paper. Now I was to write a letter to Fazul telling him to work with Abdullah and Mullah Malang, and with Daoud's father on the transfer of the money.

I wrote this. As I did, I asked myself, *Why Abdullah?* I thought they were trying to arrest him. Was he part of this? And Mullah Malang, how was he involved? He would only try to help me, wouldn't he? I was sure he was in Kabul, trying to free me. I thought about him all the time. It was all so confusing.

It was just the three of us in the room. We could overpower the Maulavi and take him hostage, but we had no weapon. They would kill us in a second. We finished. The Maulavi went to the door. It was locked. He tried to open it but it was bolted shut. All of a sudden his power was gone. He was small and vulnerable. Again, I thought of attacking him. He knocked on the door. "Now, I'm a prisoner here, too," he said. He sat on my cot. We sat on the floor. He was stuck here with us. It was eerie. "Is there anything you want to ask me?" he said.

I asked where and how he decided to live the life that he now led. He spoke as if addressing a crowd. He started this for the happiness of God, for the sake of Islam, and for jihad. He was seeing his success and prosperity in this. Therefore I was not penalized. Islam gave dignity to an old man, a gray beard like me. That is why I had been treated well. The money was already in Pakistan, he said.

What? CBS, or Ellen, my friends, or my family had sent a million dollars to Islamabad? How did they do this? Was it true? Was it possible? What kind of game was he playing? Would he get the money, if it was really even here, and then kill me? "We want to realize this quickly," he said. "We will send a suicide bomber to the exchange."

My hopes evaporated. If there was anyone there from any government, we would all be killed. I imagined walking with a dozen Taliban toward the border. They would be armed and nervous. I would be in the center, skinny, bearded, hard to distinguish from the others. We would come up to the top, on the border, and there on the other side, standing in a small valley, would be Fazul. He would be standing near his SUV.

Other men I knew would be there with him. Ellen would be there, wearing a scarf and baggy women's clothes. Or would it be my sister? She could do this. Fazul would be holding a briefcase, with a million dollars inside, and he would walk forward up the hill. A Talib and I would leave the others and walk toward him. I would turn and look back, the last time I would ever be with Pashtun fighters.

I would walk down the hill. There would be ten or fifteen men standing with Fazul, men from Afghan intelligence. Fazul would come toward me and hand over the briefcase to the Talib. He would open it, see that the money was there, and walk away. The Taliban, standing in a line on the ridge, would be watching, their rifles and rocket launchers ready. As the Talib walked back, a man in the valley would give a signal and two helicopters would rise over a hill and roar forward. As they did, a teenage boy with green eyes, who had come to watch what was happening, standing near us, would press the button on his suicide vest.

I saw this scenario twenty times. What was my guarantee that they would honor their agreement? It was only their word.

The door opened. Gulob brought in Razi Gul and Samad. They joined us on the floor. The Maulavi gave a piece of paper to Samad. He ordered him to write a letter to Abdullah stating that he must work with Daoud's father and Mullah Malang. How could they work with him if at the same time they were trying to capture him? Samad hesitated. He was nervous. He didn't want to write the letter, but the Maulavi and Gulob stood over him. Outside there would be men with guns.

He got down on his knees and wrote the letter. The Maulavi grabbed it from him. We stood up with him. He touched my chest and shoulder. I touched his arm and shoulder, as taut as a rope. "I will be watching the media," he said. "When I see that you have become Muslim, we can do some things together, in friendship." He pointed his finger at Daoud. "Make sure he studies and learns his prayers," he said. He walked to the door. "Bye, bye," he said, in English, without looking back.

I sat back on the floor. I was giddy, confused, and exhausted. "Why did they tell you about your father?" Samad asked Daoud. He was angry. I didn't trust him.

Gulob returned. "The Maulavi speaks fluent English. He just didn't want to tell you," he said. I had sensed this and knew never to say anything critical of him. I wasn't even certain that his men weren't listening now or that one of them hadn't planted a recorder in here. "The Taliban have been calling CBS every day," Gulob said. "It is very upset at you."

I hung my head. He always had a way of bringing me down. CBS was involved. Maybe some of the money was coming from there. I was a consultant, not a member of the network's staff, and it was doing this for me. Of course people there would be mad. All the trouble I was causing. How was I ever going to pay the money back? How did Gulob know that CBS was mad at me? What was going on? I asked what our guarantee was.

He said that he had promised to take me to the border, and he would do that. It was his word against four lives and a million dollars.

Thursday, March 13

Everyone was critical of Daoud. He didn't get up for prayers but got up later to drink tea and eat the parata. I didn't want to be near him. How could the Taliban receive the money? he asked. If they couldn't, we were all in danger. The others nodded. If the money was here, that meant that Pakistan and America were involved. We were paranoid and suspicious, as dark in our thinking and as worried as the Taliban. After prayers I did exercises and poured cold water over myself and washed, shivering in the cold.

Afterward I sat, my patoo around me, listening to the birds outside. It was peaceful. I was not paranoid. Rahman came to pick up the teapot and parata. Only Daoud had touched the food. "You look like a real Pashtun, not like other foreigners," said Rahman. He brought me a cup of green tea. "You have a real light in your face."

You compliment me, I said to myself, *yet I am afraid you'll kill me, and at the least you are going to steal a million dollars from me.*

I was his prisoner, his Golden Goose. How could the Maulavi preach to me when he took money from me and talked of suicide bombers? What kind of Muslim was he?

Later, Rahman brought in a few chunks of gristly meat and fat cooked in oil for lunch. Daoud took meat for himself. Razi Gul slowly took the best piece he could find, and the largest chunk of fat, and put them in front of me. He took a small portion for himself. I tore the meat in two and gave the larger piece to him. "No, no," he said, raising his voice. Back and forth we went like two men arguing over who should pay the bill. Daoud searched the bowl for more meat for himself.

Gulob returned late in the afternoon. He had been gone for two days. He carried a large cassette player. The men hugged him, and so did I, gently and warily. We shook his hand. We were happy to have him back, although again I was angry at myself for not being more reserved. He was the only one who stood between us and the wrath of the outside world.

He sat down and took off his sandals. "I've had many duties to perform, that's why I've been gone," he said. "I had to climb over the mountain and cross the border, and I hurt my feet." There were a few small cuts on them, and they looked slightly swollen. He rubbed his right foot. "The Maulavi said I was becoming too close to you, and wanted to send a long-haired man here to watch you, but I overruled him."

I sank in fear. Gulob had talked with a sense of awe, even fear, about long-haired men. They were real fighters, it seemed, more hardened than others, more dedicated and more capable. They were long-haired men who had come the other day with six men they were going to slaughter.

Gulob turned on the cassette player. The sound of a young man, with a high, lilting voice, singing a capella, filled the room. It was a Taliban recruiting cassette.

"It begins with women taunting men," he said.

"Give us your turbans / give us your swords / we will give you our shawls if you do not go on jihad." A young male chorus sang, the voices melodic and lilting, of women imploring men to fight. In Pashtunwali, if a man is a coward in war, his wife or mother will reject him when he comes home. A man has to be strong. *"We must think of the orphans and the widows."*

On and on they chanted. It was hypnotic. After a while, Gulob turned the tape off and turned to Samad. "Can one person's kidney work in another person?" he asked. Samad said yes. "I don't think so," Gulob responded, "because another maulavi's son had bad kidneys, and he went to Islamabad to exchange them, and they haven't worked. The news reported that a German in Herat had been kidnapped, and they're demanding fifty thousand dollars. Why so little?"

Gulob answered his own question. "Maybe they have taken his kidneys."

I didn't like where I sensed this conversation was going. "Do you know that the artery that goes from a man's leg to his heart sells for eighty thousand dollars in Islamabad? We will sell your arteries," Gulob said. I looked down and ran my hands over my knees. I felt myself shivering, and my stomach tightened. "Razi Gul and I are old," I said. "Young people's arteries are better." Everyone laughed, but I was scared. Gulob wouldn't have brought this up if he or others weren't thinking about it. A maulavi's son needed kidneys.

The men talked about the price of body parts in Pakistan. I had read too many stories about boys being kidnapped in Afghanistan for their kidneys and being left for dead.

"Pakistan has some good doctors, but some of them are very cruel," said Gulob. He gathered up our tea cups and the teapot. "If we have trouble getting the money, maybe we will sell your body parts." He walked out the door.

The room was silent. I could feel the energy welling up in me. "If this is true, I am leaving tonight," I said. They needed a hospital for this, Samad said. I said they didn't. They could come here. They probably had doctors who supported their cause. I imagined a small, middle-aged man walking in the room carrying a satchel and the Taliban holding me down while he injected me with a sedative. He would wash my skin, cut me open and take out my kidney, and sew me up. I would lie in the cot bleeding to death, slowly, painfully. No. I couldn't die in this dark, dirty cell. I had to get out of here. I got up and walked around the cell.

"We have to escape. I can't die here," I said. I kept repeating this. We would use the cord. I pointed to the clothesline over the pit and explained how we had to tie Gulob up or strangle him with it. "We may have to kill Rahman. We can do it at sundown. We have to get through the compound, get a rifle, and head west and try to escape over the mountains," I said.

I laid out the plan. I had been thinking of it, and others, for weeks. None of them involved killing Gulob or Rahman, unless we had to. This was different. Gulob had crossed the line. I was afraid, but for the first time in weeks I felt alive and strong. I was no longer depressed. I was no longer a victim. I thought of the passengers on United Flight 93. They didn't sit there. They acted. They had died feeling strong. That was the best way to go. They were the best of men. I felt stronger and stronger as I paced around the room. The three others watched me. "We have to do this," I said. "We just can't sit here." Razi Gul looked at me. Samad and Daoud kept their heads down. I had to be the leader on this. I realized that they might not come with me. How was I going to do this alone?

"We will go to our relatives; we will sell our land; we will borrow money; we will do anything so we don't have to sell our kidneys," said Samad. Razi Gul said that a kidney cost about fifty thousand dollars in Islamabad.

"Gulob probably walked from the markez to the border," I said. "We may be only a few miles away. We don't have to kill them. We can tie Gulob and Rahman up in here, use our scarves or towels to wrap around their mouths, and we could have a two-hour lead."

Daoud said there might be other Taliban around. How would we avoid them? Again, I said, we go at sundown or later. We had no money. I kept wondering and thinking how we could get through the mountains, past villages, avoid people, get past the border guards, the Taliban, whoever was patrolling the border, and over into Afghanistan. Even there we had to avoid the Taliban. If we were captured, who knows what they would do? Was it better to live without a kidney or to have my head cut off after trying to escape? I paced around the room.

Gulob returned that evening with dinner. I didn't look up as he placed the bowls on the ground. I was too afraid of him. Dinner lasted about ten or fifteen minutes, as we ate increasingly little. All of us were losing weight. We weren't hungry. I dipped my bread into the spinach, which Gulob said was wild, and I ate some yogurt, but that was it. I kept thinking about a man coming into the room to cut out our kidneys. It was too dark to try to escape now. Gulob was strong. I would need help from Samad or Razi Gul to overpower him.

"I won't come if you don't eat, Mamur Sahib," said Gulob. "I will just deliver your food and leave. I will stay outside." I dipped my bread into the oil, which dripped over my hands and into my beard. I was nervous. "I am mad that you would think of me as one who would sell your body parts. They beat Afghan soldiers at the markez. It's terrible what they do to them. They take the life out of them. I have refused to allow you to be transferred there." Someone had said something to him about my rantings that afternoon.

Later Gulob led us outside, one by one. When it was my turn, I walked with my hand along the wall to keep my balance. I breathed deeply. I looked at the sky. I would have to overpower Gulob, get out the compound door and past his dogs. Then, which way would I go? Where would I hide? How could I overpower Gulob? I was afraid.

I returned to the warm comfort of our cell. Samad was next and stayed outside longer than normal. I wondered why. "I have felt terrible and still do that I haven't been able to allow you outside to get some sun," Gulob said later. "Really I do." I thanked him and said I believed him. I did. I didn't know what to think of him. "I have been glad that you haven't tried anything with me. You haven't caused me any problems. The Maulavi had wanted me to chain you to your bed, like the others, but I haven't done that, in part, because you are older." Where did this come from? The Maulavi had said that he had ordered the others chained, but not me. If I escaped, I wouldn't know where to go.

Then it came.

"Don't try to escape," Gulob said. His face was six inches from mine, his voice low and growling. He was hunched over. He looked like a bear ready to pounce. "If you do, I will come at you like a dog. You won't get anywhere. There are Taliban throughout this village."

How did he know I had been talking about escaping? Daoud looked at me knowingly. There was a spy among us. That was why Samad was outside for at least ten minutes. He was talking with Gulob. That was why they no longer chained him to his bed. He had cut a deal with them at the markez. They had flipped him. Or he had been in on this all along.

I felt alone. I couldn't trust anyone. I had no friends. I hated Samad. "If you try anything, it will be difficult for you," said Gulob, his voice low and deep. "I want to resolve this as quickly as possible. God willing, the Taliban will allow you to be released soon. But don't try to escape. Don't try anything."

Samad was boiling water on the bokhari. He asked to wash my clothes. Why would this man, who had just betrayed me, want to wash my clothes, as if he were my servant? Did he feel bad, or was he trying to lure me in so I would talk more? I didn't care about my clothes. I was beyond caring. In fact, I preferred them dirty. Why wear clean clothes in this pit? I wanted them dirty when I fought Samad.

I didn't want him to touch them. I had to admit, he was good. I was a fool to have trusted him. I had an excuse. I was afraid that Gulob would sell my kidneys, for starters. No, that was no excuse. I was afraid.

That night I lay in my cot, staring at Samad. I couldn't see him; it was too dark. But when I closed my eyes I could see his face covered with blood. I lay there seething. He had betrayed me. I wanted to cross the room and beat him senseless. I was afraid I might kill him. I had never wanted to kill anyone before.

Saturday, March 15

It was midmorning. Gulob sat on the kotgai, sipping tea. He put the cup down and walked over to the pit and with his flashlight looked at the crumbling walls, a few inches high. "You must stop using the pit to wash in. You must use very little water for wadu," he said. He returned to the kotgai. "We have a problem, or, rather, I have a problem. You are sending water outside, and it is causing problems for my neighbors."

The water we used was flowing out through the hole in the

wall and eroding a neighbor's wall. We had to use less water and wash on the floor so that water could seep into it and not go outside. He had been trying to hide us, but the neighbors knew that there were more people than normal in his compound. I wondered: How could bin Laden, how could any group of outsiders, hide for long in a Pashtun village? Like us, he and his men would leave signs of their presence.

This was why Gulob was nervous. His neighbors would turn us in for money; his cousins would betray him to the authorities.

"Where do you think bin Laden is?" I asked.

"He is rich and has access to more money from Saudi Arabia and other places," said Samad. Razi Gul nodded. "But even with this, he is too big for panah."

"I agree," said Razi Gul. "He is too big to hide."

Everyone I had asked, all along the border, especially tribal chiefs, had said the same thing. Bin Laden was too big, too important to hide under panah. He was said to have Arab bodyguards around him. How could you hide all these people? It would be as hard to keep him hidden in any village as it would be for Gulob to keep us hidden for too long.

Gulob left, and we sat in the dark. Hours passed. That afternoon I watched a large insect, with its tail up, walk across the dirt floor and then onto the kilim. It was a scorpion. Samad took a stick and guided it over to my cot and crushed it. We moved our cots away from the wall and looked everywhere for more scorpions. I looked up at the brush ceiling. Gulob had said there was a snakeskin up there. I stared up at night wondering if a live snake would drop on me.

Samad returned to his cot and read the Koran, chanting quietly. Daoud put some wood into the bokhari. He wanted to make a fire to heat water to bathe. Razi Gul made the fire. When the water was ready, Daoud took our drinking pan and used that to pour water over himself. It became his washbasin.

"We drink water out of that!" said Razi Gul. "Why are you doing that?"

"You are crazy," said Samad, shaking his head.

Daoud said he forgot.

"All you think of is yourself," I said. "We all have to survive here, not just you."

Daoud finished bathing, took the small mirror that Gulob had brought in, and sat near the window and stared at himself, running his hand over his beard and through his hair. Gulob returned and went to the windowsill next to him and took a metal box and a wood box, each filled with ammunition, put them on his shoulder, and walked outside. He was going on jihad tonight.

A boy brought our dinner. While we were eating, Daoud mocked Razi Gul. "You are getting smaller and smaller," he said. I couldn't believe that Daoud, a Pashtun, would talk this way to an older man.

Razi Gul raised his forefinger. "I know," he said, "but it is not for you to tell me."

I could feel the tension in him. Daoud smiled. Razi Gul kept staring. I had to defuse this quickly. I asked Daoud how he could talk that way to an older man. He got up and went to his cot. Razi Gul finished eating, wiped his hands on our towel, and went to his own cot, like fighters in a ring going to their corners.

Wednesday, March 19

I slept off and on until noon. We were all sleeping more and more now. Our bodies seemed to have slowed down. Gulob and Rahman had been gone for a few days, and we wondered about them. I spent hours thinking, worrying, going through my life. *You can't hide from yourself in prison*, I wrote in my diary. Gulob's young sons brought food and buttermilk. We drank the buttermilk and ate only part of the food.

I was facing death. I had to be honest with myself. I had no choice. Nothing else mattered. I couldn't escape, like other people, into my family, work, food, entertainment, exercise, alcohol, sex, whatever it was that people anywhere in the world did, had, or used to keep from looking deep into themselves and at their lives. For hours and hours I sat in the dark, day and night. "For what shall it profit a man if he gain the whole world and lose his soul," it said in the Bible. Men preached that to me all the time when I was a boy. As a young man I used to think about what it meant. My soul was my very being, that deepest part of me, the truth of what I was. I couldn't convert to Islam, even if I wanted to. I hated myself for trying to fake it now. But all my life I had been looking for God, for something to give me strength and courage. I had said this a hundred times. Now here I was looking at the abyss.

For years I thought I had left my faith behind, but now God had come back to me, the God of my youth. I couldn't be dishonest before God, whoever or whatever God was, that something deep inside of me. I couldn't give in. I couldn't sell my soul. Long ago I wanted to get rid of my past, of what I felt were my sins and my failures, in the cauldron of war. They were nothing now. I was in that cauldron.

Gulob returned toward sundown. "I've been at the markez," he said, and he told us that the Taliban had shot down a helicopter in Sarkano, a district in Kunar Province. The situation was getting worse in Pakistan. Soon the Taliban and the government would be fighting in the mountains.

Gulob left. When the door opened I caught a glimpse of light, the rock gray wall of the mountain outside, the thatched roof, a bird sitting on the edge. I could hear children's voices. Tomorrow was Nowruz, the first day of spring, the beginning of a new year.

Gulob now brought in a small hand broom and a pan. I covered my mouth with my patoo, trying not to breathe too deeply, as he swept the floor, and thick dust filled the air. He left, quickly shutting the door behind him. I sat in the corner and closed my eyes, waiting for the dust to settle.

Gulob returned after a few hours and was silent. No one talked. I asked him after a while, to change his mood, if he would clarify the number of virgins who will be waiting in Paradise. I wanted to give him some authority, to show that I looked up to him and that we had talked about Islam. I was also always curious about why the emphasis was on virgins in Heaven, but I was afraid to ask Muslims about this.

"There will be twenty-four," he said. "Seventy-two for a martyr, seventy for a regular Muslim." He began to preach again. "The money we take from you, from your house and your family . . . you cannot take these things to Paradise. We came into this world with nothing and leave with nothing. The only thing that counts is Islam. A person who misses one prayer will spend two hundred thousand years in Hell."

It was tyranny. It was fear, always fear, that he tried to instill in me, as the maulavis instilled the fear of Hell in the mosque when they preached. I looked at his eyes. They were dark, wide, and certain. I lowered my head. I wanted to argue with him, but I had to be humble. He preached how I had to avoid going to Hell and the necessity of becoming Muslim. I wondered again if I would have to convert to survive.

"There is a head over my head. I can do nothing. I cannot take you out into the sun," he said, and he began to pray. We held our hands up, our palms facing upward. "Please God, release Mamur Sahib and make him a Muslim." At that moment, I again believed that Gulob wanted to help me. He had prayed to God for me. He wouldn't lie to Allah. He wouldn't dare.

Gulob took off his sandals and sat on the floor next to me.

Now what? "What do you think about when you think of the hereafter?" he asked. "What did you learn in your country?"

I hesitated and then explained the Christian message that I had learned as a boy: "I was told that if you believed that Jesus was the son of God, that he was born of a virgin, lived and died on the cross for your sins, rose on the third day, and was now in Heaven, then you were a Christian and would go to Heaven."

He shook his head. "You must not believe what you learned in church. You must learn only Islam. That is the true answer." He brought his head close to mine. "What do you think of Heaven and Hell?" he asked. I hated this. Once he started he wouldn't stop. God would punish him for not preaching to me, and if I converted, God would reward him.

Razi Gul chimed in. "On Judgment Day, God will take us by the neck and ask, 'Why didn't you teach him about Islam?'" he said. I was surrounded.

"Think about the hereafter," said Gulob. "When the wealthiest person in the world dies, he or she cannot take any of it to the grave. Think about eternity. When someone leaves this world there is no return." I kept my head down, pleading silently for the sermon to end. I looked at the dirt floor. I thought of my father preaching to me when I was a boy. I was afraid of his anger if I didn't believe. I was afraid now of the Maulavi and Gulob, for far greater reasons. I listened politely. I had to save my life.

"I look at Mamur Sahib, and I see my own father, who is a Tablighi," Gulob said. "He has been gone eleven months in Canada, Korea, and Singapore, preaching. Gray beards sit in the mosque reading and reciting the Holy Koran. Mamur Sahib is an old man, and I appreciate him."

So Gulob's father was a Tablighi, a Deobandi missionary. I had seen Tablighi in Afghanistan walking from village to village, their faces bright and happy. It was said that they never preached about jihad. The son was a Wahhabi and a member of the Taliban.

He was rebelling from his father. The Tablighi traveled around the world preaching the gospel.

"Have your father come and preach to me," I said. I had to end this.

"No, he would beat me for keeping you here," Gulob replied. The room was silent. He knew what he was doing was wrong.

"If only the other countries would leave Afghanistan, then we could destroy America," he continued. "They bombed a village in Khost today, killing children. They are building bases in the mountains on the border. The Taliban have forced the government from checkpoints here. Maybe the government will leave Bajaur entirely. The Pakistani army cannot fight them, so they deploy the Taliban up there to fight. Today the U.S. was firing across the border from where the Taliban fired. There is going to be much fighting here in the future."

I didn't know what to think, except that I was stuck in this cell. A feeling of frustration swept over me. I looked around the room, as I had a thousand times. I could dig a hole in the wall, but where would I hide the dirt? How would I cover the hole? I was stuck here.

"I am an intelligence officer for the Taliban," said Gulob. "I go to Afghanistan. Mamur Sahib is not a problem. You three are the problem. If you see me in Kabul, you will say something, and the NDS will arrest me. The Taliban will destroy all three of your houses. Animosity with the Taliban is terrible. The penalty for you is death. The Taliban wanted to bring you to the markez. It would raise their stature. They could show everyone who they had captured. I said no. They have eaten with me. They eat what I eat. I have protected you."

We were in his house. Under Pashtunwali no one could take us from here. Under panah, he was obliged to protect us, as Mullah Omar had protected Osama bin Laden. He would die to protect us. Was it true? All I knew was that again I was afraid.

Thursday, March 20

I slept little. I kept thinking of Gulob's preaching. I had to convert if I was ever going to be released, and if I didn't, maybe I would die. One minute he was nice, the next minute he was threatening us. After prayers, I worked out and washed in the pit. Razi Gul prayed for a half hour and then retreated to his cot. He turned on the radio and listened to an imam preaching. He no longer talked about his precious Amina. He talked more about God, like a man preparing to die.

Today was Nowruz, celebrated as the new year throughout Central Asia, long before the arrival of Islam. I asked Gulob why they didn't celebrate today. "We celebrate Eid," said Gulob. "In Bajaur we don't celebrate August 14," Pakistan's Independence Day.

That afternoon Daoud sat facing the window, staring into the mirror, then climbed beneath his quilt. We all slept. I was tired from working out. My energy was going. What did it matter? We could be here for months, or years. I felt relaxed, giving in. It was all in the hands of God.

I later read, for probably the sixth time, one of the books that the Maulavi had given me, and studied Pashto. It was the only thing that gave me purpose and energy. Yet I could study for only an hour at a time before getting tired. I fell asleep.

Sometime later, the door opened and I awoke, afraid, as I was every time the door opened. Gulob came in, silhouetted in the light. His hair was wet, and he had a towel around his shoulders. He held a long razor. *Oh, no. What is he going to do?* He looked at Razi Gul. "I need you to shave my head," he said. Razi Gul took the razor as Gulob sat on the kotgai. Razi Gul had said that if he came to America I should help him open a barbershop. "I am good at this," he said.

"Why are you doing this?" I asked Gulob. I assumed it had something to do with beginning a new year, but he had said that the Taliban didn't celebrate this pagan festival.

"I do it to increase blood circulation and because I have to go to Pakistan." By "Pakistan" he meant Peshawar, part of what Pakistanis called the "settled areas." One day he was Pakistani, the next day he was Afghan; one day the tribal areas were part of Pakistan, the next day they were separate. "The police think long-haired people are Taliban."

"If you copulate with your wife, you must bathe afterward," said Razi Gul. "Your children will see your wet hair and know you have just copulated with their mother. It's better to shave your head."

He carefully, gently, shaved Gulob's head. Long locks of dark black hair fell onto the floor. I went back to studying. "You shouldn't study," said Gulob. "You're an old man. Razi Gul doesn't try. Everything is preparation for the hereafter."

"It says in the Koran you should study from the cradle to the grave," said Daoud. "The Prophet, peace be unto him, said we should even go to China to learn."

I silently thanked him for his support. "Why are you worried about roadblocks?" I asked. "You said the government supported the Taliban."

"The arrangement is between the government and the heads of the Taliban. The police capture long-haired men after a bombing to show America they are fighting. They want to keep the money coming from America. They go after the low-level people."

Razi Gul continued shaving. Soon Gulob's head was bald. He looked older and more intimidating. "You should shave your head, Mamur Sahib," he said.

"If you take me to Peshawar," I responded. "We can go through the roadblocks together." Gulob smiled. Razi Gul finished his work. Gulob put on his pakool. "How do you feel?" I asked.

"I feel lighter," he replied. "I can feel the breeze. It's good for my head. Shaving your head is like burning a field. You have to clean the land to make your crops grow better."

We heard jet fighters far away. Toward sundown, Gulob appeared again, this time with a kettle of milk tea and a bowl of rice pudding. It was to celebrate that Samad was almost finished reading the Koran. He had been reciting it every day, almost from memory, looking down at it only on occasion as he sat cross-legged on his cot chanting in his lilting singsong voice. When he finished, Gulob would slaughter a goat.

Daoud complained that he was now suffering from a head-ache and asked for some aspirin. "During the time of the Prophet, peace be unto him, people did not have pills for headaches, and when they read the Koran their headaches went away," said Gulob. "People can memorize the Koran when they cannot a book. There is a powerful spiritual force in it that helps them."

Samad spit on Daoud's head to make his headache go away. As he was doing this, Rahman came in and sat near the door. He immediately voiced his approval. "When someone gets hurt or gets bitten by a snake, they spit on the wound and read from the Koran," he said. "Only special people have permission to read if it is a snake bite."

"My headache is better," said Daoud.

"If you become Muslim then the whole world will change for you," Gulob said to me. "You will be happy in this life and in the next. You can minister to other Americans, who will seem like donkeys to you." I wanted to change the subject.

"You talked about a suicide bomber," I said. "How long does it take to train one?"

"It depends on each one—some fifteen days, others three months or six months. A mullah trains them. Never a fat mullah, only very thin ones. They don't drink tea or take naswar; they completely focus on Islam and minister to the suicide bomber. I myself was trained by a mullah. There is a very large network of people involved."

He was warming to the subject. "Once suicide vests covered a person from his legs to his chest; now they only cover your arms and chest," he said. "We don't make the vests. They come from the leadership. The person chooses his target. People go to areas they are familiar with." I thought of my vision of how I would be released to Fazul and of the young boy with green eyes going to his death, age and anger destroying beauty and hope.

Monday, March 24

I worked out again. I was getting skinnier, but at least my muscles weren't atrophying too much. I could hear birds singing, chickens, children's voices, and women making bread. I sat on the floor looking at the light seeping through the dirt casting an amber glow—light, precious light. I was lucky to be here, and not at the markez, and to be alive.

Around noon Gulob brought in a metal pan of dark grilled meat and a platter of rice. It was goat pilaf, in honor of Samad. He had completed reading the Koran. Samad brought over the chillum chee and held it out. Reluctantly, I put out my hands. He poured water from the bucket with the curved spout over them, and I rubbed my hands, turning them over in the proper Pashtun style. Razi Gul handed me our dirty towel.

The other men washed their hands. I had practiced washing my hands until I got it down. In Kunar six months ago, I had sat with Daoud and our guide waiting to meet Abu Hamza, my first meeting with the Taliban. We would eat beforehand. I only talked a little. I didn't want to give myself away. Our host brought in a chillum chee and I washed my hands, thought I was doing so in the proper way, turning them over and over.

"He realized you weren't Pashtun when he saw you wash your hands," Daoud said the next day when we were back in Asadabad. I couldn't let that happen again. I had to pass completely. In the end all my work didn't matter. Here I was.

"*Bismillah ir rahman ir rahim*," said Razi Gul as we raised our hands, our palms up, in prayer. Razi Gul put pieces of meat on my bread. I put them back in front of him. "I don't like goat meat. I don't feel well," I said, touching my stomach. Gulob was upset. I ate a few handfuls of rice and broke off a few pieces of bread.

I had eaten goat meat before, but it did not agree with me. Normally I wouldn't offend my hosts, but I refused to honor Samad. I was afraid now to talk openly. I didn't trust anyone, including Daoud. I was withdrawing more into myself. I began to think of trying to escape alone. They could fend for themselves.

They were in a good mood, eating and talking. Gulob had heard the news of a Taliban attack that morning on fuel trucks waiting at Torkham, the border crossing, on their way into Afghanistan. "One man shot an RPG into a tanker. It blew up, and other trucks waiting in line to cross the border caught fire. You could see the flames far away," he said.

It had put him in a good mood. "The Taliban have been holding meetings. They would start their new program after New Year's. This was one of their first attacks," he said. Nowruz, this pagan signpost, meant something to them after all. If the story about the tankers was true, it was strange. Torkham was near Landi Khotal, and Razi Gul had said that it was under Pakistani government control. "It is very complicated," he said now. This was also near where the Pakistani ambassador was kidnapped.

As we were eating, Gulob heard something, got up, and went outside. He returned ten minutes later. He spoke in a low voice. "Taliban are here. You must not talk." My stomach tightened.

I hadn't heard a motor. Maybe they came on foot. I lost my appetite completely. They kept coming to this Taliban safe house, back and forth, probably from here to Afghanistan and back again.

It was time for prayers. We poured only a trickle of water over our hands, elbows, and ankles, but even this amount created puddles on the floor. We used the pit, still, as a toilet, but now could no longer use water freely to wash the refuse away. The room smelled worse than before.

I turned to my Pashto book. A boy came in to pick up our food. I hid the book and turned to the wall. It was getting warmer, and flies now buzzed around. Razi Gul took a rock and closed the hole that went from our pit to the outside. "To keep the rats out," he said, "and so no one can see us. The Taliban are like a river. If they kill us, where do you go for revenge? You disappear, and they are the Taliban. If a family kills your brother, you go to that family for revenge. Here a dead man disappears in the river of the Taliban."

"The only thing that counts is what we do for God," said Samad. "When we are not praying or working for God, our lives are nothing. To die for God is very good."

I didn't want to talk to Samad, but I couldn't help myself. "During jihad I never met an Afghan who wanted to die," I said. "I heard of Wahhabis from Saudi Arabia who did, but never an Afghan."

"Then they could not put on a suicide vest and become a martyr to destroy a helicopter," said Razi Gul. "Now there are tanks and such against which we must fight. Now we can fight against a tank. We have suicide bombers. It is a different way to fight the jihad."

"Would you want your children to become suicide bombers?" I asked.

"We can tell our children what to do in Islam," said Razi Gul. "We can invite them to Islam. We can teach them to pray. We can tell them what to do in life. If there is a fire, you take your children's hands and steer them away from the fire. I think it would be wonderful if they would go to jihad against America and give their lives as suicide bombers."

I felt sad, listening to this. Razi Gul touched my arm, as we sat in the approaching darkness, four of us on the floor drinking tea. "We have a proverb. Listen to what a maulavi says, but do not look to his actions."

"America has attacked Afghanistan," said Samad. "It is killing our women and children with their bombings. It invades our homes. It is as if they invaded our own homes here. We are opposed to them."

We broke for prayers. I crouched over the pit, using little water, and washed. Why was I going through this charade? It was to save my life. I did not want to become a martyr. I felt like a charlatan praying in Arabic. We returned to our conversation.

"Actions speak louder than words," I said, as I had before. "Gulob and the Maulavi are robbing me. I am a hostage. Maybe they will kill us."

"Do not look to the Maulavi," said Samad. "Look to Islam." He was a spy. I was caught in the middle. I had to listen to this hypocrite. "If a woman does not become Muslim, the maulavis say it is the fault of her father, her elder brother, her father-in-law, and her husband." He, Razi Gul, Gulob, and Daoud were required to teach me.

Gulob came in again. "Do not talk. Abdul Wali's people are here." Abdul Wali was the leader of the Taliban in this region. Fear swept over me. We sat in silence. Razi Gul paced the floor, thumbing his prayer beads. Muslims were afraid of Muslims. They were harboring me.

We sat in the dark. In the next room, on the other side of the baked-mud wall, I could hear the Taliban talking. I was upset. I was tired of being preached to. Gulob brought in a plate of rice and goat meat, a pan of goat liver, and a bowl of goat broth into which the others would put pieces of bread, let them soak, and eat with relish their beloved masta curry. I couldn't eat with them. I ate some bread and went to my cot.

Gulob returned later to check on us, and the others told him that I didn't eat. Razi Gul came over and gently put his hand on my shoulder. It was the first time he or anyone had touched me with such warmth. "Why? What happened? What is wrong?"

I waved him away. Abdul Wali's men were in the next room. They wanted to kill me. Gulob and the Maulavi and probably these men all want my money. Daoud was too self-absorbed to be of any help. *I am in this alone, and I may not get out of here*, I wrote in my diary.

Gulob went outside, returned, and came over and again touched my shoulder. "Mamur Sahib, I've brought a bowl of yogurt, and if you don't eat it I am going to be mad," he said. I was a fool. I was pouting. I sat on the floor with them.

Gulob tore off a piece of bread and placed it in front of me. "Now eat the whole bowl," he said. I wanted to smile at his kindness but couldn't bring myself to. "Don't worry about the Taliban next door," he went on. "I will be killed before you are. I promised I would take you to safety, and you will see it. I am in a difficult situation here. You are a good man. I want you to eat." He chuckled softly. I ate.

Razi Gul sat next to me, dipping bread into the yogurt more to be my friend than to eat. "Why are you so sad?" he asked.

"The men next door, if they knew I was here, would want to kill me," I said. "Gulob and the Maulavi want my money. You people preach to me and I think deep down want to kill me. Daoud lives in his own world."

They were silent. "We're just passing the time," said Razi Gul. "We are in the same situation. We are even chained to our beds." He was right. He was kind, decent, always serving me tea, giving me food, bringing water to me at the pit in the morning when I performed my ablutions, acting like my servant. I looked down, ashamed.

Gulob came in to see how I was doing. "I have to go next door," he said. He put his finger to his lips. "Be quiet." It was extremely dangerous what he was doing, juggling us and different Taliban factions. "I am not a simple man in the Taliban. I have a lot of influence. I am just in a dangerous situation right now."

Tuesday, March 25

I could hear the men's voices in the morning. We were quiet. By late morning they were gone. There was no sound of a motor. I was in a bad mood all day and tried to stay away from Samad and Daoud. They spent half the afternoon sitting on Samad's cot, talking quietly. I couldn't understand them. Razi Gul lay under his quilt.

As sundown came, Gulob appeared, in black jamay and a dark patoo. He looked dangerous in his dark clothes and shaved head. "The Maulavi has disappeared," he said. "I've been trying to find him, but no one knows where he is. There have been problems among the Taliban. Baitullah Mehsud has said that Abdul Wali is to be the leader in Bajaur. Others wanted to take over." He mentioned different names. "It's now been worked out."

"Mullah Omar is head of the Taliban in Pakistan," said Samad. "Baitullah Mehsud is under Omar. Haqqani is under Mehsud. Hekmatyar and bin Laden are separate. Bin Laden's role and Ayman al-Zawahiri's role are international. That is my understanding."

Gulob nodded in agreement. So did Razi Gul. "You are fortunate that you are here and not at the markez," said Gulob, once again.

After dinner, we sat around talking. "Isn't it hard to keep it a secret that we are here?" I asked Gulob. "Does Abdul Wali know that you are keeping me here?"

"He knows about you," said Gulob. "He said I should bring you to the markez and before the military commission, but I said no. It is secret because we are stealing from the Taliban." I wanted to ask more, but Daoud shook his head. It wasn't a good idea. I reluctantly kept quiet. Rahman came in and sat on the kotgai. We hadn't seen him in a few days.

"How are you? How is your work? How is farming?" I asked.

"Good." He wouldn't say anymore. He and Gulob talked between themselves. "I know that they stone boys and girls in America for eloping," said Rahman.

"No, that's not right," said Gulob. "I asked him."

"Here we stone them," said Rahman.

"What do you do if they run far away to a big city like Karachi or Lahore?" I asked.

"It doesn't matter how long it takes," he said, "one week or ten years."

"How do you find them?"

"We do. We pay the killer to kill them. Always we kill the girl. Always. To save the boy, his family will give two girls to the girl's family." Rahman spoke calmly, showing no emotion.

"During the time of the British reign," said Daoud, "two men went to Peshawar where one of them committed a crime and was sent to prison. They were old, and the prisoner's wife and his friend decided to marry. They returned to Kunar, where they were from. The villagers killed her and shot him in the foot."

"Why? Why do you always kill the woman?"

"Taunting. You will be taunted by others," said Rahman. "So we kill her." It was Pashtun pride and honor (eftekhar), always honor. They were afraid of appearing weak.

"Do you beat your wives?"

"Yes, in Islam and in Pashtunwali we are allowed to beat our wives," said Daoud. The other men listened.

"Muhammad did not beat his wives," I said. "According to the Koran, he treated them with respect."

"I give money to my wife to send my children to school," said Daoud. "If she doesn't, I will beat her. Women here are not educated. They don't care about sending children to school. In the West women are educated and know the value of a husband."

He could tell I was getting upset. "What about in Bajaur? Have the Taliban made any statements on women or on beating women?" I asked.

"A woman came to Abdul Wali," said Gulob. "She said, 'My husband is terrible. He is always beating me.' Abdul Wali said, 'You are not a good woman. You are a prostitute. You have come to me, and I am not your husband. We have no links. This is forbidden in Islam.' Abdul Wali called for her husband. When they were both present he told him to 'beat her until you break her arms and legs.' That night he beat her badly."

I hated sitting with these animals. Yet Razi Gul for three weeks had pined for his daughter. Samad had said he missed his daughters more than his sons. The Taliban forbade the killing of birds and demanded that people treat donkeys with kindness, but not women. It wasn't just the Taliban. A Pashtun wife calls her husband her malaak, her owner.

Razi Gul pleaded with Gulob for some fresh air. Gulob opened the door. I couldn't believe it. On the thirty-ninth day we sat there with the door open, and clean cold fresh mountain air rushed in. It was too much. I wanted him to close the door. I was afraid of the outside. Every night I wanted to return to our room after being allowed outside for a few minutes. I was afraid that someone would attack me. I was afraid of everybody, including the children. I knew they would turn me in.

Gulob again decided to sweep the floor. He sat on his haunches and moved around the room, like a duck, sweeping with his straw hand broom. I could take the cord down that we had strung across and strangle him. He was vulnerable, but I couldn't do it. A part of me liked him. He was the only person who would protect me. He had given me my sweater, my reading glasses, a pen, and a notebook. I couldn't count on my cell mates to help me. They would stop me. I sat there, frustrated.

The air was filled with dirt. It was hard to breathe. A cat walked in and began to explore the room. I watched it, fascinated. I had never seen a cat in a Pashtun house or village before. It would find any rats that were here. The air cleared. Gulob and Rahman talked about how bad it was that women now worked in offices.

"I went to a hospital in Pakistan, and I saw a doctor and a nurse kissing at two in the afternoon," said Gulob. He watched me watching the cat. "Do they have cats in America?"

"Many." I refrained from saying that I had met many women in New York who owned cats. I didn't want to tell him that some women lived without men.

"I have twelve cats," he said. "They're all pets." I asked how many dogs he had. They were considered unclean in Islam. They roamed the streets of Kabul. "Four. Last night, at around two a.m., two of my dogs were fighting and I thought you had escaped, so I took my rifle and ran outside."

He had a soft spot in his heart for animals. We talked about birds, goats, and turtles. I kept thinking that he had run outside last night with his rifle, ready to kill me. I looked at him, wondering if I had it in me to kill him. I didn't. I was unsure about Samad. I didn't like what I saw in me. I couldn't turn the other cheek.

"Have you ever eaten a pig?" asked Gulob. "It is dirty. It is forbidden in Islam."

I wondered how to answer this. "Yes, years ago, I ate some." It was true. I had been a vegetarian for about five years, but no more. Gulob actually shook in disgust. The other men squirmed. "Do you have wild pigs here?" I asked.

"Yes," Gulob said. "They have horns." He showed how they curved out. "We used to hunt them." He was afraid of them.

Gulob lay back on Samad's cot, put his hand behind his head, and began to do sit-ups. "Mamur Sahib, I know you do exercise," he said. "You can help me. I need to lose weight." I showed Gulob how to do push-ups. I would become his coach. It would draw us closer together.

"Show him how you do your bicycle," asked Daoud. I wanted to show Gulob that I wasn't an old man. I got up on my shoulders, put my hands on my hips, and pumped my legs, like riding a bicycle, for a few minutes. I felt I was home. It was comfortable. My father taught me this exercise when I was a boy.

"No one can do that in Afghanistan," said Daoud.

"I've been working hard and eating too much," said Gulob. "I can't eat yogurt. It's bad for me. We ride in cars to the markez, but when we go on jihad in the mountains we just attack and run. I need your help, Mamur Sahib."

I stopped. I wouldn't help him. Normally I loved helping people get in shape. But I refused to help Gulob. There was no way that I was going to help him get in shape so that he could better kill American soldiers. Never. I sat silently. Gulob was waiting. The others were quiet. I was nervous. I wouldn't give in. I changed the subject.

"How old are you?" I asked Gulob.

"I am about thirty-seven," he said. He looked twenty years older. He was solid, and a bit hunched over when he walked, like a football player. Rahman was a little taller, over six feet, and wiry. Gulob went outside and returned with a metal washbasin, about two feet wide and a few inches deep, and a small plastic sack with white powder. He put them on the floor. Samad made a fire, heated water in the kettle, and poured it in the basin. Daoud took off his clothes and put on another set from our plastic sack. He gave his dirty clothes to Samad, who sat on his haunches and washed them.

"I told Samad to wash his clothes," said Gulob. He loved his power. He put some naswar beneath his lower lip. It is forbidden, in the Koran, to drink alcohol. Many Muslim scholars feel this prohibition extends to tobacco, opium, hashish, and other intoxicants. "I want to quit taking naswar," said Gulob. "I know it's bad, but I can't stop." I wanted to tell him he would be able to run faster if he did, but I didn't.

Wednesday, March 26

It is a milestone. My fortieth day in prison. I was relaxed, worn down, proud that I was still alive. I hadn't gone crazy, not yet. I was no longer frustrated. I was beyond that. This was my life. I might be here for a long time. I could hear a riot of birds chirping outside. It was springtime. It would be nice to see birds again. I thought of the Maulavi. Always I thought of him.

Daoud put a tape into the cassette player. The sound of the Taliban, their voices high, chanting in harmony, reminded me, as we sat in our dark cell, of monks reciting Gregorian chants, only these men sang not just of God but of jihad, of history, of death, of martyrdom. The Taliban banned music, for it was of this world and took man away from God, but they loved the sound of young men's voices, like Samad reciting the Koran, or these men calling for war. A young man with a beautiful voice chanted alone. It was haunting and melodic.

Gulob returned now in white clothes. "There are Taliban with the Pakistani army all over the mountains," he reported. "America is building a base on top, and the goal is to destroy it. I talked with a man on the phone who said negotiations with CBS will be finished in three days."

Negotiations? CBS? Was he making this up?

Gulob listened to the Taliban chanting. "To pray while the Taliban chant is to understand complete submission to God and to his will," he said. Daoud turned up the sound on the cassette recorder. The others leaned forward listening intently. I felt afraid.

> *The clang of the sword of Afghans is the clang of the sword of*
> *   Muslims*
> *How the sword sparkles*
> *How clean the turban looks shining as the Talib fights*
> *The clang of the sword*
> *The swoosh of the arrow*
> *The pounding of the horse's hooves*
> *From the peak of Shamshad comes the voice of Bilal*
> *Calling to future generations to fight for independence*
> *Once again Khashal takes up this sword against the Mogul*

Daoud and Samad explained that Shamshad was a mountain in Mohmand Agency; Bilal a companion of Muhammad, said to have had a beautiful voice; Khashal a Pashtun nationalist poet. The Moguls were Muslim invaders from Central Asia who had ruled northern India before the British came.

> *Once again the holy sky of Asia is filled with the sound of noise*
> *   and cries . . .*
> *From East and West and North and South*
> *We send the message to the world*
> *This is the power of the nation—the Taliban*
> *In his chest burns the power of revenge*
> *Leave your sleep of relaxation and come support Islam*

Once again the youth . . . stand waiting in the battlefield
They have white swords, they are tall
And they have black eyes like eagles
When they fight the dust is on their forehead
And in the hair around their temples
With their heads in their palms
They go to the battlefield

All of us, including Gulob and Rahman, sat listening, like brothers, to this call to war against the West, this call to history, this call to Pashtun nationalism tied to Islam, this call to death, to martyrdom. I was the enemy. I was right here. Why didn't they just kill me?

I looked down. There was no place to hide. Outside the wind blew, rattling the thin tin chimney. We heard what sounded like artillery. It stopped. We heard a Predator overhead. I was worried that it would fire on us. "We are under threat from all sides: the Taliban, the Americans, the Pakistani government," said Samad.

Thursday, March 27

I lay awake for a long time, staring into the darkness. On the wall in front of me I saw a shadow of a man holding a rifle. I had seen him there before. I sat up and looked around. There was no one there. I listened for rats. Daoud said he had been hearing them. I could hear him talking in his sleep. I could hear dogs barking and wondered if men were coming. I fell asleep.

I awoke to the sound of Razi Gul praying by my cot. He sat on his knees, his face in his cupped hands. It was comforting to see him here. Next to him, Samad quickly went through his prayer. I waited for them to return to their cots, and then I got up and performed my ablutions; it was second nature now. I stood for a long time, in the Wahhabi style, my hands crossed and resting on my chest, my pants high above my ankles, my mind blank, trying to remember the Salat. I was getting dizzier every time I stood up.

The prayer finally came to me, and I took my time, happy to have no one watching me. When I finished I rolled up the jahnamaz and slowly went through my workout, after which I poured water over myself and onto the floor, which was now our sink. I still worried that too much water was going outside through the hole. I thought of Gulob cleaning our cell. I felt good toward him, but if I made a wrong move he would kill me. Death, it came so easily to mind here. Outside children were playing.

Later that morning, the men woke up again. Daoud turned on the cassette player, and the sound of the Taliban again filled the room.

They sang not just of martyrdom but of Mahmud, who in the eleventh century had raided India seventeen times and solidified Sunni Islam as the religion of Afghanistan. They sang of Pashtun poets and of Iraq. Daoud turned the tape to the other side. It was the story of a Talib talking to his mother. We listened to it for the next few hours.

Oh mother, you must not cry
I will tell you everything clearly but you must not scream
Take my books and keep them with you
The handkerchiefs that you have given to me keep these also
Kiss me quickly
I am leaving you

They play with our lives and dignity
I walk street to street and I revolt and step by step I say the word
    jihad
They have attacked our religion and our faith

They have also attacked the Holy Koran of our Prophet
With pride they attack the world's poorest nation

Do not wait for me to return
Do not be unhappy, at any time, that I have left home
If I become deceased do not wish to see me
I don't feel I will come back alive
I strongly believe I will return in a coffin
I have a wish for martyrdom

The chant ended. The room was silent. I was exhausted. I could hear the haunting chants of sadness and death singing in my ear.

Gulob came in, filled with energy. It was time for spring cleaning. He opened the door and, for once, the window. I looked at the sun shining in. Outside there was life, there was light, and maybe there were men waiting. I was afraid. Gulob swept the floor, rolled up my quilt and mattress, and took them outside. "I will put them in the sun," he said. I wanted to go in the sun. I didn't care about the quilt or mattress.

Razi Gul picked up the broom and continued sweeping. There were tea leaves, branches, toilet paper, tobacco, and dirt. I could see the light through the haze. Gulob dismantled the bokhari and took the chimney outside. It was warm now. Winter was over.

Samad stared up at the hole in the ceiling. I got up and looked also. I could see the sky. It was blue. I thought of *Fidelio*, and the prisoners' chorus, and the video they had made of me when I was first captured, and I cried briefly. No one saw me. I sat down on my rope cot and wrote in my diary. There was enough light now with the door and window open.

It was 1970. I was twenty-four. I was a student in Paris, curious and nervous about the world. I was with a group of other students one evening watching *Civilisation*, a British television series. The program showed thousands of students our age marching in Prague in 1968 against the Soviet Union. The beautiful sound of the prisoners' chorus, which I had never heard before, came on. It was a call to freedom. I was filled with joy and enthusiasm.

I wrote in my diary:

> It was in Paris I knew that I would be on the side of the oppressed and that I would be in the world. I had been brought up to shun the world. We were but pilgrims passing through on our way to Heaven. I missed that community, that love, that warmth, that certainty, but no, I had to live in the world. I knew, long ago, that I would be a traveler, that I would see the world, that it would be cold and I would be lonely, but I had no choice. I wanted to be in the world. I cried today think-ing of my video, of becoming a prisoner. Maybe we soon will be released. Everything will be different now. There is so much emotion inside of me. I will play the prisoners' chorus when I return home, and I will cry.

Once the cleaning was done, Gulob closed the door and the window, and we returned again to the comfort of our darkness. There was another part of the tape. It was the mother's response to her son who was joining the Taliban. Again we listened.

Oh my son, go and good-bye
I appreciate your stories of mettle and I want you to be victorious
Attack your enemy from the front
I want you to be brave

In Pashto poetry, and in Pashtunwali, women expect their men to be brave in battle. I thought of the Maulavi in the front of his men as they ran down the mountain toward us. Samad or Razi Gul could have killed him. Gulob leaned forward on the kotgai, lost from us. He looked at me, his eyes emotional, almost crying. "This fills me with the passion of Islam," he said. He clenched his fists and raised his arms against his chest. My stomach tightened in fear.

> *I want you to be prominent*
> *If you become a ghazi*
> *I will spend flowers on your head*
> *If you become a martyr I will put my shawl on your coffin*
> *Oh, my son, I will always be proud of your mettle*

> *I will come to your shrine every day*
> *I also have in my heart this desire to be a martyr*
> *Oh my son I suffered bringing you up*
> *I cradled you in my chest*
> *If you disappear to whom will I give the love I have for you?*
> *If you are not here who will I look at?*

The mother and son now spoke as one:

> *We were tortured before*
> *Do not torture us anymore*
> *We have cried*
> *Do not make us cry again*
> *We have been burned by fire and we are dying and mourning*
> *For how long must we cry and moan*

After it was over, I could still hear the Taliban music in my ears. There was something pure about sitting on the kilim, drinking tea, listening to the poetry. I could see why the music could draw young men in. I had gone to the movies in New York and watched the advertisement where a young man changes into a marine, holding his sword, standing straight. He was a man. Every boy wanted to be a man, a real man, a warrior.

The Taliban used poetry, appealing to a young man's understanding of Pashtun history, honor, and the desire for freedom. It appealed to the love he felt for his mother and to the glories of martyrdom. He would die a hero. The American warrior, with his sense of his own patriotism, would kill him.

Friday, March 28

Gulob brought in a radio and we listened to the morning news in Pashto on the Voice of America. A U.S. delegation had come to Islamabad to see the new Pakistani government. Gulob laughed. "They are all like a pregnant mother waiting to see if her child will be male, female, or stillborn. Will it be pro-Taliban or anti-Taliban? It doesn't matter. The bureaucracy and the ISI run the war policy here in the tribal agencies."

The announcer said that a report from an analyst at the Rand Corporation, the Pentagon-supported think tank, said that Pakistan should kill the foreigners and not Pakistanis. "By 'foreigners,' I assume she meant al-Qaeda; is that correct?" I asked.

"They are the same," said Gulob. "There are Arabs around. They know Pashto. You cannot tell the difference between them and Pakistanis. They are all together, a part of the foreign policy of Pakistan. It is unchanged. The goal is to expel foreigners from Afghanistan and to control it. Osama and al-Zawahiri are not in the tribal zones. They are being protected by institutions. Pakistan will never give them up."

"Where are they?" I asked. At other times during these conversations with Gulob I had asked Daoud to find an opening to ask him about Osama bin Laden. Always he said, "It is too dangerous."

"I will tell you another time," said Gulob. It was a start.

PART THREE

Sixteen Hours

Sunday, March 30

I woke up, grateful to be alive. I had dreamed vividly again, as I did almost every night now, of my youth, of parts of my life I had long forgotten—things, to my knowledge, I had never dreamed about. I wondered if my mind was preparing for death. Rahman came in and unchained the other men. Where was Gulob? His absence made me nervous. I washed and prayed, and prayed to God. Later, as I was sitting on the kilim studying, fingering my prayer beads, Gulob came in, shook my hand, and sat down. "I tried to call the Maulavi," he said, "but the phones didn't work. Very carefully, I will take you."

Where would he take me? When? How? What was he talking about? I knew not to ask.

He left and I went back to bed, to sleep, to escape the darkness all around me. I woke up to the sound of women making bread, the rhythm of beating the dough a sort of music of joy and happiness. Food was life. A boy brought in bread, lentils, and potatoes and later a bowl of buttermilk. I drank some, sharing a cup with Razi Gul. I wasn't hungry.

Afterward, Razi Gul turned on the cassette player. I didn't want to listen anymore to the Taliban.

Gulob suddenly walked in. He seemed lighter. He went to each man, hugging him; then he came to me and hesitated for a second, not out of a desire to keep his distance but out of respect. I could read and write, and I reminded him of his father. Gulob sat on Razi Gul's cot. "How much would you give me if I took you to Jalalabad today?" he asked me.

What was this all about, another attempt to show his power over us? Was he playing a game? "As much as you want," I said. Daoud looked at me hopefully. We were sitting on the floor. Samad, sitting on his cot, shook his head and muttered, "Don't pay any attention to him. He is playing with us." Gulob left.

A few minutes later the door opened, and the Maulavi walked in slowly, his back straight, like a king. I froze. *Oh my God, oh no. He was here.*

I looked down humbly, then up at him. He too seemed relaxed. What was he doing here? This was dangerous. Something was up. I hesitated this time. I was tired of this, but I stood up, to show respect. "*Kenna, kenna,*" he said. He took off his shoes at the edge of the kilim and sat down cross-legged in front of me, a foot away, and looked at me. His eyes were gleaming.

"Congratulations on escaping death," he said. "You are going to be released today. We have received $200,000, and tonight you will be with your wife. She is waiting for you in Jalalabad."

Was this true? Was this possible? I sat cross-legged, my head down, and looked up at him. I was calm. I was waiting for the death sentence to come next.

"Thank you. Thank you," I said. I didn't trust him. I didn't believe him, but something was up, something.

"Congratulations on escaping death." He said it again. They had been planning to kill me, after all, but someone, somewhere, had saved my life. Who? *You promised me that you would never harm me*, I said to myself, *but you were going to kill me, after all.* I breathed deeply and smiled. Maybe it was true. But I was still here. "What do you have to say?" he asked. He was smiling now, too.

"I am deeply grateful. Thank you," I said. I was still afraid. I thought it might be a joke, and after they had built me up, they would take me outside and shoot me. I was completely confused.

"We are going to be watching to see if you become Muslim, and we will be waiting to hear what you say about us," he said. It was a threat.

"Watch, listen, and read what I write," I said. "I will tell the truth. I guarantee it."

"You get to be with your wife tonight," said the Maulavi. "Aren't you happy?" I didn't believe him, and I didn't trust him. Was Ellen in Jalalabad, or did my sister come over? Did Ellen find the money and bring it over? Was it possible? Maybe this was a sign from God, and I was supposed to marry her.

The Maulavi smiled broadly, putting his hand to his lips. "I was in charge of this. It was my decision to release you," he said. "Congratulations on escaping death." He was saying it too many times, and it made me nervous. "I hope you will become Muslim. You will know the true joy of brotherhood, the joy of peace and certainty," he said.

"I've been praying to know the true God," I replied. It was true, but Islam no longer had any appeal to me. I felt nothing when I prayed; only afterward when I prayed to my own God, the God of my youth, and to the force of good, of light, did I feel better.

"How do you feel now?" the Maulavi asked. He was offering me life itself, if he was telling the truth. I was in shock and wary. I didn't feel happiness. I didn't want to talk, didn't want to say too much that I would later regret. I refused to lie. He was relishing this moment. I smiled and mumbled that I was grateful. I still wanted him to like me. I didn't want him to laugh, call it a joke, and kill me. But maybe it was true. And two hundred thousand dollars, if true, I could pay back.

He got up and put his feet in his shoes. They were black high-top training shoes and reminded me of home. The mujahideen had worn sandals. They were more authentic. He was more modern and scarier. He gathered my books and my sweater and put them in my plastic sack. He started to walk out, came back, and went over to the cassette player. "If there is music in here, you will not be released," he said.

What kind of tape was in there? I was nervous.

He pressed the PLAY button and the sound of the Taliban filled the room. His eyes were shining. "With this you can feel the pleasure of being a suicide bomber," he said, smiling, and he walked out the door.

The four of us stood up. Samad rushed to me and hugged me tightly. He was strong. I was glad I didn't fight him. I hugged Daoud slightly, though I didn't want to. Razi Gul and I embraced. He was skinny now, but his body was like steel. I didn't want to leave him. They were all filled with joy. I sat down, dumbfounded. I grabbed my notebooks and put them in my vest pockets.

Gulob came back in with a scarf, blindfolded Samad, led him outside, and did the same with Razi Gul. He returned with a light blue chadari and put it on the ground. He then blindfolded Daoud and took him away. A man with short gray hair opened the door and looked in. How many people were involved in this? Gulob blindfolded me and put the chadari over me. It was silky and felt feminine. Someone clasped my wrists together and guided me outside into the heat, into another room, and down some winding dirt stairs. It was cool, and then we walked back out into the heat. I could hear children's voices. Were they watching this? It was part of their lives. They were learning early.

Someone pushed me into the backseat of a car. The seat sagged, and the engine sputtered and shook the car. The car was old. Daoud sat next to me, in the center. The Maulavi, I sensed, was on the right, and Gulob was up front, by the window. I could hear voices all around us. A crowd was watching. We were in a village.

Gulob was right. It would have been hard if not impossible for us to escape unnoticed.

We began to drive. My blindfold was loose, and I tried to push it up to peek outside. I wanted to see something so I could tell where we had been. I desperately wanted to see something. Someone, probably Gulob, kept pressing his hand on my head over my eyes to make sure the blindfold was in place and that I couldn't see out. They wouldn't leave anything to chance.

It was hot and suffocating inside the chadari. I heard a siren briefly in front of us. Was a police car leading the way, clearing the crowds? We were in a bazaar. I could hear murmuring voices all around me as we crawled forward. Four times I heard the siren. I would later ask Daoud if he heard it, and he said no. I didn't believe him.

We drove slow, fast, slow again, turning here, there, driving on a dirt road, paved road, gravel, turning, slowing down, going fast again. Then we slowed again and I heard voices. We were driving through a village. It was too hot. Gulob kept putting his hand over my face. I was getting sick. I could feel it. I felt hotter, claustrophobic, and I could hardly breathe. I cried out, in Pashto, "Why, God, why, why?" After all I'd been through, why was I getting sick now? I said it was hard to breathe.

Someone, I think Gulob, rolled down the window. I leaned outside. "Lower your head," said Daoud. "You must act like a woman." I lowered my head and kept gasping for air. Finally, I started to vomit. Again I moaned, *"Wali Allah?"*—angry at myself for getting sick now. They would think it was a plot and get mad. I couldn't help myself.

The Maulavi had had enough. He cocked his rifle.

"Quiet, or you will get us killed, Sir Jere," said Daoud.

I wanted to die, forced myself, pleaded with myself to hold on. *Don't get sick, quit moaning.* I leaned my head against Daoud's shoulder, and for a few minutes it stopped swimming around in torment. Why now, of all times? I had hung on for so long, and now, at the last moment, I was going through this. *Why, God, are you doing this to me?* I was angry at my weakness and afraid.

We kept driving on different types of roads, and I was afraid every minute that I would throw up. About two hours later we stopped, and two men took me by each arm and pulled me out of the car. Someone took off my chadari and then my blindfold, and the light was overwhelming. I covered my eyes, breathing deeply and slowly. I lowered my arms and my eyes gradually adjusted. We were in a field. There was no one around. I saw open fields, gray silent mountains, a wide-open plain with a stark white mosque and a mud-baked house about a mile away in the center.

I stumbled forward, feeling like an old man. Razi Gul and Samad were sitting on their haunches, blindfolded, in a ditch in front of us. I walked toward them. Gulob untied them and undid their blindfolds, and they covered their eyes. We began to walk slowly on a goat path up into the mountains. I could barely keep up. Samad took my hand, our fingers entwined as if we were a couple, and we walked forward. He was my friend. He was helping me. I tried to walk alone, halted, kept going. Razi Gul took my arm, and we kept climbing. I didn't think I could make it. Yet I knew this was where we had come down from the mountains six and a half weeks ago, blindfolded, and where they had put me in the car.

A man with a white prayer cap, three donkeys, and a boy came toward us down the mountain, smiling, greeting us. I said, "*Estale mache*" (may you not be tired), remembering the greeting the mujahideen used years ago. I shook hands with the man and continued onward. He didn't notice anything. For a second I was happy. Life was going on. I felt light.

We climbed for about half an hour in the sun, and then the path leveled off and we were in a small, wide, rocky gorge. We stopped in the shade beneath a rock. Gulob told us to sit down and walked ahead, carrying a rifle and a bundle, a patoo tied together at one end, over his shoulder. I assumed my cameras were inside. He had promised to give them back to me.

He sat on a rock twenty yards ahead and above us, watching us and the path in front. I was sick again. I was too weak to walk, and I laid my patoo on the path and sat down. Behind and above us I saw the Maulavi, in his black turban, his gray patoo blowing in the breeze, his Kalashnikov over his shoulder, standing on a ridge, his head up, like a hawk, staring ahead. This was his land.

I took out my notebook. *The land is silent,* I wrote. *The wind comes and dies down. We are waiting. For what? For those to come pick me up?*

I fell asleep. Five or ten minutes later I woke up. There were men behind us, carrying rifles, their faces covered, with only their eyes showing. I saw a man with a prayer cap leaning down, fumbling in a sack. He waved his hand, telling me to look away.

Was he preparing the suicide vest? Were they going to take us to a spot high on a ridge where they would shoot us and dump our bodies where no one would find them? Were we waiting for a group of armed men to come and take me? Was this the exchange point? Would there be a shoot-out? What kind of plans did both sides have? I looked at the mountains. There was no vegetation. There were booming sounds far away—artillery fire. Were we going to attack a U.S. base? It was silent again.

Gulob climbed higher up the rocks, looking all around, and then came down behind us, keeping his distance, and joined the Maulavi. "Gulob is afraid of us," said Daoud, chuckling.

Ten minutes later, it was time to go. Gulob took the lead. I threw my patoo over my shoulder and we walked down through a gorge. The rock was slate, and I slipped and stumbled forward. My body and legs felt skinny and weak. I knew everyone was watching to see if I could keep going. I would show them.

I was the runner I had been as a boy. We walked for hours. Daoud kept falling farther behind, and we had to stop to wait for him. This time I was glad. I could rest. I wanted to lean forward and put my hands on my knees, but I didn't dare show weakness. We kept going, all of us changing order as we walked along. Two Talibs were always behind us. We passed a young man, his face covered, holding a rifle, sitting on a rock. He rose and walked with the men behind us. Razi Gul carried my plastic bag. I wore my vest with my notebooks in them. We kept walking up and down through the mountains. The sun was starting to wear me down.

We came down a rocky hill, and in front of us were three or four tall narrow caves and a village. We had passed through this village on our way north. It was comforting to see it again, but we had come by a different path. We didn't pass the spot where the Maulavi and his men had attacked and surrounded us, where I had been certain I would die. I didn't want to see that spot again, not with them. I watched the Maulavi from behind. I could come up on him, grab his rifle, and take him hostage. It would be easy. It was a fantasy. Everyone would surround me, and I would be dead.

We came down and walked through the village. A boy watched us pass. "We'd like to come back and stay with you tonight," Gulob shouted to him. "We don't have a hujra," the boy shouted back.

I had never heard of a Pashtun village that was too poor to have a guest room where travelers could stay. Clearly, Gulob didn't know this area or these people. It made me wonder, how could the CIA ever insert a spy here or into any other part of the tribal areas and not be discovered? How could bin Laden ever hide here? Everyone in this village was related to one another or knew one another closely. The women had sensed immediately when we walked through here a month and half ago that we were new or different. They had turned and watched us.

Everyone in this village was part of the same tribe, the same clan, the same subclan. They had banded together centuries ago for protection. Pashtuns married their cousins—Gulob, Samad,

Razi Gul, Daoud—all of them. Each clan was woven together tightly, like knots in a rug, and they lived according to their ancient rules. Even the Taliban followed Pashtunwali. "What is your father's name?" they had asked me.

Daoud could tell that the Maulavi had a Kunar accent. Razi Gul said he could tell a Shinwari accent in Landi Khotal from one from Jalalabad, not forty miles away. A CIA agent in this region would have to speak perfect idiomatic Pashto, with the proper accent, know how to walk, dress, eat, pray, wash, and be related or be discovered as an outsider.

If he were invited in, he would be putting his family at risk. His cousin would probably turn him in. That was Tarburwali. Gulob was armed when his cousins came to visit.

Gulob's neighbors knew within a month that more people than normal were living in his house. We had to pour water on the floor. We couldn't let it flow outside. Gulob was worried about his children talking. The boy shouted back at him that they didn't have a hujra. We were outsiders; Gulob and the Maulavi would have to find another place to sleep tonight.

It was growing dark. We kept going. Up ahead, we saw a group of men standing together. Who were they? The Maulavi took his rifle off his shoulder and walked forward. He wore a black turban. He was the Taliban. I admired his courage, walking toward those men. We waited. He walked to the circle, talked with the men, and signaled to us. We walked forward, twenty yards apart, all of us keeping our distance from one another.

"They invited us to eat with them," said the Maulavi, coming back toward us. He said it was getting late and we had to walk faster. We walked on, the Maulavi in the lead, passing the men, greeting them. No one was armed. Only we were. We were the Taliban. We stopped a few hundred yards beyond them, on a ridge, above a small narrow stream. Hills rolled off to the west, becoming jagged, rust-red mountains. The sun had set, and it was quiet and beautiful. The men put down their patoos and faced southwest toward Mecca. It was time for prayers.

There was a spot next to the Maulavi, but I didn't want to be near him. I didn't want to be near Gulob or anyone with a rifle. I laid my patoo down and went through the motions of praying. I was afraid not to pray. I wanted to show the Maulavi that I knew what to do. I knew everyone was watching me. I prayed in Arabic and silently in English, asking God to protect me.

I was afraid that I was being a hypocrite. But no, I had prayed to God. *Al-Lah* means "the God" in Arabic. I wasn't a hypocrite. I wasn't when I prayed in prison. I hadn't prayed in decades, but I had in prison. It was comforting.

We got up and walked on. It was getting darker. "We have to walk faster," said the Maulavi. We pushed on. I was running a race now, and it just got hard. I was getting dizzy, and my chest was burning. I desperately wanted to sit down. I was getting worried. My legs felt weak and I wondered how long I could hang on. I had never been the one to hold others back, and I couldn't do it now. I would have to dig down inside. I couldn't show weakness, not here, not with these men.

A breeze came up, kicking dust into our faces. Daoud was falling farther and farther behind and we had to wait for him. I was never so happy to sit down. I breathed deeply, quietly thanking Daoud. The men laughed. "Daoud is weak," said one of them.

We kept going. We had been walking for about six hours, and I realized that we hadn't seen a single Pakistani soldier. Where were the ninety thousand soldiers who were supposedly guarding the border? We came down along the stream. It was almost the exact spot where we had stopped to eat six and a half weeks before. Gulob and another man told us to go into a gully. They made us sit bunched together in a row in a hollowed-out rock. It was a perfect place to kill us. I looked up. "Look forward," said Gulob. *This is where they are going to do it*, I thought. We couldn't move; there was no place to run. My stomach tightened. I put my head down. Nothing. I looked up and saw a man crouched on a rock above us holding a rifle.

I put my head in my hand, waiting. "Tell Mamur Sahib not to be unhappy," said Gulob. Maybe they weren't going to kill us, after all. I was a wreck. Daoud joked and laughed with Gulob. Why was he so relaxed and friendly? Was it because he felt that we were being freed? What did he know that I didn't? Razi Gul and Samad talked, but they didn't laugh. "Where are the others? Are they praying?" I asked Samad. He said they were. I felt better.

I looked up again at the man on the rock. I recognized him. I half smiled, waving. He grinned and nodded. He had held a rocket-propelled grenade launcher at my head and later talked to me in Nuristani. Maybe we would survive. I breathed easier.

We got up and walked over a grassy spot. I stumbled more than I walked. I was dizzy. There was a pool of rancid water in front of us. I knew not to drink it but I needed some water. I sat on my haunches and washed my neck and face and arms, trying to absorb water this way. I took a few small sips. The water in prison was cool and good. This was a sewer. I sat next to the Maulavi. He was putting on his shoes. "Did you pretend you were sick in the car so you could look out or cause trouble so someone could see us?" he asked, half smiling. "It was very dangerous there for all of us."

I told him I truly had been sick, that I had gotten sick in cars when I was a boy. He looked at me, nodding, but I wasn't sure if he believed me. "I was afraid you might kill me," I said, "but then I said no, not after all of this. You said you wouldn't harm me." I was saying that I trusted him, but what I was *really* saying was, "I trusted you, and if you are a man of your word, a man of honor, you won't kill me now. You will free me."

"I had a bullet in the chamber," he said, "but I took it out when I cocked the rifle."

I smiled. I felt myself shaking inside. I believed him, but had it really been dangerous for all of us? I thought of the sirens I swore I heard. If we were all in danger, that meant that Gulob was telling the truth. They had done this secretly, keeping it even from other Taliban. If the government was in control, they were bandits. Yet the Maulavi had worn his black turban, and there had been people, especially children, all around when they put us, blindfolded, into the car.

Were the other men really blindfolded, or was it just a show? It was impossible for me to know. I saw Gulob blindfold Daoud, Razi Gul, and Samad and lead them out of the cell, but did they take their blindfolds off when they were outside? Did they take them off in the car, only to be blindfolded again before we stopped? All I knew was that when my own blindfold came off, I saw the other men blindfolded. I really didn't know anything.

We walked on. The man who was on the rock above us came up next to me. "Remember me? I spoke to you in Nuristani," he said. He gave me a big, friendly, rough grin.

"Of course I do," I said. "How are you? How is your health?" I put my arm on his shoulder, trying to be his friend. It was as hard as a rock. Why was I doing this? After all that I had been through, I didn't want him to kill me. I had watched him walk in the cell, chewing on a piece of straw, looking at us, through us, not seeing us. His eyes were cold. This, I knew, was the Maulavi's best fighter, the man he relied upon the most in battle.

"I hope you will become Muslim," he said. "I hear you've been praying."

"I have," I said, taking my arm away. "I've been praying five times a day."

"Good," he said, smiling. "We will be watching. I hope you will come back."

I didn't want to talk to him anymore. A part of me liked him, and I didn't want to lie. I wanted to be far away from him. I walked ahead.

Time passed. It was dark now, and I started to falter. It was becoming harder and harder to see ahead. I was exhausted. How much longer did we have to go? I began to stumble. Twice, three times, four times, I don't know how many times I almost fell. I put my hands on my knees, kept going. My chest was burning.

When would this ever end? I stumbled forward. I had nothing left. We lost our way, backtracked, and began to climb, thrashing through high weeds. I couldn't go any farther. I couldn't climb. I had to go on. I couldn't do it. I kept going, afraid I would fall down. We kept going and going and I hung on, and my throat was burning, and then, finally, blessedly, we stopped. I sat on a rock, my head down, trying to catch my breath, hoping some strength would return. We waited for Daoud. He finally arrived and collapsed on his back. The Maulavi and Gulob sat on a rock. Their men and the four of us came over and sat with them. I kept my head down, my heart pounding. Then they stood up, and I slowly went over to them. It was night and I could barely see them.

"We are going to release you here," said the Maulavi. "We are going to be watching you. Do not say anything to any government. If you do, we will kill you. We know where your families are; we know where your houses are; we know all about you. Now go."

"You can have my knife," I said to Gulob. "You wanted it, and I promised it to you."

I then turned to Daoud. "Where are my cameras?" I asked. "Gulob promised them to me. I thought he was carrying them with him in the sack." Gulob looked at me, his eyes cold. He didn't have the cameras.

"I don't know anything about this," said Daoud. He didn't care.

I looked at Samad and Razi Gul. I couldn't make out their faces in the dark. It was hopeless. We had to get out of here.

"We will be watching you," said the Maulavi. "I hope you become Muslim."

I didn't respond. "Good-bye," I said.

He and I embraced in a formal hug, baghal kashee, touching each other on the chest and placing a hand on the other's shoulder. I did the same to Gulob, but he didn't respond or look at me. I felt sad.

We walked on. I waited for someone to shoot me in the back. Was it possible? Were we actually free of them? I couldn't believe it. I couldn't believe it. I felt lighter, almost smiling. I was exhausted, but I knew I could keep going.

Razi Gul took the lead. He knew where he was going. It was pitch-black. He veered left, and we walked down through high brushes and soft, sandy dirt toward a river. It was the Kabul River. We had crossed somewhere near here before. We walked through a poppy field, whose plants were almost up to my waist. I fell in a ditch, but Samad pulled me up and wanted to take my hand. I said no. I stumbled forward, fell again, and got up. Razi Gul walked easily in the lead.

I thought I heard a whistle. I saw a light flicker and go off. It was a small flashlight. A few minutes later I saw it again. We walked toward the light. There were no bushes around now. Again it went on. Five men in white, with white skullcaps and carrying guns and ammunition, came out of the dark and approached us. A man hugged Razi Gul. A moment later an armed man appeared out of the dark, wearing white, and hugged me gently, welcoming me, too. I sighed in relief. They would not kill me.

We followed them down to the riverbank. A man turned on his flashlight for a second and switched it off. He did it twice. A light flicked on across the water and then off again. We waited. Then a small motorboat came across the water and pulled up into the sand in front of us. "No English," whispered Samad. We got in, and I drank some water from the river as we crossed. No one spoke. We reached the other side, climbed out onto the sand, and walked up a hill. Again, I felt the exhaustion hit me. I wondered how far I could walk. I wanted to lie down in the sand and sleep.

The others walked and I stumbled through the soft sand south along the water about three hundred yards, and a pickup truck appeared, parked on the road. It was the same road we had come down weeks before. My companions told me to sit in front, but I knew I would be sick in there. I climbed in the back. A man brought a pan of water and Samad took a drink and so did I. There were a dozen men around us, all of them armed. They moved quickly.

The truck started up and we drove up and onto a paved road. We drove fast, around bends, and I got sick again. I vomited and kept vomiting, but it was all bile. There was nothing inside of me. I knew I shouldn't have drunk that rancid water. We kept going, and my head was swirling. I leaned over the side of the truck. A half hour or so later we reached a small village. Samad helped me out, took my arm, and we walked up a hill toward a group of buildings. "No English," he whispered. We walked into a compound, and he put me on a rope cot. I lay down and fell asleep. A few minutes later I woke up and heard men's voices all around me talking softly. I saw a cup of green tea sitting on a stool next to my cot. I drank it. The sugar gave me some energy.

I lay back down, covering my eyes with my arms, trying to hide. I was afraid that someone would recognize me and kill me. A young man poured more tea for me. I got up on my elbow, and as I drank the tea I looked around. There was a row of men, all of them armed, sitting on cots like mine against the wall. A roof came out about five feet over them. I saw Samad sitting with them, hunched over, looking at me, holding a rifle. He didn't smile. He was far away, with his men, his clan, his tribe. I lay down on my back and closed my eyes. The men got up and began to walk down a small hill to what looked like a white tent or modern building. "Do you want to eat?" someone asked me. I said no. I lay there looking at the stars, wondering if this was where we took the car after we crossed the border. I closed my eyes. The world spun around. I heard voices again. The men were coming back. I put my elbow over my face.

I was half asleep when I heard Daoud's voice: "Sir Jere, Sir Jere. Wake up." I raised my head. Daoud was crouching on the ground next to me. "There is a man who wants to talk to you," he said. I pulled myself up.

"Sir Jere, this is Abdullah," Daoud said.

I looked at the man sitting on the cot by my feet. Abdullah? It hit me. I tried to sit up but couldn't. I had to whisper. "Where have you been?" I said. "What happened?" I looked at him. He wore a white prayer cap, like some of the other men, and had a thick black beard and a stocky build. He seemed to be about forty-five years old. I looked at him closely. His eyes were level, almost kind. He didn't have a hard, angry face.

"I've been running and hiding for the past month," he said, softly. "I was trying to free you, while I was being hunted by the people who had you, and by your people who wanted to capture me. I haven't seen my children in a month."

It was true, then, what the Maulavi had said, that Abdullah was trying to release me and that they were trying to capture him. Or did they agree that this was the story they would tell me? I thought back to the car ride weeks earlier, when someone had written in the palm of my hand "Abdullah" and held my hand tightly. Yes, he would come and rescue us.

Razi Gul had told me that we had been about twenty minutes away from reaching Abdullah's compound before we were captured. I believed him. We were that close. But this was Abdullah's territory. I learned in prison that it wasn't Samad who wrote "Abdullah" in my hand, as I first thought. "I did," said Daoud. "I was sitting next to you." How did he know he was sitting next to me when I couldn't tell who was sitting next to me? Maybe he could. I was the skinny one. Still, I was confused and dazed.

"Do you want to go on the trip we were going to take before?" asked Abdullah. "I can take you now." Was he crazy? Did he actually think I wanted to travel with him now? The truth is, my first thought was, *Yes, let's go.* I still hadn't been to Waziristan, not since 1981. I could see Jalaladin Haqqani. Who knows who else I would see.

"I can't," I said. "My wife is waiting for me in Jalalabad." I had mixed emotions about leaving. Abdullah looked at me kindly. "Did you try to arrange for us to go to Waziristan, and to see Jalaladin?" I asked. I thought of Mullah Malang, who had told me, "Abdullah can get to Sirajuddin. You can't, but he can." (Sirajuddin was Haqqani's son, said to be one of the leaders of the insurgency in eastern Afghanistan.)

"I talked to Sirajuddin," Abdullah replied softly. "He said if I brought you to his area that you and your translator would be killed. My life would be in danger for working with a foreigner." I sighed. If only he had talked to Jalaladin, the father. "When I was planning our trip, I went to Waziristan and talked to Baitullah Mehsud," Abdullah said. "He said if I brought you there he would behead you. It would be dangerous for me also."

I was confused. Daoud, who was translating, had just said that Abdullah was ready to take me to Waziristan. But now he said it was impossible for me to go. My mind was reeling. I was weak. I wanted to clarify this but didn't have the courage or the strength to ask him.

"I know you had to pay a lot of money," Abdullah said. "I am sorry about that. I have some property in Jalalabad that I can sell to pay you back."

Again, I was confused. Why would he say this? Did he feel bad that he had extorted money from me, if he actually had? Or had he been trying to find me and free me so I wouldn't have to be ransomed? Was he acting or being sincere? I wanted to tell him to sell his property, but I didn't. "No, thank you," I said. "Let me talk to my wife. I don't know what has happened." All I knew was that Ellen was supposedly waiting for me in Jalalabad. CBS was also likely to have been involved in getting me out. The Maulavi said the Taliban had received $200,000. Ellen had probably raised the money. But the Maulavi had lied to me about other things. I didn't know who or what to believe. "I don't know what to say," I said. "I don't know what to think. I can't travel with you now. We'll talk later about selling your property."

There were a hundred questions I wanted to ask him, but I didn't know what they were. I couldn't formulate them. I was afraid of him, of Samad and the other men sitting against the wall. I was their guest, in their compound, but I didn't trust anybody. Abdullah was polite, almost humble. Maybe he felt bad about what had happened to me. He was Mullah Malang's friend. Mullah Malang had trusted him, and therefore I had trusted him. I lay back on the cot and closed my eyes. My head was swimming. I was too weak to think. I didn't get to Waziristan. I didn't see Haqqani, but I was alive. I was still alive. I sat halfway up again.

"What are we going to do now?" I asked, half expecting them to shoot me.

"We're waiting for another truck," Abdullah said. "It will be here in about half an hour. We're going to take you across the river. We can't go into Afghanistan, but we'll take you to the border." We had been in the compound about an hour, maybe longer.

I lay down and closed my eyes. I knew I should ask Abdullah more questions, that this was my only opportunity, but I couldn't. I liked him. He was nice to me, even kind in the way he looked at me and talked. I didn't think that he might have orchestrated my kidnapping.

I looked up at the sky. The stars were bright and the air was dry and balmy. It came time to go. Someone I didn't know helped me up, and we walked from the compound. There were twenty men around me, all of them armed, it seemed. We walked to a pickup, and a few men asked me to sit in the cab, up front with Abdullah, but I wanted to feel the breeze and I was afraid I might be sick again. It had to be close to midnight. Maybe it was already the next day. It would be forty-five days now. I got in the back with Samad, Razi Gul, Daoud, and six armed men. We rumbled on, the truck bouncing and swerving around turns, and I got sick again. I threw up all the tea I had just drunk. I kept throwing up. It was the rancid water now. I leaned over the side. We drove about a half hour or so and down onto a wide sandy beach.

The Kabul River, here the border between Pakistan and Afghanistan, flowed by again. We walked to the shore. A man flashed a small light. A light flashed on the other side. One of our men talked to a man across the water. A light flicked again, and a pickup on the other side drove down to the water, flashed its lights, and turned them off.

Abdullah, his men, and I waited for the ferry—two boats lashed together—to come across the water. Abdullah kindly asked if I was okay. I was too tired to stand up, and Razi Gul gave me his patoo to sit on. I needed to go to the bathroom. Razi Gul took me in the dark to a gully away from the beach. As he escorted me, he walked easily and was strong and confident. He carried a rifle. He seemed distant. He could shoot me here. I was afraid.

We walked back to the beach. I knew, but at the same time it didn't fully register, that Razi Gul would probably get some of the money the Taliban had taken from me. He had robbed me. But I liked him. We had been through a lot together. He had cried in prison and had always given me the best pieces of meat. And yet I couldn't forget that he was a member of the Taliban.

The ferry docked, and the men with their rifles, Daoud, and I rode it, feeling the breeze, silently across the water. It stopped and Samad gave me a hug. "We can't go any farther," he said, "because of animosities." They couldn't enter Afghanistan. Abdullah gave me a hug. I barely hugged him, or Samad, in return. Razi Gul came close to me and gently pulled on my beard. No one had ever done that before. I felt violated and deeply close to Razi Gul at that moment. "Please help me," he said. He was afraid. Or did he want money and for me not to come after him? He was being a supplicant. I hugged him good-bye.

Daoud and I walked off the ferry; we were back in Afghanistan. A man got out of the pickup, came up to us, and told us to climb in. We got in the back. Who were the two men? Where were they taking us now? We headed west on a rough and bumpy dirt road. Dust flew over us but I was oblivious. The truck stopped after half a mile. The man in the passenger seat came back and asked if I wanted to climb in the front.

I did and was grateful for the soft seat. We rode for about an hour, bouncing, dipping, and turning in the night. There were no lights, no signs of anyone. We passed poppy fields now and then, but mostly the land was gray, eerie, and empty. I clung to the side of the truck, exhausted and sick. We came upon a dark baked-mud settlement. A man stood in the road waving a small flashlight, like a lantern.

What now? The truck stopped, and the man with the light talked to the driver, as other men watched in the darkness. The man in the middle of the front seat said he had to get out. I opened the door and held on to it as I stepped on the ground. I could barely stand up, but I couldn't lean against the truck. I had to look Afghan. I tried to hide my face, pretending to be nonchalant.

The men came around to the side of the truck. One of them held out a card. It said CBS and showed Fazul Rahim's picture. I sighed. The man handed me a letter. I opened it but was too tired to read it. It didn't matter. I followed the man toward a house and saw a white SUV, hidden in the dark, parked next to it. Behind it was another one.

I climbed in the backseat of the first SUV. The man who had handed me Fazul's card got in the front passenger seat. His driver started the car and we moved slowly forward. I looked up front and saw a Kalashnikov on the floor, with its barrel pointed up facing me, next to the driver. I sat back, wary, too tired to talk. The man in the front passenger seat was in his forties, thin, nicely dressed, distinguished-looking. He handed me a bottle of water. I trusted him.

We drove over dark, empty, bumpy dirt roads. I saw more poppy fields, the plants as high as a man's chest. There were no houses around. I got sick again, opened the window, and leaned down. I looked back and saw the other SUV behind us and a rifle pointing out the window. The men inside were bodyguards. I was relieved that they were there.

I kept throwing up for the next half hour or so. The man in the front passenger seat handed me a box of tissues.

We came to a graded dirt road and headed east. My instincts said we should be going west. A half mile later the road ended. This was dangerous. Who were these people? Why didn't they know the way? We turned around and headed in the other direction. We stopped ten minutes later at another junction. The men got out to talk with the men in the other SUV. I got out of the car and staggered forward. I wanted solid ground beneath my feet.

I was dizzy and almost fell but walked slowly up the road about thirty yards, away from the direction of the headlights. I wanted to be sick where no one would see me. I came back to the vehicle and leaned against it. Daoud, who was in the other SUV, walked up close to me and pulled on my beard. I hated it. Twice now within a few hours two men had pulled on my beard. Daoud was scared. I wanted to push him away. He was too close.

"They have a tape recorder and are asking me questions," he said. "You must help me. I want to ride with you. You said you would protect me."

I crossed my arms, put my head down. I wanted to be far away from him. *What do these people know that I don't? Is Daoud a part of this? Did he betray me?* I thought back to my talk with Abdullah. Daoud seemed so relaxed sitting there, as if he and Abdullah were old friends.

I tried to move away from him. I didn't want anyone to think I was close to him, but I was too tired to move. All I wanted to do was sit on the ground. I was leaning against the vehicle for support.

"We have a pact," he said. "You agreed that your neck is my neck." It was true. But still, had he betrayed me? "I want to ride with you. I don't want to be with those people."

I was too tired to resist. It was time to go. I got in the backseat, and Daoud got in the other side. We drove on. I got sick again. When would it stop? Would this ever end?

An hour later, we came to a village. We got out and walked to a compound and into a dirt courtyard where there was a rope bed. I lay down and looked up at the stars. A man brought over a bottle of Mountain Dew. I said no. Another man brought over a glass of green tea. I took a sip and lay down. A cell phone rang. I hadn't heard a cell phone since leaving Jalalabad over a month and a half ago. The leader came over and handed me the phone. *What? For me?* I took it.

"Jere, this is Fazul." I recognized his voice. "Are you okay?" I said I was fine. My voice cracked. "I will see you in one hour," Fazul said. "Fraidoon will take care of you."

I lay down and breathed deeply. One more hour.

The phone rang again. Fraidoon brought the phone over to me again. "Jere, this is Andy Clarke," said the voice. I assumed he was calling from London, where he was the CBS deputy bureau chief. I began to realize that others knew about my situation. I heard later that a group of people had set up a task force in Islamabad, working for weeks around the clock to find me. I heard stories of helicopters ferrying people from Afghanistan to Pakistan and back; of Pakistanis traveling in the tribal zones, knocking on doors, chasing after people; of Afghans tracking down people, interrogating them; of the involvement of a retired Pakistani general; of Afghan officials using their tribal networks on both sides of the border; of American intelligence networks and the FBI being involved; of a NATO spy being the first to report that a foreigner had been kidnapped; of one man placing hundreds of thousands of dollars all over his body, evading all airport detection, and traveling halfway around the world to bring money into Pakistan. I would hear Andy's name come up, as I would hear other names, but everything was murky. I was the first foreigner kidnapped in Pakistan since Daniel Pearl, and the dragnet was wide and deep, and people were afraid for me.

"How are you?" Andy asked.

"Andy, is that you?" I said. I started to cry. "I'm okay. I'm fine. I'm a little tired, but fine." He asked if I was hurt or injured. "No," I said, "they didn't torture me." By then we were both crying. "I'm fine," I repeated. I didn't know what else to say. I was exhausted, overwhelmed, humbled, ashamed, grateful, and happy all at once. "I'll see you soon, Andy." I didn't know where or how. I didn't think about that. I ended the call. I didn't want to talk about myself. I didn't like being the center of attention.

I wondered where the tears had come from. I didn't know what I had pent up inside of me, what had been inside for weeks. Two other calls came, and I felt the warmth of knowing that people cared. I wasn't alone.

Dark shadows began to move around me. Men were walking. Daoud said we had to go. I walked slowly to the SUV. We drove for an hour on dark, bumpy dirt tracks, gunmen riding behind us. I leaned out the window, sick again. Daoud wrapped his arms around my waist. He was trying too hard to show that he cared.

We passed poppy fields and giant clods of dirt and boulders, occasionally a tree, a baked-mud house, all a blur. I didn't know that the man in front of me, Fraidoon Mohmand, was the tribal leader of this area and a member of parliament. I didn't know that as soon as I had climbed into this SUV I was safe. I was told he had given his word that after he took possession of me he would release the money to Abdullah.

We pulled up in front of another compound. I saw some men standing around another vehicle, and other men walking toward the compound. Daoud climbed out, and I moved toward the door.

Fazul appeared and hugged me. "You're safe, Jere, you're safe," he said. I cried briefly, my emotion and gratitude coming out. "Don't cry, Jere, be happy," he said. I smiled. I was safe. I was safe. It was over. I saw Ahmed Jan, another friend, holding a camera. He was filming this. Of course he would. "Ahmed Shah is waiting for you in Jalalabad. He couldn't come here," said Fazul. Ahmed Shah was Fazul's cousin. They were all my friends, Tajiks, from the north, risking their lives, deep in Pashtun country, to save me. That's why I cried, because so many people had helped me.

There was movement all around us. We stayed in Fraidoon's SUV. Fazul give Daoud a hard, dark look. He didn't want him in the car. "We think he was involved in this," Fazul whispered to me. I didn't want him there either, but I didn't have the strength to tell him to get out.

We started to drive through the night. I sat next to the window, Fazul next to me.

"How are you? Are you sick? Are you injured?" he asked. He was so concerned.

"I am fine," I said. "I am fine. I drank some bad water. I am throwing up all the time."

Fazul took from his vest a cellophane bag with pills in it. He had come prepared. "Take this," he said, handing me a pill. I resisted, but he insisted. I took it, for him. There was nothing around us, only darkness and land that looked in the night like a moonscape. We could be attacked at any moment. "Who do you want to talk to first, your brother or your sister?" he asked.

So my family knew about this. "Either one," I said. Then I thought about it and decided to call my brother first. He had always been there for me, when it counted, and we had come to Afghanistan together, so many years ago.

Fazul took out his cell phone and a piece of paper and dialed my brother's number. "This is Fazul Rahim," he said. "I am calling from Afghanistan. I'm with CBS. There is someone here who wants to talk to you." He handed me the phone.

I said hello. Sarah, my niece, was on the line. I had sent to her my last e-mail from Jalalabad before I crossed the border. I had thought of her the night after the Taliban had shot the videos. She was my tie to home.

Sarah was happy that I was safe. She cried briefly, and so did I. She said the rest of the family was at church, that she was home alone.

"You're supposed to be happy," Fazul told me. What he was saying was "Don't cry. Be strong, be a man." I understood, but I didn't want to laugh and joke. I didn't have it in me. I didn't want to be the tough guy anymore, as I had to be in prison.

Fazul then called my sister, introduced himself, and gave me the phone. There she was, on the line. She too cried, but I didn't. "Are you all right?" she asked. I told her I was fine. "It's been sur-real," she said. "The FBI and the State Department and CBS have been calling." So the government did know. The kidnappers didn't know that. We talked for a minute, and then the phone cut off. Fazul called the number again. "We didn't tell Dad," she said. "We were told not to talk to anybody." She paused. "Are you okay?"

I said I was fine. I knew what she was asking. "They didn't tor-ture me," I said. I didn't know then that there are two types of tor-ture, psychological and physical. I was happy that she hadn't told our father. He would be ninety-five soon. The news might have killed him.

Fazul and I talked like the friends that we were for a few

minutes, and then I didn't want to talk anymore. I didn't like it that Daoud was there. Fazul wouldn't look at him. I didn't know what to think. I leaned out the window and was sick again. I was too weak to think.

Suddenly we were driving on a paved road, past rows of baked-mud houses and shuttered shops. We had reached Jalalabad. I was free. I was truly free. The car behind us disappeared. Fazul called a man named Joe on his cell phone. "He's a real nice man," he said. "We've been talking for the last few hours. He's going to meet us at the PRT."

PRT was short for Provincial Reconstruction Team. We were going to a U.S. military base. I had been trying since I had begun my work to stay as far away as possible from the U.S. government. I had wanted to operate underneath its radar. I had wanted to stay away from everyone. Now I was going from the Taliban to the heart of America here. We came to an intersection, silent at night. There are no traffic lights or crosswalks in Afghanistan. A man with a rifle stood in the center. Fraidoon got out. We drove on.

Fraidoon, I was told later, would soon authorize the money to go to Abdullah. He would keep his word. If he didn't, he would lose his standing as a tribal leader. Abdullah was probably a thief and a criminal, but they had an agreement. Fraidoon's honor was at stake. It was part of Pashtunwali. The Taliban, or those behind them, no matter how hard they tried, could not destroy this ancient tribal system. They were a part of it. Islam was not always stronger than blood.

We drove around past more baked-mud houses, and now open sewers, looking for the right entrance to the PRT. We came upon bright lights shining everywhere, a high cyclone fence with concertina wire on top. A soldier, standing in a guardhouse surrounded by sandbags, lifted a bar at a gate, and we drove onto the base as a few American men and women, unsmiling, in civilian clothes, watched us coldly. A man opened another gate, and we drove into a garage and someone shut the door behind us.

Two men came around and opened the door, and I climbed out and they grabbed me. I had trouble walking. They guided me into a brightly lit room and I sat down at a table. There was a woman in her late twenties or early thirties at one end, and a man about the same age with her. They were in civilian clothes, but he wore a pistol. Another man, a few years older, with longer hair, in civilian clothes, also carrying a pistol, walked in, stood on the other side of the table, and looked at me hard. He had strong, almost gleaming eyes. He reminded me of the Maulavi in his intensity. "Where do you want to go, Bagram or Kabul?" he said.

I didn't know. Why was he asking me this? Who was this man? Who were these people? What was going on? Was I under arrest? Bagram was the U.S. military base north of Kabul, built by the Soviet Union in the 1980s. I remembered being there in 2001 and seeing the Cyrillic lettering on a fuse box in a hangar. It was ironic that the United States was now there.

I looked at the soft drinks and a few cans of beer in front of me. The soft drinks were American and made me think of home. I had heard the U.S. military didn't allow its people to drink alcohol in Afghanistan. Maybe the beer was for special guests. They were being good to me. I looked at one soft drink can closely. It was America. It was home. I was so glad I was American.

"I've been sick," I said as I took the can and popped open the lid.

"Be careful," said the older man. "Drink only a little bit at a time." He was right. He was being kind. I was grateful to him. I wasn't under arrest.

"Do you know where you want to go yet, Bagram or Kabul?" he asked again. I said that I didn't care, that either one was fine. I was in no rush to go anywhere. I just wanted to rest. "You have to make a decision," he said. "Think about it." He walked out. I didn't understand what was going on.

Daoud sat at the end of the table across from me. I had mixed emotions about having him there. He wasn't American, and I kept thinking of what Fazul had said, and of him tugging on my beard.

The woman gestured toward two plastic containers on the table. "Do you want some food? We have this for you."

"Thank you, no food. I'm not hungry," I said. I was too sick for food.

She asked Daoud if he wanted some food. He shook his head. He took a can of soft drink and opened it. The woman moved her hands and couldn't sit still. "They wanted a woman here, to remind you of home," she said to me. "What can I do? I want to help you. I don't know what I can do." She was pleasant, but I felt strange sitting in this bright, clean room at a table with fluorescent lights overhead. I asked her what day it was. She looked at me and hesitated. "March thirty-first," she said. I had counted the days but had forgotten dates. It was around 3:30 a.m. Sixteen hours ago I was in a dark, frightening prison listening to Taliban tapes. Now I was in a bright, well-lighted room smiling and talking with an American woman with a ponytail. The young man with her was a medic. He took my blood pressure, checked my heart, asked me questions, and wrote my answers on a clipboard.

I was grateful to the military, or whoever these people were a part of, for providing all this to me, but I was embarrassed, giddy, and calm at the same time. I asked the woman if she was in the military.

"I'm in the navy," she said.

"How did you decide to join?" I asked. I was curious. She seemed too friendly, kind, and decent to choose a career, which, at heart, was dedicated to killing people.

"My family has been in the navy for a long time," she said. I understood now.

"What's your name?" I asked. I was trying to be friendly. I just wanted to talk to someone but, as with Gulob, I had gone too far.

She hesitated. "Sally," she said and walked away.

I had talked to various Special Forces soldiers in Afghanistan since 9/11. I liked them, but they always gave out a first name, which sounded fake. They were afraid, it seemed, to say their real names, or they didn't trust journalists, or they had their orders. I wished that I hadn't spoken to the woman. I didn't trust these people.

The medic finished checking Daoud. I talked a little bit about prison, but the medic didn't respond. He didn't seem to care. I suspected it was because I was a journalist. I looked like I was a member of the Taliban. I had been kidnapped and imprisoned by them, but I was, in some way, in his mind, a part of them. The navy woman, if she felt this way, had hidden her feelings. She did seem to care.

I said that I had been in the army a long time ago, hoping he would be friendlier.

"Really, what did you do?" he asked. He smiled and was friendly. "When were you in?"

"It was during the Vietnam era. I forget my title exactly." I knew my title, Movements Control Specialist, and my service number, like every other GI in America, but I didn't want to explain to him my military career, that I had been a Spec 4, worked in the mountains in Germany, but had also run track. He wouldn't understand.

"Must not have meant that much to you if you can't remember," he said disdainfully. His true feelings toward me had come out. I was a journalist, had gray hair, a long beard, and had been with the Taliban, consorting with the enemy. He was like Daoud mocking Razi Gul for losing weight and being illiterate.

Fazul came in and sat at the table. The older man came in again. "Who are you?" he asked Fazul loudly. There was a tone of contempt in his voice. Fazul, relaxed, smiling, was taken aback. Before he could say anything, I explained that Fazul was the CBS representative in Afghanistan. I would build Fazul up as much as I could to protect him from these people. I didn't know then that he hadn't seen his wife or children in a month, that he had been working nonstop, from Kabul to Islamabad, to save me. The older man looked at me. "Which do you want to do? Have you decided? Bagram or Kabul?" he demanded.

I didn't like this man, but I was afraid of him. I was afraid of everyone. I wondered what the U.S. government was going to do to me. I thought: *Bagram. I haven't been there in five years. I can see how much it has grown and return to Kabul from there.* "I haven't been to Bagram in a few years," I said. "That's fine." I looked at the man as I said this.

He stared back at me. "We know all about you," he said. He did hate me. I wondered if it was because of what I had written. I had written a paper for the U.S. Army War College on Islamic fundamentalism in South Asia and about the U.S. military's long ties to the Pakistani army and about U.S. and Pakistani ties to the mujahideen in the 1980s. I had also written about American tactics in the current conflict, breaking into people's homes, frisking women, humiliating everyone, creating enemies, of U.S. convoys going down the center of roads with soldiers screaming at people to get out of the way, calling them "hajji," just as soldiers of my generation had called Vietnamese "slopes" and "gooks." I didn't like this dark side of America. The United States would never win over the Afghans like this.

I looked at Fazul. "We would have to drive from Bagram back to Kabul," he said. I wanted to do what was easier for Fazul. "I'll fly to Kabul," I said reluctantly. I didn't know I was in the middle of a turf war.

The man walked out of the room. A few minutes later he

returned. "It's time to go," he said. "There are some people waiting to see you."

We walked back to the garage. I was no longer sick, so I climbed in the front seat of the SUV. The man climbed in the driver's seat and made a phone call. Fazul and Daoud got in the backseat. Behind us, men with pistols on their belts and women, all in civilian clothes, opened the gate and we drove out. They looked at me and then away.

We drove through the base. "I was in the army a long time ago," I said to the man. I wanted him to like me and respect me. I was acting toward him as I had acted toward Gulob. I was still in prison. I had told myself that if I survived I wouldn't have to put up with anything ever again. Already I had given in.

"I was going to go on an embed with the army after I finished my other research," I said. He didn't say anything. I hated myself for trying to win him over. I felt guilty. I had been with the Taliban. I had caused all this trouble.

He drove us to another part of the base, parked the car, came around to my door, calling me "Sir," and took me by the arm and led me past groups of men, Humvees, and SUVs standing in a row, their engines running. Fazul and Daoud followed close behind. He then gave me to two other men, wearing armor and holding rifles. I turned to say good-bye but he was gone.

PART FOUR

America

Monday, March 31

The two men shook my hand warmly and introduced themselves, Joe and Jim, both with the FBI. "Come on, climb in," said Joe. "We're going to see a doctor and get you something to eat. Do you want some breakfast? We told the mess hall to open up early for you." Fazul, Daoud, and I climbed in their SUV. The FBI agents kept talking, being friendly. What did they want?

I only half-listened to them, my mind wandering as I looked around at all the activity, the buildings, the lights, at exhaust fumes pouring out from a row of military vehicles ready to move out to fight the Taliban. I could feel the energy. I was back in America. I had tried to avoid the army until I was ready. Now I was in the center of it. The base reminded me of pictures and films I had seen of U.S. military bases in Vietnam. I hadn't been on a base since I left the army.

The FBI agents drove us past another check post, down a gravel road with trees on either side, and parked next to a row of Humvees. There were truck containers and rows of small sheds made of plywood. Jim took Daoud and me inside a shed and into a room filled with boxes, medical equipment, large canisters, body armor, helmets, and other gear. Fazul and Joe didn't come in with us. A friendly man in shorts and a T-shirt greeted us. A clock on the wall said 4:10 a.m.

I told the doctor to check Daoud first. He asked Daoud if he had any problems. Daoud pointed to his head. He had bad headaches and got sick. He had pointed to the same side of his head in prison. The doctor, holding a pen, asked him to explain. He said he had a stroke when he was eighteen. The doctor looked pained. That was so young. It was unusual to have a stroke at that age.

I glanced at Daoud as he put his left hand to his head. He had told me that he had hurt his head on a water pump, which I thought strange. Women and children drew water from wells, not men. Or perhaps he had said "struck" just now instead of "stroke." But he didn't correct the doctor. I kept thinking of what Fazul had told me about Daoud.

I kept talking, still giddy. Jim looked over. "You did break the law," he said. I nodded. He just brought me down and made me worried. Yes, I had crossed the border without a visa.

Joe came in with a camera and took our pictures. I wondered how much like the Taliban I must have appeared to him and the other Americans. As I stood there, I felt vaguely like it was a mug shot. I also wondered where Fazul was.

We finished our checkups and walked outside. Joe pointed to a building that looked, in the dark, like it was made of brick and had been there for generations. It had been a Russian officers' retreat in the 1980s. He thought I'd like to know that. It housed a movie theater and recreation facilities.

I half paid attention. That was a long time ago. I was numb, tired, and groggy.

We entered the mess hall. There were signs in English and men in T-shirts and fatigues, a small cafeteria, and picnic tables. I knew I stood out. A soldier in a T-shirt and long shorts brought me a large tray of eggs, bacon, pancakes, fruit, and cereal. He smiled and gave me a simple nod, which made me feel better. To him, I wasn't the enemy. I insisted to Daoud that he take some food. He took a banana. Fazul came in and sat across from me far away from Daoud. He was smiling, watching me.

I was now giddy, talking, and wide awake. I picked up a piece of bacon, realizing it was offensive to Fazul. He was a good Muslim. I looked at it, felt guilty, but I ate it. It reminded me of my youth. I wasn't Muslim. I could eat only a little.

We all walked back in the dark to what Joe called our hooch, a term from Vietnam. Once, it meant a thatched-roof dwelling. We walked into a large, lighted plywood shed. Inside there were thin doors with locks and small rooms, like cubicles. I opened the door to my room. There was a small cot, and it was covered with neatly folded clothes—some mine, some new—soap, a toothbrush, newsmagazines, a new backpack, power bars, and there, in the center, were my old beat-up running shoes. I kept looking at my shoes. They were home, my youth, my life; they were me more than anything else. They made me feel warm and comfortable. I glanced at the bottles of water and the fruit bars spread out neatly with other items on the floor.

"We wanted you to have everything you needed," said Joe, "and to make you feel at home." The FBI was being too good to me. It was hard to accept the kindness of these two men. What did they want from me? I preferred to sleep on a mat on the floor. Joe asked if I wanted to take a shower. I said no. I wasn't ready to be clean. I didn't want to leave where I had been. I had to go slowly. Daoud took a towel from Joe, who took him outside and across the gravel to the bathrooms. Fazul came to my room with a large sack. He and Maria, the CBS manager in Pakistan, had bought some clothes for me in Islamabad. I was supposed to be released there. I thanked him. I saw them in my mind walking into stores, picking out clothes for me. I put my hand on his shoulder.

Fazul left to have a cigarette, and then he would go to sleep. I lay on the cot and looked through the magazines. I was hungry for information. It was America, my country and culture, but the articles meant nothing to me. I didn't feel part of America.

I couldn't sleep. The room was hot, and I preferred the cool of the mountains. I drank some bottled water. Gulob, the Maulavi, and the others would be getting up now for prayers. I wondered where they had slept. Soon they would be walking through the mountains, back to their homes.

I heard Daoud moaning in his room and trying to vomit, just as he had in captivity. Why was he doing this? He would wake up the soldiers. Was he trying to show the FBI that he really was sick, or was he pretending? I felt he was showing off. Finally he stopped.

I got up an hour or two later. It was daylight. I hadn't slept a minute. I still didn't want to take a shower, but I also didn't want to appear any weirder than I felt I already did. I didn't want to leave Afghanistan behind. I reluctantly took the clothes that Fazul had brought me and walked across to the bathrooms. I stood, dizzy from lack of sleep, staring at a strange man in the mirror. My eyes were hollow, my face was gaunt, and my hair and beard were long and unkempt.

A soldier with short hair, an army T-shirt, and long shorts came up, looked at me, and moved away. He kept looking at me. I wanted to say something with my American accent, to put him at ease, but it would be contrived. I was in the wrong room. I went back outside and upstairs and into a shower room. There was an empty stall, and I stood in it enjoying the hot water running all over me, but I didn't want to be there.

I didn't want to join civilization. I wanted to be back in the mountains. I didn't want to wash and wear clean clothes and be normal. I washed my hair slowly. I stood in the changing section drying myself with my old clothes. I glanced at the other soldiers, a few with tattoos all over their backs and arms. No one looked at me twice. It felt good fitting in, but I knew somewhere deep inside of me that I had just washed off the mountains and that my time with the Taliban, my life in Pashtun villages and mud hovels, along rivers, through quiet farmland and soft pathways, was over. Something that was very much a part of me had gone and would never come back.

I walked back to my hooch and sat on my bed. A soldier opened the door but stood in the hallway. "Sir, are you Jere Van Dyk?" he asked. Yes, I said. He looked at me, keeping his distance. He had found a man outside who didn't have any ID but said that he was with me. Daoud stood behind him. I said he was with me. "Just checking," the soldier said. I nodded, and he glanced at me again, as if to ask, *Who in the world are you?* He walked away.

"Come outside, let's look at the sun," said Daoud. I went out into the morning heat and stood facing the sun. It was bright, hot, and hard on my eyes. Daoud was smiling and wanted to talk. I was too exhausted, and wary, but I sat with him. Joe and Jim brought over plastic containers of breakfast for us. I ate some fruit. Fazul joined us. Daoud said he wanted to go to his family in Peshawar, across the border. Fazul gave him some money.

The doctor who had examined us, now in uniform, came over and gave me some medicine. "Boy, you look different," he said. He smiled openly. I looked more American, and he felt more comfortable.

We gathered our gear and packed it into an SUV. Other men appeared, in T-shirts and baseball caps, carrying rifles. I didn't know who they were, but I assumed they were bodyguards. They put some gear into the back of a pickup.

I shook hands with Daoud and agreed that we would be in touch. We had been through so much together. I couldn't grasp that he might have betrayed me.

I said I didn't have any money to give him. I wanted to pay him for his work in Jalalabad before we crossed over, and for interpreting for me in prison. He waved his hand. "Fazul gave me some money to go to my family," he said. I had never seen him so relaxed about money.

Our bodyguards reappeared, and we climbed into our respective vehicles. Fazul and I rode in the back of our SUV and Joe and Jim were in front as we left the base. In my mind I now reentered Afghanistan. Fazul was on his cell phone.

We reached the main road and stopped. There was an SUV waiting on the other side. A man jumped out and came over to our vehicle. It was Ahmed Shah, one of Fazul's cousins. He smiled, shook my hand through the window, and handed me the pack that I had left with Daoud's father. Fazul and I shook hands. He was going to drive back to Kabul with Ahmed Shah. He wanted to see his wife and children. He smiled. He was happy. He had helped save my life. "I will see you tomorrow at the embassy," he told me.

As we left Fazul and drove down the highway, I looked at the eucalyptus trees, the palm trees, the motorized rickshaws with their loud, polluting, yet comforting lawn mower engines, men in turbans sitting in the shade drinking green tea, a boy leading two water buffalo, a girl carrying a water jug on her head. Afghanistan, this land I loved. Life was going on and would continue to go on.

We turned off the main road, drove up a gravel road, waited as a guard pushed a button lifting a bar, and drove onto another U.S. military base. We parked our SUV among a group of other dirty, gray SUVs with no license plates, Humvees, and trucks small and large, and locked the doors. There were hundreds of soldiers all around. Beyond was an airfield. Two helicopters were lifting off. Joe pointed to a small white airplane sitting far on the other side of the airfield. "That's our plane," he said.

One of our bodyguards, a man in his late forties, in a T-shirt and holding an M-4 rifle, stood next to me. We introduced ourselves. I asked who he worked for. He hesitated. "DOD," he said. The Department of Defense. I thanked him for coming with us. "I was coming over here anyway. Happy to help out," he said. I asked where he was going now. "We're going up to Nuristan for ten days to look around," he replied.

I smiled inside; the Afghans had thought I was from there.

"Want a smoothie?" asked Joe. I said sure. It was America. All I really wanted was to get out of the sun. Jim handed me a hundred dollars, expense money. I thanked him. Joe, Jim, the DOD man, and I walked down a road as military vehicles came and went. There were soldiers everywhere. I saw how big the U.S. military presence was in Afghanistan. I felt strange walking with these men and looking at the soldiers. I was American but felt distant from all of them.

No one, it seemed, paid any attention to me. I felt relieved. We walked into a small shed. There was a television on, soldiers hanging around, and two young Filipinos making smoothies. We all ordered one and went back outside and walked toward the runway. I could drink only part of the smoothie. It was too much. We got our gear from the SUV and waited while Jim went to see about our plane.

"I helped clean out your room at your guesthouse in Kabul," the DOD man said quietly. This operation was bigger than I thought. I realized that I wasn't going back to my room. I liked this man. If he had cleaned out my room, he knew all about me. We were quiet for a second. "We're glad to have you back," he said. I felt emotion well up in me. He cared about me. He didn't judge me because I had a long beard and looked like I belonged to the Taliban. He didn't hate me.

"Thank you," I said. I looked at him. "It's good to be back."

"If you ever want to write anything about how you survived and how you think we could learn from you, I know a lot of people down at the Kennedy Special Warfare Center and School at Fort Bragg that would like to read it," he said. I said I would be happy to. I liked that we were talking. He took out a card and gave it to me. It was from a private company. Jim returned and said we were ready to go. The other men took my gear and we walked across the two airport runways and to our plane.

The pilot, a South African, took our gear. Joe and Jim took out the clips from their rifles. I shook hands with the DOD man. "It was nice talking to you," he said. I smiled. I would write that article for him.

There were about ten seats on the plane but just the three of us and another man, with a pistol, as passengers. As we flew north to Kabul, I stared out the window, looking at the rolling green and brown land. It meant nothing to me. We landed at the Kabul airport, and when we taxied to a stop three SUVs were waiting, and men stood around holding their rifles.

They smiled, and we all shook hands. A man put a flak vest on me and sat me in the center, in the backseat of the middle SUV. As we drove through the streets of Kabul, I felt strange and overly protected in the government vehicle. "These people will never modernize," said the driver, as he skirted around people walking in the road. "Never."

I looked at the Afghans in the streets. Once I used to walk among them. Kabul looked far away now. A man next to me mentioned the Final Four. We talked about college basketball, and I felt I was trying too hard to show that I was American, so I stopped talking. We passed guards and check posts and entered the U.S. Embassy grounds. "We've got a room for you," said Joe. We parked the car, and I stepped outside and smelled the familiar air of Kabul, a combination of burning wood, garbage, a hint of sewage, and mountain air.

The men took off my flak vest and I felt freer. I wanted to go outside the gates and be in Kabul, but I was afraid. I knew too that this was impossible—I was now in the embrace of the U.S. government. Joe and Jim took me to my room. There was a refrigerator, a television, bunk beds, a shower, and Internet access, everything I needed.

That afternoon Joe, Jim, and their boss, Brian, whom Joe later called the "mayor of Kabul," because of his contacts and friendly nature, came by. They took me to get a haircut, to shave my beard, and to have a pizza. I didn't want to get a haircut or shave—not yet. I wanted to sit on the floor and eat Afghan food with my hands and talk quietly. I wanted food cooked over an open fire. I was comfortable with men with beards, but this was a different world.

We drove across the street to the International Security Force of Afghanistan headquarters, with its flags of many nations blowing in the spring air, walked past shops selling trinkets, a restaurant, men in different colored berets and camouflage uniforms, and came to the barbershop. I felt like I was in a European tourist village. The barbershop was closed, so we went to the pizza place. Westerners were sitting outside eating and drinking as if they were on vacation.

We ordered pizzas from a menu and sat inside. I ate the pizza quickly, not realizing how hungry I was. The FBI wanted information about my captors. "We're going to go after these guys," said Brian. I thought of the Maulavi's last statement: "If you talk to any government, we will kill you." I was afraid of him, and I had given my word, but I was now talking to the U.S. government.

We returned to the embassy. Joe took me to the FBI office, where Fazul and Ahmed Shah were waiting for us. Fazul gave me a packet of mail. We took photographs of me with each of them. I watched them watching me. I was talking fast. I was still too giddy, still running on adrenaline. Fazul gave me my cell phone back. He had got it from Daoud's father. It was a question and a statement.

"We tracked him down," he said. "I went to see him. There is a lot I have to tell you." His eyes were bright. Today he was rested and happy. I wanted to know all that he had done and what he had learned, but he didn't want to talk now. I asked about Ellen, the wife I created. Did she come over? "No, we made that up," he said.

I wanted to ask about a ransom, but I was too embarrassed. I also wondered about Daoud.

Jim came in and said some men were there to see me. Did I have a few minutes? Fazul stood up and said he would come back tomorrow. I would talk to them then. I hugged him and Ahmed Shah, and they left. I felt closer to them than to the Americans all around me. They were Afghans but part of my family.

Three men, in their thirties, in sweatshirts and jeans, entered. They carried notebooks and pens. I sat on the sofa and briefly explained what I had been trying to do in crossing the border, and why and where I had been, and what I had learned. They took notes but didn't ask questions. Their faces were blank. I didn't know if they knew much more than I did or if they didn't know what to ask. I talked quickly. After a while, Jim ended the conversation. The FBI was in charge. It was in charge of all kidnapping cases involving Americans, anywhere in the world.

It was getting late. I went to the computer in another room to see if I could remember my password and gain access to my e-mail. I knew I was rushing too fast back into Western life, but I didn't understand that I was too wound up to act normally. Another man, in a suit, came to see me. He turned out to be the deputy ambassador. We began to talk. I tried to slow down and measure my words. I said the United States was apparently building a new base along the border. The people who had held me said the Pakistani army would use the Taliban to destroy it. "They'll find themselves impaled on it," he replied firmly. I explained how complicated I felt things were. "This is a brother war," he said. I knew what he meant. Men from the same tribe, on different sides of the border, were killing one another. It was like brothers from both sides of the Mason-Dixon Line killing one another in the Civil War. I liked this man. He didn't seem upset that I had long hair and a full beard, but I wasn't sure. I felt that everyone in the government who knew about my case hated me. I was the enemy. I had been with the Taliban.

"When was the last time you had a really good whiskey?" he asked, smiling. "Why don't you come upstairs, and I'll give you one and we can talk there?"

I didn't feel strong enough to talk with him like a normal person. I wanted to learn from him, but another part of me was wary, and I didn't want to give away what I knew. I didn't want to tell him all the places I had been. I kept thinking of what Jim had said in the doctor's office. He was right, I did break the law. I broke it five times, each time I had sneaked across the border through the mountains, without a visa, into the tribal areas of Pakistan. I wondered what they really thought of me. Who was I, really? What was I up to? I didn't want to say too much to the deputy ambassador. "Thank you," I said. "Let me think about it."

He said to let him know and then left. It was getting late. I told Joe and Jim that I was tired and wanted to be alone. I went back to my room and called Nazaneen. She was the one who had told me to memorize some of the Kalima. She had helped me. I thought of the evenings I had spent in her living room, talking, eating dinner by a fire. She answered and heard my voice. She was silent. "You are alive?" she asked.

"Yes," I said, "I'm in Kabul."

She laughed gently. I could hear the warmth in her voice. "It's so good to hear your voice," she said. "I never thought . . ." She didn't finish the sentence. "Where are you now?" I told her I was at the U.S. Embassy, under the control of the FBI. They had brought me back from Jalalabad. "I've been calling for weeks," she said. She was quiet. "Are you okay?"

"I'm fine," I said. "They didn't torture me." I didn't realize what I was saying. "When can I see you? Can you come over now?" I asked. I had thought of her the first two weeks in prison, counting the days when she would return from India and would know, because she couldn't reach me, that something was up.

"I can't," she said. "There are people here. I'll come tomorrow. How do I find you?" I said I would tell the FBI. She could reach me on my cell phone. I was back in the modern world. I hung up. I could marry her and settle in Afghanistan. No, I didn't want that. I didn't want to live in Afghanistan anymore. The Taliban would kill me. They would know I was here. They were everywhere, some shaven, some with beards, in the army, in the government. I had to go home.

My life is not my own, I said to myself. I wanted to see Nazaneen. Talking to her gave me energy and a feeling of warmth. I wanted to talk with the deputy ambassador now, but it was too late. I read, tried to sleep, and couldn't. I finally slept for a few hours. I woke up at dawn and went out for a walk. It was April 1. The weather was cool and brisk.

Coming back to my room, I noticed a laundry room a few doors down. An Afghan attendant gave me some soap, and I put my Afghan clothes in the washer. Joe came by and took me to the dining room for breakfast. We sat outside by the swimming pool, eating quickly, and then we walked over to the barbershop.

We passed the deputy ambassador on his way to his office. I thanked him again for the offer to talk. He shrugged. I had my chance. A young man waiting to see the barber gave up his place for me. Joe took my picture. We wanted a before and after. The barber cut my hair short and trimmed my beard to a more urban crop. We walked back toward my room and saw Brian talking with some other men. He smiled brightly and gave me his card. He seemed friendlier and more at ease with me now that I looked more like a typical American.

We returned to the FBI office. Joe and Jim asked if I would see a man who had come down from Bagram. I said of course. The man said he was from the Defense Intelligence Agency and had a large notebook with a number of questions. He politely began to ask them, and I answered, explaining some of what I had learned.

I talked quickly, everything spilling out, and the DIA man wrote quickly. After fifteen or twenty minutes Jim said that was all the time I had. The DIA man put his hands in the air, as if to say, "I'm just beginning." He rose and we shook hands. I wanted to talk to him more, but Jim said that we had a plane to catch in a couple of hours.

A young woman came in and introduced herself as the consular officer and handed me two sheets of paper. "We want to issue a statement to the media, but we need your signature," she said.

I looked at the form. *So the world will know about this soon.* When I made that decision to go with Razi Gul across the border, I didn't think anyone would know. Now the world would know. I signed the paper. Joe, standing in the room, picked it up. "I'm no friend of the media," he said, "but shouldn't CBS have the right to announce this?"

Before that moment, I hadn't thought clearly about the possibility that it was CBS, at least it seemed according to Joe, that had gotten me out. I knew very little, but I did know that I could now tell the world what I had been doing and what had happened— and that it was over. I was going home. I had to call CBS. I told the State Department woman that I wanted to think a minute. I looked up, and I saw Nazaneen, with her long curly hair, looking around the doorway, smiling. People were all around me. We had a plane to catch. What was I supposed to do? I went outside with Nazaneen, sat by the swimming pool, and called the CBS bureau in London and asked for Andy Clarke.

The receptionist said that he was in Islamabad. He was in Pakistan? I reached Andy's boss in London, told her about the statement, and asked her advice. "It's up to you," she said. She said that the State Department had wanted to have a news conference in Washington but that the idea had been shot down. *This has become complicated*, I thought. All the happiness I felt, all the joy of being released, began to go away.

Everything was being kept quiet. Reluctantly, I told Joe to tell the State Department no. I was sad and angry, but he was the FBI. I deferred to him. I didn't know what was going on, and I felt I should defer to CBS, too. I knew the network was involved in some way. Somebody, maybe a great many people, had saved my life. I was indebted to them. The only moral thing to do was to put my own feelings aside.

I walked back to my room with Nazaneen. We hugged each other. "I knew something was wrong when I couldn't reach you," she said. "I sensed it. What happened?" I briefly told her the story. She put her hand on my knee. I relaxed. She was quiet. I didn't want to leave Afghanistan. I wanted to go back to her house and to have her fix me some tea and sit in the garden and talk.

"Nancy told me that the FBI had cleaned out your room," she said. Nancy was Nancy Dupree, widow of the late Louis Dupree, a famous and remarkable American expert on Afghanistan. "Nancy said they clean out the rooms of people who've died." Nancy thought I was dead. So did Nazaneen. I had put her name on the list I had given to Daoud. She would have been able to raise the money in Kabul. She would have done whatever it took. I kissed her on the cheek. We had only a few minutes together. Joe would be here at any minute. "I'm afraid you'll never come back to Afghanistan," she said.

"I'd like to stay, but I can't," I said quietly. "I don't control any-thing here." I told her that the FBI was going to try to find the men who kidnapped me, and that my captors said they would kill me if I talked to the government. Gulob said that the Taliban were throughout Kabul. I believed him. They would find me. I had to leave. CBS was expecting me back. I couldn't diminish all that it had done for me by staying here. I had to see my family.

Nazaneen and I hugged again. She helped me pack my bags. I had only a few things; the FBI had all my gear. Joe knocked on the door. "It's time for lunch, and then we have to go," he said. "There is a place here with really good Afghan food. You'll love it."

He took us across the embassy compound to a dimly lit restaurant filled with Afghans who worked at the embassy, but I wasn't hungry and it wasn't Afghanistan. We went to the main dining room, bought tea, and sat outside by the pool. Two Gurkha guards, fully armed, walked by. A group of embassy employees sat in the shade on the other side of the pool.

"They are clueless about what is going on here," said Nazaneen. Fazul appeared and joined us. He and Nazaneen smiled and shook hands. I had never seen an Afghan man and woman shake hands before. They were both Tajiks, both from northern Afghanistan, both modern, and they knew each other, but still I saw a warm, smiling grimace on Fazul's face. Nazaneen, whose family had fled Afghanistan when the Soviets invaded and who had lived in America for twenty-three years, becoming an American citizen, shook his hand firmly.

We chatted for a few minutes, and then we all walked quickly to the front of the embassy, where I stood for photographs in front of the great seal of the United States. I was humbled by all the attention. I was welcomed. I was part of America. I was American. I also had my picture taken with Fazul and with Nazaneen. I put my arm around each of them. I shook hands with other FBI agents, all of them friendly.

Then someone put a flak vest on me, and I climbed in an SUV, along with Joe, Jim, and a pair of armed guards. We drove through Kabul, passing cars, as policemen waved us by and we rushed to the airport. Joe gave our tickets to an Afghan, who got our boarding passes.

We sat on plastic chairs outside on a lawn. I faced the sun. It was the best waiting lounge I had ever been in. I saw a man I knew, Doug Wankel, formerly with the Drug Enforcement Administration, now a consultant in Kabul. I went over to say hello. He stood up. "Jere, I heard . . . Did you . . . Were you . . . ?" he stammered. I nodded yes.

On the plane, I sat next to the window. The FBI agents sat next to me. They would escort me to New York. We flew south over an endless sea of rolling, brown mountains, and here and there were patches of snow, the outlines of villages, and then desert. I looked down at the mountains and the desert and wondered if I would ever come back here.

We landed in Dubai, and I was afraid. I wondered if the Taliban were here and knew that I was on this flight. I stared out the window, looking for them. The Taliban were in Dubai; they got money from here.

The next day, April 2, we flew to New York. CBS put me in first class, so I could rest, but I couldn't sleep. I stared out the window, read magazines, ate, and wrote in my notebook. Joe and Jim rode in business class. They debriefed me on the plane for a few hours. They also told me that someone from CBS would meet me at the airport. There would be FBI agents there and maybe a camera crew. I tried to work out what I would say to the media.

When we landed in New York, four FBI men and a half dozen policemen met our flight. We walked down a long hallway, and I held up my pants. I had lost weight. I was escorted through customs, as people stared at me, and brought to a conference room where I sat at a big table. There were about fifteen of us. A man next to me put his hand on my chair and said, "You're safe, Jere. You're safe."

"Thank you," I said. I hadn't thought of that. I was fine. I wondered if I really was safe. I looked at everyone looking at me. I wondered what they were looking for. Maybe I looked strange. "It's nice to be home, thank you," I said without thinking. Home.

Another man said that the FBI wanted to help me in any way it could. The FBI wanted to talk with me about my experiences and to learn from me. I would be happy to help. "One thing," said a man across from me. "There are three messages from the Taliban on your answering machine. I advise you not to answer the phone for a few days. When you do, we'd like to know if you recognize the voices."

They had followed me back here. I wasn't safe. I asked if the Taliban had sent a fax here. The man nodded. "We know where they sent the fax from. You can throw your answering machine away if you want," he said, smiling. "You've had it for a few years." I smiled. He was right. It was more than twenty years old, like my television. People commented on them, but they worked fine. We sat there a few minutes and talked. Before we got off the plane, Joe had given me an FBI cap and Jim had given me a Joint Terrorism Task Force pin. "Where's your cap?" Joe now asked. I put it on and we walked out into the arrivals terminal.

We waited a few minutes, the FBI and airport officials in dark suits and raincoats. Then I saw Ingrid Ciprian-Matthews, the CBS News foreign editor, coming out of the crowd. She smiled and came up to me and gave me a long, warm hug. I hugged her back. I was home.

The two of us rode into the city. Ingrid told me a little bit about what had been going on. I began to realize all that she and so many others had done to save me. She didn't want me to talk yet. She wanted me to recover.

Ingrid took me back to my apartment and came upstairs with me. Ellen had gone to Europe for a few weeks. The apartment was still officially hers until August. I didn't even have a place to live. I looked around. It was home. I saw the red light blinking on my answering machine.

Ingrid sat with me on the sofa. She stayed for a half hour and asked if there was anyone I could have dinner with. I said there was. As she left, she smiled and told me not to lose my key. It was the spare key. Ellen had the other one. I smiled back. It was good to smile.

That night I woke up twice, afraid. Were the Taliban coming in the door? Where was I? I looked around. I was in my apartment, in New York. I woke up before dawn and took the elevator downstairs. The doorman said hello, as if I had never left. I went for a slow run in Central Park. As I ran, following a route I always took, I kept looking around. I was afraid that someone would attack me.

I came back and looked at the answering machine. The red light was still blinking. I couldn't listen to the messages, not yet. I saw Gulob and the Maulavi and the others walking back through the mountains. They would be home by now. I kept thinking of them.

Author's Endnote

Although this is the true story of my captivity, for safety reasons certain names and details have been changed or withheld. The names of my immediate captors and accidental cell mates are those I was told at the time, but I do not know whether they are real names or noms de guerre.

This book is primarily based on my recollections and the diary I was allowed to keep during my captivity. Although I have asked many questions since my release, I have received no definitive answers about exactly who was responsible for or complicit in my kidnapping or about the precise roles of any government agencies or private parties who may have been involved in securing my release, including whether any ransom was paid and to whom. As a result, the questions and suspicions I had during the unfolding of my captivity, which I report in this book, remain unresolved.

Acknowledgments

I wish to thank Paul Golob, the editorial director of Times Books. I could not have undertaken this project without him. I thank him for taking a chance on me, for his support, and for his intelligent editing. This book is his vision as much as it is mine.

I am grateful to Nicole Dewey, the director of publicity at Henry Holt and Company, for her warm, enthusiastic support for the book, and Maggie Richards, the director of sales and marketing. I would also like to thank Stephen Rubin, the president and publisher of Henry Holt, and his predecessors John Sterling and Dan Farley.

Joel Rosenthal, the president of the Carnegie Council for Ethics in International Affairs, provided an office for me where I could write much of this book. I thank Joel, his assistant Melissa Semeniuk, and his staff and my colleagues at the Carnegie Council for their help and friendship.

Wendy Weil, my literary agent, supported this project from the beginning, and her able assistants Emily Forland and Emma Patterson listened quietly as I sat in her office, a few days after I returned, and told my story. I especially want to thank Emily for suggesting the single word that became the book's title.

I wish to thank my family for their love and support, especially after I returned. Their warm welcome and their hugs meant everything to me.

In February 2002, Daniel Pearl, a reporter for the *Wall Street Journal*, was kidnapped by militants and beheaded in Karachi. Almost exactly six years later I became the second American journalist kidnapped in Pakistan. A great number of people, most of whose names I do not know, and probably never will, worked hard, often tirelessly, sometimes in dangerous circumstances, to do all that they could to try to prevent a second Daniel Pearl. Unfortunately, I cannot mention most of the names of those I know who were involved. I must protect them. I can name some, however, and the first is Michael Semple, whom I wish to thank publicly, not just for all that he did, but for his friendship and humility in giving credit to others. I wish to thank Fazul Rahim, whom I have known since 2001, who risked his life for me, and who is the best friend a man could have. Sami Yousafzai, who knows what it is like to be in prison, took risks on my behalf. Maria Usman, a friend since 2003, will be my friend for life. Mullah Malang not only warned me in advance but also summoned one of the kidnappers to his house and demanded that I be released and not be harmed. Fraidoon Mohmand, a member of parliament in Afghanistan, and a chief of the Mohmand tribe, worked quietly among his people and gave his word, which counted more than anything else. In the best Pashtun tradition, he kept his honor and brought me to safety.

I want to acknowledge Samiullah Sharaf, Sean Langon, David Rohde, Tahir Luddin, John Solecki, and most of all I wish to honor the memory of Piotr Stanczak, who, unlike us, did not get out alive.

I wish to thank President Hamid Karzai for the long talk we had one evening about Afghanistan, Pakistan, and the tribal regions; and the many tribal chiefs, village elders, and common Afghans who fed me, gave me a place to sleep, took me on dangerous trips, and talked to me at length about the border region. I met men I had not seen in twenty-five years. I wish I could have written about them, but this book is not the one I thought I would write.

My thanks also go to Ekram Shinwari, Enayat Delawary, Peter Lewis, Arthur and Sherry Hill, Ana and Miguel Real, Nancy Dupree, Roshan Khadivi, Peter and Hassina Jouvenal, and the staff at the Gandamack Lodge. Henry Kaufman was especially helpful in providing legal advice.

Often I think of the young woman, with long, dark, curly hair, whom I watched that September morning leaning out the window high up, before the first tower began to crumble and those of us below, on the ground, started to run. This book, finally, is in memory of her.

Index

About the Author

JERE VAN DYK is the author of *In Afghanistan: An American Odyssey*, an account of his travels with the mujahideen in the early 1980s, when they were fighting against the Soviet Union's occupation of Afghanistan. Since then, he has covered stories all over the world, mainly for the *New York Times*, CBS News, and *National Geographic*, that required him to visit places where few Western reporters had ventured before. He lives in New York City.